The Archaeology of Race

The Archaeology of Race

The Eugenic Ideas of Francis Galton and Flinders Petrie

Debbie Challis

B L O O M S B U R Y

LONDON • NEW DELHI • NEW YORK • SYDNEY

Bloomsbury Academic
An imprint of Bloomsbury Publishing Plc

50 Bedford Square	1385 Broadway
London	New York
WC1B 3DP	NY 10018
UK	USA

www.bloomsbury.com

Bloomsbury is a registered trade mark of Bloomsbury Publishing Plc

First published 2013
Paperback edition published 2014

British Library Cataloguing-in-Publication Data
A catalogue record for this book is available from the British Library.

ISBN: HB: 978-1-7809-3420-4
PB: 978-1-4725-8749-7
ePDF: 978-1-4725-0220-9
ePUB: 978-1-4725-0219-3

Library of Congress Cataloging-in-Publication Data
Challis, Debbie.
The archaeology of race: the eugenic ideas of Flinders Petrie and Francis Galton/Debbie
Challis.
pages cm
Includes bibliographical references and index.
ISBN 978-1-7809-3420-4 (hardcover: alk. paper) – ISBN 978-1-4725-0219-3 (ebook (epub) –
ISBN 978-1-4725-0220-9 (ebook (epdf) 1. Eugenics–History. 2. Race–Philosophy.
3. Archaeology–Philosophy. 4. Petrie, W. M. Flinders (William Matthew Flinders),
1853–1942. 5. Galton, Francis, 1822-1911. I. Title.
HQ751.C53 2013
305.8001–dc23
2012045742

Typeset by Newgen Imaging Systems Pvt Ltd, Chennai, India

Contents

Figures

Abbreviations

BAAS   British Association for the Advancement of Science
EEF   Egypt Exploration Fund
ILP   Independent Labour Party
NGA   National Gallery Archive
NOA   National Olympian Association
NHM   Natural History Museum
PEF   Palestine Exploration Fund
PMA   Petrie Museum Archive
RGS   Royal Geographical Society
SRBM   Society for the Recognition of the Brotherhood of Man
UCL   University College London

Foreword

With a passion for measurement verging on the obsessive, Francis Galton (1822–1911) possessed all of the Victorian enthusiasm for classification and improvement. However, rather than seeking to classify natural history specimens, or to restore ancient churches, Galton's focus was on improving human populations and selective breeding. His interest in geography and travel led to mapping sections of the African interior in the early 1850s on a tour that was self-funded but had the support of the Royal Geographical Society – an expedition that gave many opportunities for testing his eccentric inventions designed to make life easier for the gentleman explorer. Inspired by his tour of Africa, Galton's considerable energies and private wealth were then concentrated on seeking ways to improve the human race and his activities around measurement had this end in view.

Galton's influence on nineteenth-century society is tightly interwoven with wider fears of degeneration of the population, over-crowding and the growth of the criminal classes. Coining the word 'eugenics' for the first time in 1883, much of his work was focussed on finding laws of heredity, and examining physical 'types' from groups within the population, and involved collecting vast amounts of personal data. Galton collected photographs and physical and behavioural information from hundreds of individuals, ranging from Jewish schoolboys, inmates of Bethlem Lunatic Asylum, women suffering from tuberculosis and convicted murderers. Perhaps inevitably, his assumptions about race and class can be perceived in his findings.

Galton's collection and archives are held at University College London (UCL), where Galton re-located his Anthropometric Laboratory in 1904, forming the Eugenics Records Office. An earlier version of this laboratory opened as part of the 1884 South Kensington International Health Fair. Many of the measuring tools, including head callipers and other apparatus designed to categorize individuals into types, are preserved as part of a research collection, along with extensive archives of photographs and forms showing anthropometric measurements. This collection is available to the public by appointment and remained little known until the preparations to celebrate the 2011 centenary of Galton's birth began at UCL.

Viewed as a controversial figure in UCL's history, the Galton Centenary raised the level of awareness of his influence on twentieth-century bio-medical research at UCL. As the plans for the centenary began, it became evident that the legacy of Galton and the associated Nazi taint of his early work in eugenics were by no means dead to the collective memory. Colleagues from departments varying from Geography, Art History and Archival and Information Studies entered into discussions with UCL Museums & Collections and the Library Services about how to manage the centenary, with the aim to acknowledge fully any of the university's history now deemed unsavoury.

As custodians of the artefacts and archives relating to Galton's life and work, both the Galton Collection, of which I acted as a Curator during this time, and my colleagues within the Museums department and that of the Library Services had a unique responsibility for the ethical challenges thrown up by the Galton centenary. Despite the interest provoked by Galton's work, a more traditional 'celebration' seemed inappropriate – yet, neither did it seem justified to shy away altogether from the difficult questions being raised, indeed to do would be a lost opportunity. Eventually, the two primary projects chosen to focus on were the project of digitizing UCL's extensive history of genetics material (in association with the Wellcome Trust), and to examine Galton's influence on his contemporaries, especially that of the most famous of archaeologists, Flinders Petrie. Providing digital access to information created further ethical challenges, especially involving placing online personal and medical information about people who lived in the late nineteenth and early twentieth centuries, and a consultation on this issue is ongoing as the digitization of the history of genetics continues at UCL. Examining the eugenic thinking of Flinders Petrie at his own museum proved that museums can provoke discussion by providing a more balanced space for debate, even when current archaeological discourse is being challenged.

Examining the elements of Galton's work that provokes uncomfortable responses in a modern audience allows us both to get a clearer understanding of the works of other eminent Victorians, and to situate them within the complexities of nineteenth-century thought. Unlike Galton's cousin, Charles Darwin, and his cousin-by-marriage, Florence Nightingale, Galton had little sympathy with the dignity or rights of the individual, which he would not hesitate to sacrifice for the common good. This book examines the relationship between Galton and Petrie for the first time, uncovering the connections between the development of modern eugenic thought in the work of Petrie, and Petrie's own contribution to the research on eugenics and biometrics at University College London, where the legacy of these two compelling personalities still reverberates strongly today.

Natasha McEnroe
Director, Florence Nightingale Museum

Acknowledgements

A number of people assisted with *Archaeology of Race* and *Typecast*, the exhibition on which it is partially based, and there is only room to list some of them here. Natasha McEnroe, Stephen Quirke, Kate Nichols, Sally-Ann Ashton and Gemma Romain have given thoughtful advice on my ideas and on the ethical implications of some of the ideas in this study. I am grateful to Carole Reeves, Amara Thornton, June Challis and Kate Sheppard for reading and discussing parts of this book with me.

Alice Williams was indispensable at assisting with research in the Egypt Exploration Society archives. Felicity Cobbing (Palestinian Exploration Fund), Tine Bagh (Ny Carlsberg Glyptotek), Peter Brand (Memphis University), Jaromir Malik (formerly of the Griffith Institute, Oxford) and Nicholas Donaldson (National Gallery) have also helped with archive enquiries and shared their time and expertise. I am also grateful to them for allowing references to their respective archives or work in this book.

Colleagues from UCL Museums – in particular Jack Ashby, Mark Carnall, Subhadra Das, Sally MacDonald and Nina Pearlman – and the team at the Petrie Museum – Tracey Golding, Susi Pancaldo, Edmund Connolly and Tonya Nelson – supported the original exhibition idea. Margaret Serpico, Jan Picton and Ivor Pridden pointed me in the way of important information and source material. Staff from UCL Library Services made the Galton centenary constructive, particularly Gill Furlong, Kate Chaney and Elizabeth Lawes. Sarah Chaney, Phoebe Harkins, Niall Boyce, Caroline Bressey and Matthew Sweet all assisted with making the Galton Centenary memorable and thought provoking.

Natasha McEnroe and Kate Sheppard have generously contributed to the writing of the book with their respective Foreword and Afterword, while Alice Williams assisted with the compiling of the table for Appendix A. Any faults are my own.

I would like to remember the academic Dominic Montserrat, who died in 2004 and whose work has deeply influenced me and this book.

Archaeology of Race is dedicated to Simon Guerrier.

Introduction

Half of history seems incredible to one who looks at all things through modern spectacles.

(Petrie, 1911: 122)

The contention of William Matthew Flinders Petrie from his book *Egypt and Israel,* quoted above, is the contention of this book. Petrie's point is a truism that verges on cliché. *Archaeology of Race* goes a step further than Petrie to argue that all of history, ancient and modern, is viewed through the spectacles of our present day concerns and assumptions. It is understanding this vision that is important. This does not make history pointless, but adds to our understanding of how the past is presented and used in scholarly and popular discourses. Understanding how different visions of the past are framed and observed is particularly pertinent when working with objects and archive material in a museum environment. Museum objects have a collection history and provenance. The people who collected them and their reasons for doing so become part of the museum in a manner that used to be rarely made public in galleries and exhibitions. In addition, archaeological and anthropological objects usually record people from different cultures and time periods to that of the museum that houses them. These objects have been in turn collected by different people also, usually, from different cultures and time periods to the one in which the objects were made and used. Chris Gosden, Frances Larson and Alison Petch ask the question 'What is a Museum?', in the introduction to their book on the people and the collections of the early history of the Pitt Rivers Museum in Oxford (Gosden, Larson with Petch, 2007). They contend that a museum is made up of the histories of the people behind the scenes of the collections and their agendas as much as the objects themselves.

A popular and articulate exponent of thinking about people and history through objects is Edmund de Waal's *The Hare with Amber Eyes. A Hidden Inheritance* (2010). In de Waal's work, 264 Japanese netsuke miniature sculptures become characters themselves; tying together personal, familial and material biographies. Objects can be seen as transformative and active agents. They can take a role in collecting people as much as being collected:

> In one sense, of course, the objects in the Museum have been collected by people, but it is also possible to see that the people associated with the Museum have been collected by objects. [. . .] It is not just that objects illuminate the relationships that created the Museum, but that many of these connections were created through objects and because of them. (Gosden, Larson with Petch, 2007: 5).

Each chapter in *Archaeology of Race* begins either with an object or collection of objects in a museum or archive, usually in the Petrie Museum of Egyptian Archaeology at University College London (UCL). The object acts as a way into understanding an aspect of racial science or eugenic thinking in ideas about archaeology and society. I often explore Petrie's description of an object and place that description in context. I am also looking at these objects myself and positioning myself in context as a museum professional, as well as part of an audience, working in the early twenty-first century, looking back one hundred years or more. The object considered remains, essentially, the same in terms of physical structure. However, its ancient and modern purposes are changed by different viewpoints, while my relationship to the object, Flinders Petrie and the museum has been transformed by considering the intellectual histories of these different antiquities, displays and photographs.

This book is a history of a certain way of looking at the past. It investigates a once wide-spread methodology that is uncomfortable, even distasteful, to contemporary museum professionals, archaeologists, historians and visitors to museums. Yet it is an important one and, as *Archaeology of Race* illustrates, is necessary for understanding how some collections of objects have been formed, presented and archived, as well as how many academic disciplines were established. 'Eugenic thinking' describes a form of intellectual inquiry that prioritizes ideas about racial difference and genetic inheritance; by genetic here I mean the traditional idea of 'bloodlines' or genealogy, rather than the modern scientific definition of genes as based on DNA. It considers the relationship between a gentleman scientist, Francis Galton, and a professional archaeologist, Flinders Petrie, at a time when disciplinary boundaries were not formed and the distinction between amateur and professional was not absolute. The personal and professional relationship between these two distinguished men – they both received knighthoods – has not been fully considered before. I argue that Galton's support for Petrie assisted him enormously in his early years as an archaeologist and his ideas influenced Petrie until his death in 1942. In turn, Petrie was a prestigious advocate of Galton's anthropometic data gathering and racial science in understanding ancient Egypt and archaeological evidence, as well as a backer of Galton's eugenic vision in contemporary society. The relationship between these two men further illustrate the crossovers between anthropology, archaeology, sociology, statistics and biological sciences, while all these disciplines were being formed in universities. Galton and Petrie belonged to a network of different societies and institutions, such as the Anthropological Institute or the British Association for the Advancement of Science, through which practitioners in these fledgling disciplines met, presented evidence and took part in discussions. These disciplines were formed and related meetings took place against a background of British imperial expansion, political change and social upheaval in the late nineteenth and early twentieth centuries.

Race is not a biological but a social construction. This does not negate the devastating consequences that this construction, and the perception that it was intricately linked to biological and related ethical differences, has had for people (Malik, 1996: 71). It is, therefore, vital to understand the way in which discourse around race and inheritance was formed, used and changed in archaeology and ideas about the ancient world. Throughout this book I use the term racist to describe the point of view in which a biological concept of race is systematically used to be the main determining factor in explaining the actions and characteristics of a person or group of people. This form of thinking considers race to determine 'the workings of society and politics, the course of history, the development of culture and civilization, even the nature of morality itself' (Biddiss, 1976: 245). This racism is often derogatory and 'racist' in the sense that we understand it today. *Archaeology of Race: The Eugenic Ideas of Francis Galton and Flinders Petrie* is the result of an exhibition *Typecast: Flinders Petrie and Francis Galton* that was held at the Petrie Museum during 2011; the centenary year of the death of Francis Galton. Natasha McEnroe was involved in the centenary programme and I am grateful for her thoughtful guidance last year and for providing the 'Foreword' to this book. The exhibition and this book is informed by the research that I had been carrying out on the use of racial theory in ideas about classical sculpture, in particular, the ancient Greek body, for a number of years (Challis, 2010). *Archaeology of Race* is also influenced by my experience and critical reflections as a museum professional working on interpreting ancient civilizations through objects and collections for a variety of modern audiences. My experience of visitor responses in the museum as well as online reactions to *Typecast* and presenting related talks, including one on Youtube, means that I need to state clearly that to write about 'eugenic ideas' is not to condone them. Neither am I an advocate of either Petrie's or Galton's ideas about race; nor do I deny that eugenics had devastating consequences on people across the world during the twentieth century. This book occasionally refers to painful examples and atrocities within the legacy of eugenics, but it is mainly about the justification for and influence of 'eugenic thinking' among a relatively small group of intellectuals, not its practical consequences for thousands, even millions, of people.

The four races

An anti-racist educational initiative in France, called Nous Autres (or 'We'), uses an artistic rendition of the ancient Egyptian 'Four Races' from the Book of the Gates in the Tomb of Seti I (Dynasty 19, 1290–1279 BC) as one of the images on its publicity material. Hosted on the campaigning website of former footballer Lilian Thuram (www.thuram.org), the educational programme is designed to act alongside the recent exhibition on ideas about the 'other', the growth of racial science and 'human zoos' that was co-curated by Thuram at the Musée du quai Branly in Paris: *L'invention du sauvage: Exhibitions* (29 November 2011 to 3 June 2012). The use of this image could presuppose that the ancient Egyptians considered race in much the same way that people have comprehended it in the modern period (namely over the last two to three hundred years). The Egyptian depiction of other peoples – Libyan, Nubian and Asiatic alongside an Egyptian – is here used to celebrate the cultural diversity of different peoples while also stressing peoples' physical similarity. The division of the world into 'four races' based on physical difference that was related to climate and geography was enshrined in the modern period by Immanuel Kant in 1775 (Bindman, 2002: 158–9). Arguably the 'four races' in Seti I's tomb fitted the philosophical, political and aesthetic world order of modern Europeans when it was discovered by Giovanni Bapttista Belzoni in 1817.

An illustration from the footrest found in the tomb of Tutankhamen that shows the profiles of different conquered peoples across the background image of a DNA Helix forms the 1994 paperback cover of Steve Jones' *The Language of the Genes. Biology, History and the Evolutionary Future* (1994). This cover nicely contrasts the popular modern image of genetic difference, the DNA helix, with that of an ancient one. In 1887, Petrie photographed one of the facial profiles of the 'four races' in Seti I's tomb as a means of identifying different races in Egypt and the ancient world at that time. Petrie took these photographs as part of his *Racial Photographs* project for a committee of the British Association for the Advancement of Science. The project was personally and professionally supported by Francis Galton and is detailed in Chapter 4. This book is not about how the ancient Egyptians did or did not define race, nor is it about what racial or ethnic group they were. The depiction of different groups of people in ancient Egypt have become iconic images of differing racial identities in the ancient world. Whether used to celebrate cultural diversity, or to forensically pinpoint physical differences based on an assumed racial hierarchy, or to contrast with modern scientific definitions of genes; different uses of ancient Egyptian images only tell us about the assumptions of the user and their social context.

The ethnic identity of the ancient Egyptians and their relationship to other cultures is a highly charged issue. Martin Bernal's *Black Athena: The Afroasiatic roots of classical civilization* (1987) unleashed a furious debate on the identity of ancient Egyptians, as well as the racist scholarship of orientalist and classical scholars during the nineteenth and twentieth centuries. Academics have pointed out the problems with Bernal's ideas, not least because race and racial ideas is a modern construction, and how they can feed alternative politically influenced constructions of the ancient world that are also based on biological models (Snowden, 1996; Bard, 1996). Bernal's work and reactions to it were situated in the 'culture wars' that took place in the United States, and elsewhere, in the 1980s and 1990s and contemporary political conditions still influence readings of it (Goff, 2005: 16). Bernal's study has had a limited influence on the understanding of 'the role of Classics in the modern West'; yet it could assist in building a constructive scholarship that reassesses the influence of the discipline and associated areas and its relation to racial and imperial ideologies over the last two hundred years (von Binsbergen, 1997; Bradley, 2010: 17). The physical anthropologist S. O. Y. Keita has carried out useful and distinctive work that undermines the emphasis on biological constructions of race and ancient civilizations (Keita, 1992). What cannot be denied though is the fact that Egyptologists and Classicists have consistently treated ancient Egypt as distinct from the rest of Africa and, until recently, rarely tried to understand the 'complex reciprocities of ancient north-east Africa out of which Egyptian pre-history re-emerged' (van Wyck Smith, 2001: 81). Chapter 7 considers how Akhenaten and his family have been used as Afrocentric role models, as well as Petrie's ideas about the Pharaoh as a Semitic Messianic leader, and the problems with both readings. Race and identity in the ancient world was about more than skin colour and neither are skin colour or physical characteristics necessarily signs of genetic origins (Fluehr-Lobban and Rhodes, 2004: xxii–xxvi). The importance of understanding more about how ethnic and racial identities have been assigned to the ancient Egyptians is bound up in understanding racism and the colonial legacy over the last two hundred years.

Classical physiognomy

An exhibition in 2012 at the National Museum of Denmark in Copenhagen, *Europe Meets the World*, explored how the idea of Europe and European has been created since Classical Greece. The exhibition was timed to coincide with Denmark's presidency of the European Union (Christensen Grinder-Hansen, Kjeldbaek, Rasmussen, 2012). The probing questions the exhibition asked about Europe's relationship to Classical Greece, the rest of the world and the idea of borders (geographical, migration and financial) seemed particularly apt in the current context of the debt crisis in modern Greece, global economic melt-down and anxiety about migration and social welfare. A thread linking the different chronological sections together was the ancient Greek idea of a 'barbarian' and foreigner. While pointing out that the classical Greeks did not have the same idea of race and racial distinctions as those in the modern world, the exhibition showed how European cultural identities have been formed partly on distinctions around the 'other', that in the modern period has been predicated around racial difference (Lape, 2010). The Greeks did not think of themselves so much as a race, but a nation and a buffer between Asian Persia and the rest of Europe (Bindman, 2002: 25). It was this idea that the art historian Johann Joachim Winckelman was following when writing on Greek beauty in sculpture and it being part of their intrinsic nature as a 'nation' (Bindman, 2002: 90–1). David Bindman has shown how many eighteenth-century writers on aesthetics defined beauty by racial type or features, often unwittingly leading to the creation of racial hierarchies that positioned the European face of the *Apollo Belvedere* at the top of a physical ideal and the 'negro' at the bottom (Bindman, 2002). The ideal of Greek sculpture, the perception of it as ethnically based and the adulation of ancient Greek culture more generally was part of later nineteenth-century efforts at social and cultural self-definition within Europe (Donohue, 2005: 100). Such self-definitions include, for example, the philosopher Georg Hegel praising the whiteness and purity of Greek sculpture or emphasizing that only 'true' history took place when certain 'advanced' political conditions (based on those in Europe) were present (Pluciennik, 2006: 3). There is no doubt that Romantic Classicism in the late eighteenth and early nineteenth centuries played a part in forming European national, cultural and racial self-definition.

In the 1770s and 1780s, the Swiss clergyman and poet Johann Casper Lavater rediscovered physiognomy, which was based on work by classical authors such as Aristotle, and created an anthology of facial types in silhouette that purported to show inward behaviours and emotions (Swain, 2007). Lavater reinforced the ideas that the skull and the face indicated hidden tendencies that could be measured, which heavily influenced nineteenth- and twentieth-century racial theory. These profiles were different to Winckelmann's Greek ideal and Lavater's anthology of facial types created a 'nexus of racial and visual typology' (Bindman, 2002: 123). Lavater was impressed by the idea of the 'facial angle' that had been created by the Dutch physician and anatomist Petrus Camper and used it to measure against his facial profiles (Meijer, 1999: 116). Camper's facial angle showed the profiles and angles of the forehead, brow, nose, mouth and chin of different faces, most notably comparing the face of the ancient Greek Apollo to that of a Black African. Camper's aim was to illustrate the similarity of the races as he was a monogenecist, that is, he believed that all races were part of one human species, and an anti-slave trade campaigner. However, Camper's angle, as is shown in Chapter 1, was later used by racial scientists to illustrate difference and make parallels between Black Africans and great apes (Meijer, 1999: 139–44).

Camper's angle- or scale-reinforced Eurocentric ideals of beauty as presenting the face of the *Apollo Belvedere* as the universal ideal (Bindman, 2002: 209). Johann Friedrich Blumenbach had proposed five different types of humans in 1776 in *On the Genesis of the Native Varieties of Humans*: Caucasian, Mongol, Ethiopian, American and Malayan. Blumenbach based his studies on facial differences and skull measurements. He defined Caucasian as people west of the Caucasus mountains and based them on what he considered to be the most beautiful skull shape (and thus face) – the Circassian Georgian (Meijer, 1999: 169). In addition, he contended that the Jewish type could be recognized by their features and peculiar skull shape. Blumenbach's influential idea was a forerunner of anti-Semitism as a scientific practice, as we shall see in Chapter 6 (Carcos, 2005: 47–8). By the time the anatomist Georges Cuvier reinterpreted Camper's angle, it was being used to determine cranium size for humans and animals. The cranial size was considered to reflect 'the development of internal faculties under self control' (Meijer, 1999: 175). Racial difference and hierarchy was considered to be based on scientific observations and analysis by the 1820s and 1830s, of which Dr Robert Knox, as we shall see in Chapter 1, considered himself to be playing an important part. It is into these traditions and history of creating a science of race that the eugenic thinking of Francis Galton and Flinders Petrie is positioned.

Reading and breeding the face

In the early nineteenth century, Franz Joseph Gall and his student Johann Gaspar Spurzheim became famous for applying the physiognomic principles of Lavater to reading inherent moral traits of the heads of individuals. Often crudely termed 'bump reading', the practice of phrenology had a sensationally successful and popular period in the 1810s to 1830s (Kemp and Wallace, 2000: 111). George Coombe and his brother Andrew, both physicians, established a leading phrenological society in Edinburgh. The involvement of George Coombe with the American skull collector and racial theorist Samuel Morton is briefly considered in Chapter 1. As a result of phrenology and its physiognomic principles, casts of heads of notable individuals and death masks of criminals were collected. Such a collection exists as a sub-section of the Galton Collection at UCL; the Noel Collection of casts and busts dates from the early 1800s and was given to Francis Galton later in the century (Cowling, 1989: 286). Although, phrenology was scientifically derided by the end of the nineteenth century, collecting casts, skulls and head measurements of people was not. Old Melbourne Gaol Museum in Australia still displays plaster casts taken from executed prisoners, including that of Ned Kelly who was executed in 1880. The interest in the criminal face has been seen as the more 'extreme end of reading the signs' inherent in the face, but it was not the only form of reading the face (Wallace and Kemp, 2000: 122). The idea that characteristics that made people more susceptible to criminal behaviour could be read in the face was only part of the widespread use of physiognomy in the nineteenth century.

Physiognomy is reading the face and determining what peoples' facial features are and what these features say about their personality. It was common practice to refer to physiognomy throughout the nineteenth century, whether as a passing comment and can be widely seen in written works – particularly in 'setting up' characters in novels – and 'suggests a mode of perception which is peculiarly remote from our own' (Cowling, 1989: 9). (Yet, in many ways the idea that deviant behaviour can be read in the face and facial expression has never entirely evaporated, as any scan of stories about crime in newspapers demonstrates.) Art and literature of the period used facial and physical descriptions and it is today impossible for us to recover the same 'appreciation of their meaning' (Cowling, 1989: 5). This anthropological physiognomy was applied everywhere and was behind the creation of the enormous crowd scenes by painters, such as W. P. Frith for example, as we shall see in Chapters 2 and 3. At the same time as the idea that race could be scientifically identified, the importance and utility of reading the face was emphasized. Race was interwoven with social class and the term 'type' was 'loosely interchangeable with race, species, variety' all of which were given a physiognomic basis (Cowling, 1989: 184). The face could be seen or read as a series of signs that pointed from physical characteristics to combined moral, racial and intellectual traits.

It is these ideas – physiognomic, aesthetic ideals and European cultural self-definition – that founded the basis on which Francis Galton predicated eugenics rather than anything in the ancient world, as we shall see in Chapters 2 and Chapter 3. Plato and Aristotle, among others, articulated practices that might be described as 'eugenic', or breeding and preserving the 'best type' of people, but Galton never mentions these classical antecedents (Galton, 1998). There have been various major studies of eugenics and its legacy in Europe and America and the influence of race science on physiognomic prejudices and supposed intelligence tests (Gould, 1981; Kevles, 1995). Racial science has too often been ignored or dismissed as 'pseudo scientific' and therefore unworthy of notice. Saul Dubow argues that:

> Moreover, to dismiss racial science as bogus is to suggest that it was somehow peripheral to mainstream investigation. This assumption is often misleading [. . .] eugenics can be seen in some respects as a forerunner of modern genetics – no matter that many of its key premises and unwarranted assumptions have since been shown to be misguided or reprehensible. It should also be remembered that many racial scientists were prominent intellectuals who occupied influential positions and generally conformed to the accepted standards of academic rigour of the day. (Dubow, 1995: 3)

In his study, Dubow illustrates the intellectual and practical impact of scientific racism on the peoples of South Africa and how this is linked to racial thinking and eugenic practices elsewhere. Both Robert Knox and Francis Galton developed their racist ideas while in southern Africa and clearly the diverse mixture of different peoples there influenced their thinking. Britain never enacted the programmes of sterilization that were carried out in some states of the United States, Australia, South Africa and European countries, including Norway, Denmark, Germany and Sweden, which, for example, sterilized about 60,000 young women deemed 'mentally defective' between 1935 and 1976 (Galton, 1998: 266). The success of the eugenics movement in Britain was more social than legislative and can be measured by the 'way in which eugenic ideas of decay, degeneration, struggle and selection pervaded social and cultural life in this [Edwardian and Interwar] period' (Stone, 2002: 100). It was a movement that Galton created and Petrie advocated.

Genetics, as Dubow points out, is in some ways a product of eugenic science, yet also different since it is based on the study of the formulation of genetic codes and the human genome. This is not to say that genetic medicine and practice is not controversial. It is one of the most ethically fraught areas in science today, partly due to the legacy of eugenics and decisions around the transmission of disease within families and the stimulation of cells in molecular genetics for gene therapies (Galton and Galton, 1998). The study of environmental changes that have long-term biological consequences on individuals, families and communities is a fairly recent form of genetic study and has been termed epigenetics (Carey, 2011: 6–7). Gathering the statistical and environmental evidence for epigenetics (not the cellular genetic evidence) has some precursors with the evidence that Karl Pearson and his assistants collected at the Eugenics Records Office during the late nineteenth and early twentieth centuries, as we shall see in Chapters 8 and 9. Interestingly the main popular book on the subject, Nessa Carey's *The Epigenetics Revolution,* makes no mention of Francis Galton, Karl Pearson or eugenics. The most accessible book on elucidating the differences, scientific and cultural, between genetics and eugenics as well as bringing the ethical dilemmas relatively up to date is still Steve Jones' *The Language of Genes* (1994). People still read faces, we do it all the time, but hopefully we apply less derogatory value judgements in our readings.

Exhibiting eugenic thinking

Eugenics and its legacy is a difficult subject to address. The decisions I made in curating *Typecast* during the 2011 Galton Centenary at UCL were influenced by approaches to 'challenging history' and guidance from within the museum and heritage sector (Kidd, 2011). In addition, as McEnroe mentions in the 'Foreword', I was assisted by a small team of librarians, academics and curators from within UCL. Ultimately I decided to eschew the constructivist approach I had intended to make to the exhibition – giving all or a variety of audiences a voice – as I realized there was a risk of repeating prejudice (Sandell, 2007: 78). A focus group participant pointed out that it was also unfair for me to ask others leading questions on eugenics while not putting my own views forward or admitting my own prejudices. I therefore decided to present my research and ideas in a more traditional academic manner, while making the step of identifying myself as curator. This identification was to try to make the point that mine was just one voice and many others were affected by the legacy that Galton's and Petrie's ideas had. The exhibition and events programme asked leading questions about museum history and practice and about what people thought, with opportunities for feedback.

There have been other exhibitions on eugenics. *Deadly Medicine: Creating the Master Race* is a touring exhibition by the United States Holocaust Memorial Museum about the application of eugenics and medical experimentation by the Nazis from 1933 to 1945. A 2005 exhibition in California, *Human Plants, Human Harvest: The Hidden History of California Eugenics,* directly addressed the sterilization of over 20,000 people in the US state and, though the State Governor apologized to the victims, the exhibition's message was downplayed by the political authorities (Brave and Sylva, 2007). McEnroe details in the 'Foreword' to this book that there was a feeling among the group of UCL staff that the Galton Centenary should both draw attention to the achievements of this extraordinary scientist as well as address his ideas in eugenics and racial science. There were two exhibitions at UCL. As well as *Typecast* in the Petrie Museum of Egyptian Archaeology, *An Enquiring Mind: Francis Galton 1822–1911* was on display in the Main Library at UCL. This was an overview of Galton the man and scientist. Alongside this exhibition were a series of talks, a 'stand-up' lecture by writer Dan Maier (at UCL and at the National Portrait Gallery) and we decided to publish the fragments of Galton's unpublished novel *The Eugenic College of Kantsaywhere.* In 1910 Galton had written this novel about a professor of statistics, I. Donoghue, who is stranded on an island on which eugenic living is practised and combines science fiction and Utopian fantasy in a manner not unlike H. G. Wells. He sent it to his publisher, who rejected it for publication, and shortly before his death Galton gave directions for it to be destroyed. His niece Millicent cut out offending passages – mainly the views on sexual relations – and it was feared that the novel could damage Galton's reputation. Publishing *Kantsaywhere* today raised very different concerns, not least that by publishing it we approved of eugenics and made content available that groups with racially prejudiced ideas could use to vindicate their opinions. We therefore asked writer and broadcaster Matthew Sweet to write an introduction positioning the novel in social and political context. Sweet described eugenics as one of the most 'toxic' words in the English language, but also drew attention to the long-term and overlooked implications of eugenics in British society (Sweet, 2011). The publication of Galton's novel was picked up online by so-called race realists, whose websites I shall not flatter by listing, which further positioned it within the late nineteenth- and early twentieth-century literature of 'white crisis' (Bonnett, 2008: 18–19).

The decision to explore Galton and eugenic thinking through Galton's relationship with Petrie was not entirely new as it had been considered in studies by academics before (Silbermann, 1999; Sheppard, 2010). However, *Typecast* and this book is a more thorough exploration of Petrie's relationship with Galton. *Archaeology of Race* draws on the content in the exhibition to consider the position of race science in Britain; Galton's (and others') early thinking on inheritance and race improvement; how Petrie's relationship with Galton was formed; how it developed; the scientific and anthropological societies or networks to which they belonged; and the social context of the time, through reference to literary, artistic and political developments. It also investigates how race and face analysis informed the reading of archaeological evidence through examples of objects in the Petrie Museum. The approach taken by myself in this book, and my colleagues at UCL during the Galton Centenary, is that museum ethics is not about protecting institutions from contentious or damaging histories, but about embracing 'radical transparency' (Marstine, 2011: 14). This 'radical transparency' is equally applied when possible to practical museum processes; conversations between myself and museum colleagues (mainly with Stephen Quirke, the museum's curator) are occasionally referenced. This transparency is not radical but forms part of our, as I believe, responsibility to the different audiences that the Petrie Museum serves. The museum staff and UCL are responsible for the preservation of and access to a collection from a different culture and time period to that of twenty-first-century Britain. The way in which the collection was formed and the ideas surrounding that formation are important not just to the history of archaeology or museums, but to how all of us comprehend it today.

Egypt in museums

In recent years there have been a number of exhibitions addressing 'hidden histories' and contentious issues found in objects stored in museums and institutions. One of the most recent, at the time of writing this book (2012), was *L'invention du sauvage. Exhibitions* at the Musée du quai Branly in Paris. *L'Invention* considered how ideas of race and 'otherness', around physical disability for example, were formed and the role of race science in this (Planchard, Boetsch and Snoep, 2011). The spectacle of looking at how people were looked at was saved from becoming like the 'freak shows' the exhibition problematized through various audio–visual interventions recording visitor comments, or giving alternative points of view. In one section, the gallery had mirrors surrounding the images of people being exhibited so that the observers were themselves being observed. *L'Invention* detailed how anthropological museums, medical collections and academic archives were built from the display of actual human beings in zoo-like conditions and the ethical legacy of this, as well as how attitudes to difference have been formed. *Archaeology of Race* refers, on the whole, to a small part of the collection of objects from ancient Egypt excavated or acquired by Flinders Petrie and now in the Petrie Museum. This study therefore touches upon a number of key issues involved in the display of archaeological objects and Egyptian antiquities. I have highlighted a few here rather than in the main text of the chapters.

The main issue where attitudes have dramatically changed in the last few decades is to the display of human remains. The passing of the Human Tissue Act in 2004 and the release of Guidance on the Care of Human Remains for museums by the Department of Culture, Media and Sport (DCMS) in 2005 reflected changes around perceptions of human remains in museum, both within the museum profession and among visitors. The ethical treatment of human remains in museum collections has been highly important for decades, especially since first nation groups in Canada, America, Australia and New Zealand challenged the storage and display of their ancestors' remains in museums and other institutional collections across the world. Museums in Britain have made reparation of the remains of people, usually to their successors or kin, from indigenous groups. These usually relate to groups of people external to Britain and whose land may have been colonized or governed within the British Empire. A notable exception to this is the case of Charles Byrne, the so-called Irish giant, who is on display in the collections of the Hunterian Museum at the Royal College of Surgeons, London. The Royal College of Surgeons is also where the head of Flinders Petrie is stored, as we shall see in Chapter 10. Byrne's skeleton played a part in linking acromegaly with the pituitary gland and so understanding why 'gigantism' occurred. Byrne had been a performer who, apparently, did not want to continue being exhibiting after his death in 1783 and is said to have asked to be buried at sea. The surgeon John Hunter managed to acquire Byrne's body and his skeleton is still on display today. Byrne's skeleton has clearly been beneficial to the cause of medical science, but its continuing benefit is now disputed and there have been calls for his body to be given the burial he, apparently, requested (Doyal and Muinzer, 2011).

The case of Charles Byrne is a complex one, not least due to the lack of documentation about what his actual request was. At first the same ethical issues do not appear to apply to archaeological collections yet, as Mary M. Brooks and Claire Rumsey point out, both the Human Tissue Act and the DCMS Guidance reference ancient human remains, albeit with less detail (Brooks and Rumsey, 2007: 346). Before this guidance was issued the Petrie Museum put on a touring exhibition, *Digging for Dreams* in 2001, in which visitors were asked and given a choice as to whether or not they wanted lift shrouds covering mummified, or desiccated, remains (Brooks and Rumsey, 2007: 350). Tiffany Jenkins has been extremely critical of this new approach to human remains in museums. Jenkins, with particular reference to an experimental approach to covering up Egyptian mummies in the Manchester Museum during 2008, argues that it is the case of museum professionals attempting to change public attitudes and address public concerns that, for the majority, are non-existent:

> This attempt to extend the problem to uncontested human remains is an example of how certain professionals in the museum sector continue to try and target human remains as an issue. However, there were important limits to their success in doing this. In this instance the lack of claims-making group to support their actions, strong professional and firm and publicized negative public reaction to the act of covering up the remains, halted their attempts to problematize these particular human remains. (Jenkins, 2011: 129)

In fact, much of the concern around displaying ancient Egyptian human remains has come from some Egyptologists, who have pointed for the need for greater respect for the bodies due to the importance the ancient Egyptians placed on the body and the religious practices involved in protecting the body from desecration (Alberti, Bienkowski and Chapman, 2009: 140–1). A workshop at the Petrie Museum on 'How do we display human remains with respect?' in 2011 heard that visitor feedback at the Petrie Museum and the Grant Museum of Zoology, UCL, as well as in exhibitions at the Museum of London, seems to be fairly split about the display of human remains, but generally agree for the need for 'respect'.

The issue regarding human remains in this book is more to do with the nature of the collection of a particular of the body: skulls. Chapters 5 and 8 consider why skulls were removed from mummies or burials and how this related to eugenic thinking. Ann Fabian has written on the use of skulls by racial scientists in the United States during the nineteenth century and beyond (Fabian, 2010). Fabian's book usefully considers the reasons for skull collecting and the political implications of this practice, as well as the emotional and ethical consequences for the people involved. Petrie collected skulls for the Eugenics Record Office in order to add data from ancient 'races' to their records. This collection is no longer in UCL but has been used in recent studies on ancient disease, and so is clearly useful. However, the collection of these skulls, their previous and current use needs further research. The ethical dilemma, that was explored in *Typecast* and needs further work beyond this book, is around the intended use of the skulls at the time of collection and their value to science today more than the display of human remains in museums.

Part of the *Europe* exhibition in Copenhagen explored 'The white man's burden' and the idea that Europeans brought 'civilization' to the rest of the world, while colonizing territories in Africa, Asia and Latin America and controlling their natural resources. The Petrie Museum's history is bound up with Britain's colonial history, as is the case with many museums containing archaeological and/or anthropological objects. Flinders Petrie went to Egypt just before the British sent an army there, bombed Alexandria from their naval ships and established a 'Protectorate'. This book touches on the use of eugenic thinking in imperial assumptions and how the sense of the 'white man's right to rule' was established in scientific societies and disciplines. The hierarchy of races postulated in the eighteenth century translated into a 'right to rule' during the nineteenth century. Petrie himself had a great respect for many of his Egyptian workers and relied heavily on a number of individuals, such as Ali Jabri, whom we encounter in Chapter 3 (Quirke, 2010). However, Petrie believed that there were limits to what modern Egyptians could do intellectually, as we shall see in Chapter 8. Donald Reid has shown how the control of Egypt by France and Britain, both before and particularly after the British protectorate in 1882, effectively stopped Egyptians from learning about their own heritage and being formerly trained as archaeologists and Egyptologists themselves (Reid, 2002: 172–212). In addition, Paul Sedra has critiqued both Petrie's *Social Life in Ancient Egypt* (1923) and *The Making of Egypt* (1939) and shown how these works were bound up in Petrie's imperial and racial ideals about 'head' and 'hand' workers (Sedra, 2004).

This book concentrates on Petrie's eugenic thinking as applied to archaeology and British society, but he was part of a scientific community that justified imperialism and, within colonized countries, the restriction of educational and other human rights on the grounds of racial science. At the time of writing this book, Egypt is on the brink of change after the 'Arab Spring' of 2011 and it is chastening to reflect on the role of Britain and Egyptology in the long history of repression in that country. Stephen Quirke argued in his inaugural lecture as Edwards Professor of Egyptian Archaeology, the latest successor to Petrie, that in order to properly judge objects from ancient Egypt, connection needs to be made to and with the right environment. He suggested that we [Egyptologists and other academics in the West] need to 'turn ourselves inside out' in order to get at the missing histories and names of people in Egypt, ancient and modern (Quirke, 2012). Museums that preserve ancient Egyptian objects need to reflect and be responsive to the multiple voices, visions and needs of Egypt itself.

A problem with examining the history of nineteenth-century personalities through exhibitions for contemporary audiences can be briefly summed up with the word 'ego'. Galton and Petrie clearly thought that they were near perfect examples of humanity. Their ideas about genealogy and kinship only further enhanced this point of view, as Chapter 2 and 3 illustrate. In many ways, both Petrie's eugenic manifesto *Janus* and Galton's eugenic novel *Kantsaywhere* are about them. The memoirs of the philologist A. H. Sayce, considered in Chapter 6, display a similar lack of modesty. Understanding this sense of ego is important for understanding Galton, Petrie and eugenic thinking. It is necessary to believe in yourself as belonging to the top of the social, racial and intellectual hierarchy if you advocate the 'right to rule' and the ability to direct peoples' behaviour. *Archaeology of Race* seeks to understand this way of thinking not to make either Petrie or Galton into villains (Sheppard, 2010: 29 and Afterword). This book points to a number of Galton's and Petrie's contemporaries that had parallel ideas about race and a recent study has similarly considered the work of the Egyptologist James Henry Breasted (Ambridge, 2012). Although both Galton and Petrie lived into the twentieth century, their lives, work and ideas need to be considered within the context of the nineteenth-century obsession with 'great men' and heroes as exemplified with the work of Thomas Carlyle and the establishment of the National Portrait Gallery in 1856.

The end: 1911

There are references to the period and events beyond 1911. When eugenics and race science are considered, there is an immediate connection to the activities of the National Socialist government in Germany around 'race improvement' during the 1930s, followed by their persecution and genocide of Jews, Gypsies and other groups of people during World War Two. A review of *Typecast* in the magazine *Minerva* finished with reference to the role of eugenics in the Holocaust, though I did not reference World War Two or the Nazis at all in the exhibition (Beresford, 2011). My reason for not referencing the Holocaust was in order to focus on eugenics in Britain and not let the legacy of eugenic thinking and race science in British society be overshadowed by the crimes of the Nazis. In 1944, before the horrors of the Death Camps and other activities were widely known, Hannah Arendt pointed out that racism was not peculiarly German:

> If race-thinking were a German invention, as it is now sometimes asserted, then 'German thinking' (whatever that may be) was victorious in many parts of the spiritual world long before the Nazis started their ill fated attempt at world conquest. Hitlerism exercised its strong international and inter-European appeal during the 'thirties' because racism, although a state doctrine only in Germany, had been everywhere a powerful trend in public opinion. [. . .] Racism was neither a new nor a secret weapon, though never before had it been used with this thorough-going consistency. (Arendt, 1944: 36)

Arendt continued by tracing the roots of 'race-thinking' in the eighteenth century across other countries through to the 1940s. Studies of archaeologists, academics and Egyptologists have illustrated their complicity with the Nazi regime and involvement, or at least collusion, with atrocities (Arnold, 1990; Pringle, 2006; Meltzer, 2012; Schneider, 2012).

An object in the Galton Collection illustrates the link between the eugenic thinking advocated by Galton and Petrie and the programmes of the Third Reich. Dr Carole Reeves and myself supervised work by Masters' students Lucy Maxwell, Suzannah Musson, Sarah Stewart, Jessica Talarico and Emily Taylor on a hair colour and texture gauge, a Haarfarbentafel (Galt040) as part of a course in museum studies at UCL. They found that this object was likely to have been collected by Karl Pearson and bought from the German race scientist Eugen Fischer (Maxwell, Musson, Stewart, Talarico and Taylor, 2012). Fischer had established an institute of racial hygiene in Berlin in 1908 and in the same year went to southwest Africa, current day Namibia, where he studied the racial ancestry of a group of mixed-heritage people called the Basters. He later advocated for and carried out sterilization of some of these people. The Haarfarbentafel was one of the objects Fischer designed and had manufactured to help him determine the racial and hereditary characteristics of people. Fischer was later appointed Rector of the Frederick Wilhelm University of Berlin by Hitler in 1933, retiring in 1942, and carried out sterilizations of mixed-heritage people, as well as being linked to the Hadamar Clinic where the murder of the 'incurably sick' was carried out. The work of these Masters' students showed the importance of understanding the history, both intellectual and physical, of objects in collections, particularly around challenging areas of history. This study does not finish in 1911 to avoid the hideous consequences of eugenic thinking. On the contrary. The problem is that these consequences did not finish in 1945. Sterilizations and the impact of 'negative' eugenics continued into the 1970s as the 2011 inquiry on eugenics in the US State of North Carolina illustrated. In 2012, the compensation for victims of this process was shelved in the State, arguably illustrating the continuation of eugenic thinking, or, at the least, an inability to admit the horrific nature of its consequences (Severson, 2012).

The main area covered by *Archaeology of Race* finishes in 1911 with the death of Francis Galton. It is a good place to finish as it is shortly before the outbreak of World War One, after which Britain seems to enter a different historical landscape, both domestically and internationally. The eugenic movement within Britain and elsewhere also changes dramatically. In addition, the role of Egypt in the war and the increase of Egyptian nationalism and political demands for independence alter the situation there and this has an impact on archaeological practice. Kate Sheppard takes the story of certain ideas within race science forward through an examination of diffusionism in the work of Petrie and his assistant Margaret Murray in the 'Afterword'. A further reason to finish this study in 1911 is due to a large blow to inherited political power in Britain. In 1911 the Terms of Parliament Act legislated for the end of the power of the House of Lords, composed of bishops and hereditary peers, to block finance bills passed by the House of Commons, composed of elected representatives. The Act also allowed the Lords to vote against a bill passed by the Commons three successive times, but after that the bill became law anyway despite its third rejection by the Lords and some of the legislation blocked by the Lords is detailed in Chapter 9. The death of Galton, the beginning of the end of hereditary political control, the ascendancy of Petrie as an archaeologist and his involvement in Edwardian politics is a good place to conclude *Archaeology of Race*.

1

Races and Men: 'All Is Race'

A dummy figure of Dr Robert Knox is displayed in the Surgeon's Hall Pathology Museum, part of the Royal College of Surgeons, Edinburgh. It features in the reconstruction of Dr Knox's study from his house, that is nearby at No. 8 Surgeon's Square. This reconstruction includes some of Knox's specimens, his desk, writing tools, violins, a Dutch painting, an engraving of John Barclay and, as described on the museum label, 'two African "Bantu" figures'.

Dr Robert Knox was a conservator in the medical museum from 1825 to 1831 (Figure 1.1). According to his biographer Henry Lonsdale, Knox turned the museum from a 'poor affair' with a collection of medical instruments and collection of about 300 specimens of 'medical deformities' to an important pathology collection that incorporated much of the collection of the surgeon Sir Charles Bell as well as cataloguing what was there and preserving more anatomical specimens (Lonsdale, 1870: 36).

However, Robert Knox is not notorious for his prowess as a museum curator, but rather as the surgeon who received the bodies of the victims from the notorious killers William Burke and William Hare. For about a year, until being charged with murder in October 1828, Burke and Hare brought to Knox's surgery and teaching room their murder victims for dissection. The museum now references this infamous affair as well as mentioning the 'two African "Bantu" figures', which were illustrative of the fact that 'the races of men were of particular interest to the anatomist'. Yet Knox, apparently, did not approve of the collection of human skins or their display (Bates, 2010). The label elaborates on Knox's work on race by quoting from the *Lancet's* obituary for Knox; reference is made to his book *Races of Men* (1850), as the 'impress of a highly original

Figure 1.1 Reconstruction of Robert Knox's Study at No. 8 Surgeon's Square in the Surgeon's Hall Pathology Museum, Royal College of Surgeons Edinburgh. Photograph taken by Debbie Challis, 2008

though very erratic mind, which dares boldly to grapple with long-standing dogmas, and in not a few instances, lays bare their hollowness'. Alongside this quote and text is a photograph of the tombstone which was placed on Knox's formerly unmarked grave in Brockwood Cemetery, Surrey, in 1966.

This first chapter explores Robert Knox's complex and frequently contradictory views on race, antiquity and Egypt as a means of illustrating how racial theory developed during the nineteenth century. Knox was considered an extreme exponent of the separation of different races, particularly with his very negative opinions on 'Jews' and 'Celts'. The Surgeon's Hall reconstruction of Knox's study makes no mention of the racist controversies over Knox's theories, though there has been a good deal of scholarship on Knox and his role in ideas about race in the nineteenth century. A medical museum obviously exhibits human remains, but when I visited Knox's study in 2008, I found the display of the remains of two South African people uncomfortable. The term 'Bantu' was used as a general term for all Black Africans in South Africa, most notoriously by the Apartheid governments. The term replaced 'Kaffir', another derogatory term used in the nineteenth century and by Knox himself, but 'Bantu' has been long regarded as extremely offensive and it is strange to see it used today (even in parentheses). Arguably, these human remains have a very different historical and cultural context to that of medical specimens. Samuel Alberti has described how there is a 'subtle process of objectification' in the movement from 'a person to a thing' in medical museums, though this can often be complicated by traces of identity that are distinct (Alberti, 2011: 100–1). Given the content and history of Robert Knox's work, the function of these people within the display and their distinct identities should make the creation of them as objects more complicated than usual.

However, in many ways, the Surgeon's Hall display must be considered in the context of the mixed response to Knox among historians. Some historians of the history of medicine, such as Andrew S. Currie, considered Knox to be a 'martyr' to the cause of anatomy with little support from the University of Edinburgh and Royal College of Surgeons (Currie, 1932). In 1966, there was a campaign for a proper memorial stone for Knox so that his importance as an anatomist would be recognized. This view of Knox is influenced by the feeling that he was a scapegoat in the 'Burke and Hare affair' and a victim of out of date legislation around the use of bodies for dissection. The Surgeon's Hall Museum appears to reflect the view that Knox was an overlooked martyr to the cause of medical reform. On the other hand, the historian Ruth Richardson has pointed to Knox's culpability in the 'Burke and Hare affair', albeit in the context of the problems of acquiring bodies for dissection and against the backdrop of a parliamentary enquiry and the 1832 Anatomy Act (Richardson, 1987). Maclaren recognized the problems with Knox's racial theories that had come from his study of the indigenous races of South Africa, while pointing out the contradictions within his ideas:

> Quite apart from their lack of scientific validity, these theories might be held to be almost as obnoxious as the racial theories of Nazi Germany or the socio-political concept of Apartheid. On the other hand, it is likely that those who would most vehemently object to Knox's view of the ethnic inferiority of the African peoples, would applaud his strongly expressed condemnation of the effects of European colonialism upon Africa. (Maclaren, 2000: 39)

Elsewhere, Douglas A. Lorimer feels that there is too much focus on Robert Knox and his legacy and not enough on other contemporary racial theorists; arguing that 'we need to be wary of the tired game of intellectual history in which we try to trace commonplace ideas to specific authors' (Lorimer, 1997: 218). Other historians have written about Knox's contribution to comparative anatomy, his politically Radical ideas and how this connected to his racist philosophy (Biddiss, 1976; Richards, 1989; Young, 2008). While recognizing the validity of Lorimer's concerns about giving Knox too much importance for articulating ideas and assumptions already circulating in certain intellectual and medical circles, I contend that a nuanced understanding of Knox is important mainly because he brought these ideas and assumptions to a wider public audience.

My troubled reaction to the reconstruction of Dr Knox's study at the Surgeon's Hall Museum has made me reconsider issues with the wider public understanding of Knox today and how his racial ideas had an impact on the people he wrote about. The recent *Burke and Hare* film (2010), starring actors Simon Pegg and Andy Serkis with Tom Wilkinson as Doctor Robert Knox, played the gruesome story of the murders for dissection for laughs. The questionable taste of portraying the murder of a dozen people in this way was not assisted by the fact that the film was one of the dullest and least funny I have ever seen. Knox is either played for laughs, as in a 2004 Doctor Who spin off CD *Medicinal Purposes* in which he is played by actor Leslie Phillips, or as profoundly sinister, Knox is said to be the inspiration of the character of Dr Thomas Potter in Matthew Kneale's novel *English Passengers* (2000). None of these twenty-first century popular characterizations adequately addresses Knox or his legacy.

The way in which Knox broadcast his views, and their later publication, is crucial for understanding their wider circulation. He also spoke in a period when attitudes to ideas about race shifted sharply. Knox's views around race were seemingly contradictory and an exploration of his work sums up the difficulty of assessing characters from a different era with cultural attitudes that can easily be misread. In the context of understanding Francis Galton's and Flinders Petrie's ideas about race and antiquity, it is pertinent to understand Knox's focus on defining race in antiquity and his use of monuments and sculpture from ancient Egypt and Greece in assessing racial attributes. Knox was a generation older than Galton and two to Petrie and neither shared his Radical politics or background in medical science and comparative anatomy, though Galton began in that direction. Few archaeologists and anthropologists in the 1880s and 1890s directly attributed their ideas to Knox, but his influence on what became the Anthropological Institute was profound. Knox's emphasis on the importance of both material culture and of ancient Egypt permeated archaeology, anthropology and racial science during the nineteenth century. Furthermore, Knox placed great emphasis on reading race through the face, an idea that was central to Petrie's interest in racial types and ancient portraiture.

Robert Knox: Biographical sketch

Michael Biddiss draws attention to the complicated nature of Robert Knox's character and writing (Biddiss, 1976). Biddiss points out that there were three curiosities about Knox's thinking on race; first Knox 'propounded a racism with substantial traces of benevolence':

> The second is the high degree of systematization to which his racism aspires. Finally there is the fact that his contribution, developing between 1825 and 1850, comes remarkably early in the history of any fully fledged European racist philosophy. (Biddiss, 1976: 245)

In essence Knox was a 'savage Radical', the description used by the *Medical Times* to describe him in his obituary. This meant that Knox was a Radical as regards politics and highly critical of the political establishment. A position that was not unusual among scientific or literary men in the 1810s and 1820s, particularly in Scotland, in the midst of an economic recession following the end of the Napoleonic Wars (Lenman, 2009). He was an atheist, and publicly scathing about Christianity and the power of the Church, whether Established or 'Dissenting'. Knox's opinions were uncompromisingly Radical, and included fiercely anti-slavery and anti-colonial views. Later disciples of Knox's writings around race frequently ignored these forcefully argued aspects of his work.

Robert Knox was born in 1791 in Edinburgh, Scotland. He studied medicine at the University of Edinburgh and undertook further studies in surgery at St Bartholomew's Hospital in London. He became an assistant surgeon in the army and was stationed in Brussels after Waterloo. During the Cape Frontier

Wars (1817–20), he acted as army surgeon at Cape of Good Hope in South Africa. It is widely believed that his interest in ethnography developed while he was in South Africa; though a dispute, possibly to do with his anti-colonial beliefs, led him to leave the army and return to Europe. Knox spent the year 1821 studying in Paris with leading French anatomists and surgeons, Georges Cuvier, Cuvier's rival Étienne Geoffroy Saint-Hillaire, and Dominique-Jean Larrey. Cuvier also applied ideas about the 'hierarchy of race' to understanding comparative anatomy. He was opposed to the idea that human beings evolved, in part because the mummies from Egypt showed the same human physique; these ideas can also be found in Knox's theories around race. Saint Hilaire, on the other hand, had described a unity of 'vertebrate body plan' and 'postulated the existence of laws regulating development cross the animal kingdom' (Bates, 2010). Known as Geoffroyan transcendental anatomy, this system considered that animals developed from lower forms through natural laws rather than being created separately. It was also used in politically Radical ideas to argue for progressive self-advancement, regardless of class in society. Anatomy and Zoology appealed to Radicals as these natural laws appeared to erode the established modes of social class and religious beliefs.

Knox resettled in Edinburgh in 1822. The city was one of the world centres of medicine and surgery in the eighteenth century, and attracted medical students and scientists. Although there was competition from London and Glasgow by the beginning of the nineteenth century, it was still a significant city for teaching anatomy (Lawrence, 1988). Significantly, it attracted several figures who were key in the development and promotion of racial theories. Samuel George Morton, later a skull collector and exponent of scientific racism in the United States, partially trained as a doctor in Edinburgh in 1820 (Fabian, 2010: 21). It was also home to the phrenologist George Coombe in the 1820s. His 'science', promoting the 'important materialist premise that the brain was the organ of the mind', led to greater importance being placed upon brain and cranium size. Distinctions were then made between different ethnic groups (Fabian, 2010). In 1828 Coombe published *Constitution of Man*, setting out the 'laws of nature' in phrenology and encapsulating a 'reformers' manual' built around social reform while following the 'natural laws'. Coombe discusses the nature of inheritance and the need to avoid marriages between unsuitable parties, even considering the necessity of legislation to prevent such marriages. David Stack argues that, despite this discussion, Coombe was not a 'proto-eugenicist'. He was conscious that knowledge about inheritance was imperfect and still considered the environment for the mother and child an instrumental factor in intellectual and emotional development (Stack, 2008: 88–9). Coombe may not have been a 'proto-eugenicist' but it is significant that such ideas, particularly those connecting inheritance to facial characteristics, circulated at such an early date.

While in America on a lecture tour in the late 1830s, Coombe assisted Morton with the publication of a key work in racial science, *Crania Americana,* promoting it in both Britain and America (Fabian, 2010: 25). Coombe and Morton differed over slavery but agreed on the essence of a racial hierarchy with White European people at the top and Black African people towards the bottom. Knox held a similar view, additionally pronouncing, like Blumenbach, that specific environments were suitable for the races native to them. Knox went further on slavery, describing the 'Saxons' in America as hypocrites who claimed to be 'nature's democrat – the respecter of law when the law is made by himself' (Knox, 1862: 11). Despite their anti-slavery views, both Coombe's and Knox's ideas were later used by American racial scientists for the maintenance of slave ownership. Although Knox's ideas about reading the face paralleled Coombe's in some respects, Knox dismissed phrenology. It is striking, however, that Knox and Coombe developed related ideas in the same city at roughly the same time and later had similar (mis)readings of their theories.

Knox became notorious when, between 1827 and 1828, the murderers Burke and Hare supplied Knox with the bodies of 16 victims they had suffocated for use in his dissection classes. Knox was later criticized for not noticing marks and blood, indicating murder, on the bodies delivered to him. Yet he applied the observational principles of aesthetics to anatomy even when dissecting. Knox's biographer Henry Lonsdale, who studied with him, describes a class during which the body of Mary Paterson, a prostitute who had been murdered by Burke and Hare in April 1828, was being dissected:

> The body of the girl Paterson could not fail to attract attention by its voluptuous form and beauty, students crowded around the table on which she lay, and artists came to study a model worthy of Phidias and the best Greek art. (Lonsdale, 1870: 101)

Mary Paterson's body had been preserved in whisky for three months. Prior to the dissection, Knox sent for the artist John Osbourne to sketch Paterson as Venus with a 'perfect human figure' (Richardson, 1987: 135). Knox's approach illustrates how anatomists responded to an ideal beauty. Like other anatomists he was influenced by the construction of beauty in Greek sculpture, which was studied for representations of anatomy (Bates, 2011). Greek sculptures had provided models for anatomy for some time. This is pertinently illustrated by William Pink's cast of a flayed man, 'Smugglerious' (a prisoner hanged at Tyburn). Created for the surgeon William Hunter in 1775, the figure was presented in the pose of the famous classical sculpture *The Dying Gaul* (Richardson, 1987: 37–8; Kemp and Wallace, 2000: 87). There were various 'anatomical Venuses' in the form of sculpted Renaissance and Classical Venus, often made from wax with removable parts and organs. Anatomical Venuses could be eroticized by positioning them on beds or in clothing. The point with these objects was the presentation of a dissectible work of art with anatomical perfection, distinguishing them from real corpses (Bates, 2008). In his classroom, Knox turned Mary Paterson into an anatomical Venus from real flesh, adding a particularly eerie edge to his later claim that women with the features of a Greek Venus could regularly be seen walking around London.

The murder of Mary Paterson cast some suspicion on Burke and Hare; a student in the class, who had only recently spent a night with Paterson and could not believe she died of natural causes, sought Burke out. However, the pair continued to murder until 31 October, when the dead body of Mary Docherty was discovered. Only shortly before the pair had murdered 'daft Jamie', removing his head and feet as he was a well-known and popular figure in Edinburgh. The discovery of the murders caused widespread anger. Knox was threatened; crowds hung his effigy to show their anger that only Burke was convicted and hanged for the murders (Hare became a King's Witness and so was acquitted). Knox also became the bogeyman of popular ballads and, though later officially exonerated, his reputation was forever tainted by his involvement with these murders.

Despite his notoriety Knox remained in Edinburgh for a number of years. He was gradually frozen out of university life due to various quarrels and the impact of the anatomy reforms. He resigned from the College of Surgeons in 1831, shortly before the 1832 Anatomy Act was passed that eased the problems for medical practitioners of acquiring bodies for dissection. The Act enabled medical schools to acquire paupers' bodies for classroom use, but the legislation gave control of the anatomy schools to government (local and national) and inadvertently allowed the poor to be targeted for medical purposes. Knox had a difficult personality, which did not assist his tainted profile in Edinburgh, while his radical beliefs about politics and in particular religion offended many. He finally left the city in 1842 and based himself in London from 1846. Evelleen Richards borrows the phrase 'moral anatomy' from Lambert Adolphe Jacques Quetelet's *Sur l'Homme et le développement de ses faculties ou essai de physique sociale* (1835) to describe how Knox applied a form of social dissection to society and culture that was bound up in radical politics and comparative anatomy (Richards, 1989: 373). Knox moved in radical and reformist circles in London and was similar to his fellow Edinburgh doctor Robert Grant in his combination of comparative anatomy with politically Radical ideas. However, unlike Grant, who found a place at University College London, Knox never had full institutional support.

Knox: The lecturer and lectures

Knox's public lectures are an example of the complex nature of Victorian beliefs about race and reflect the events and anxieties of the period. The lectures and the writings Knox produced during this period incorporated a marriage of sculpture analysis and racial theory which influenced later 'scientific' racial literature. They are central in understanding the context out of which Galton and Petrie's racial theories developed. In the late 1840s, Knox embarked on a series of lectures on the races of men to earn a living and to expound on his political beliefs. Knox was unusual in systematically using the term 'race', while other theorists frequently used 'type' or 'breed'. Knox was a polygenist, believing that races were separated into different species in a progressive scale of intellectual and cultural abilities. White European races were at the top of this scale (Biddiss, 1976: 245–50). His lecture series and book *Races of Men* was as much about cultural characteristics as physical ones; in fact, Knox believed the two were intertwined (Young, 2008: 78). He was mainly concerned with European races and did not consider white races to be part of the same group, separating them according to different racial 'types' such as Norman, Celtic, Saxon and Sarmatian (Young, 2008: 83). Knox saw the problems of the day as entirely influenced by conflict between these racial 'types'; for example, he saw the famine and the struggle for nationalism in Ireland as a Celtic versus Saxon conflict. Knox did not think the achievements and arts of antiquity had connections with the peoples who continued to live in those geographical areas. He differentiated between the 'Russ' race, which he identified as living in parts of Russia and the Balkans including modern Greece, and the ancient Greek race; although he considered both to belong to the 'fair races'. He argued that the ancient Greeks were the finest race while 'no fair race was ever sunk so low in the scale of humanity' as the Russ (Knox, 1862: 366) (Figure 1.2).

Knox placed the Saxon at the top of his racial hierarchy and identified the Saxons as still living in parts of Britain (Lowland Scotland, Northern England and parts of Southern England), areas in Germany and Northwest Europe:

> The Scandinavian or Saxon [. . .] was early in Greece, say 3,500 years ago. This race still exists in Switzerland, forming its protestant portion; whilst in Greece, it contributed mainly, no doubt, to the formation of the noblest of

[The modern Greek and the Muscovite, or Sarmatian; both of the Caucasian race ! Mark their resemblance !]

Figure 1.2 Richard Westmacott Jr, 'The modern Greek and the Muscovite, or Sarmatian', Robert Knox, *Races of Men: A Fragment* (1862), p. 44

all men – the statesmen, poets, sculptors, mathematicians, metaphysicians, historians of ancient Greece. But from that land nearly all traces of it have disappeared; so also from Italy. (Knox, 1862: 46–7)

The Saxon race nevertheless were not blameless but were merciless in 'exterminating the coloured man' in South Africa in their attempt at colonialism there and elsewhere in Africa:

A wish to serve Africa forms the excuse for an expedition to the Niger, the real object being the enslaving of the unhappy Negro, dispossessing him of his lands and freedom. I prefer the manly robber to this sneaking, canting hypocrisy, peculiar to modern civilization and to Christian Europe. (Knox, 1862: 43)

Although, Knox considered the Saxons in this context to be merciless and in disharmony with the natural environment, he also thought that 'non-progressed races' in this way reached 'the time appointed for their destruction' (Knox, 1862: 43). He considered the philanthropic mission of the English Ethnographic Society to save Aborigine and first nation people to be pointless. It is therefore unsurprising that some of Knox's work and arguments were later used for conservative and pro-imperial ends from the 1850s and even more so after his death in 1862.

From the mid-1840s Knox gave lectures on the 'races of men' in towns across England, including London, Newcastle, Liverpool and Manchester. He entered a public lecturing culture that attracted thousands of people and publicity in the local press. Knox's lectures on race were later published as *The Races of Men: A Fragment* in 1850. As stated earlier, the ideas in the book are in many ways contradictory and perplexing (Desmond and Moore, 2009: 236). It illustrates 'unsystematic thought' because it is essentially the text of Knox's lectures which he relied on for income (Richards, 1989: 377). The 1830s and 1840s are considered the zenith of popular science lecturing in local institutions and these lectures attracted the growing middle-class population in urban areas (Hewitt, 1996: 75). London's Egyptian Hall and mechanics' institutions around the country were popular lecture venues. Far from dry textbook affairs, these lectures drew on multiple layers of visuality; lecturers donned formal dress and used blackboards and large illustrations to enhance their presentations. Knox was also known to have exhibited people as 'props' in his lectures. On

5 November 1847, the *Liverpool Mercury* reported Robert Knox giving a lecture at the Exeter Hall in London on 'the Bosjemanns or the Bush People of South Africa'. This lecture used two men, two women and a baby that were on display at private exhibition in the Portico Gallery on Bold Street. Knox is described as 'the celebrated lecturer on the human race'. Despite its appearance Knox's use of human 'props' was not uncommon. However, this newspaper notice illustrates both scientific curiosity towards the San people as well as the use of human beings as props in the creation of racial spectacle (Legassick, 2006: 65). Knox later used so-called Aztec children as props in a lecture in 1853, generating a certain amount of controversy by arguing that ancient lineage or blood from 'lost races' could reappear in embryonic development. Knox's use of people as theatrical spectacle to illustrate different races was part of a growing form of popular entertainment.

Science lectures attracted publicity in local press. The *Manchester Times and Gazette* reviewed Knox's fifth lecture at the city's Athenaeum, observing that the talk on beauty in race, given to an audience of between 400 and 500 people, lasted two hours and ten minutes. The paper describes how Knox drew on the work of German art historian Johann Winckelmann to talk about beauty but broadened his definition of beauty beyond youth. He commented that he believed that Greek statues were copies of 'living originals', such as he has himself seen 'among his own pupils':

> Dr Knox concluded with some remarks upon the necessity for spreading throughout the nation copies or originals of the great Grecian sculptures, in order to develop the public taste [. . .] Dr Knox, at the conclusion of his lecture, and frequently during its course, received the warm applause of the audience. ('Dr Knox on the Races of Men', *The Manchester Times and Gazette*, 28 September 1847)

Knox's lectures were not, however, universally applauded. In the summer of 1847, before the Manchester lecture, Knox entered into a lengthy correspondence in the *Manchester Times and Gazette* with 'Toleration', who objected to the anti-Semitic views Knox had expressed.

In 1851 there were approximately 35,000 Jews in England and Wales; with 20,000 in London and, outside the capital city, the largest concentrations were in Liverpool, Manchester and Leeds (Feldman, 1994: 21). 'Toleration' or

'T. T.' objected to Knox coming to Manchester to lecture on race, arguing that Knox was intolerant, his views linked to phrenology and 'devoid of historical explanation'. ('Toleration versus Dr Knox', 18 June 1847). Knox responded with the claim that only the Ancient Greeks were a superior race, he made no claims for others. In his view, there could be no artistic comparison between the *Iliad* and the Old Testament, while it was mainly men of 'mixed' Jewish blood who could take credit for achievements ('Dr Knox Responds to criticism from T. T.', 26 June 1847). Toleration continued his criticism in a letter in early August objecting to the way Knox spoke about the Celtic character as well as Jews. Providing a list of Jews 'who were great men', he argued that Knox's assertions about the Copts in Egypt were 'unhistorical' ('To the Editor of the Manchester Examiner', 3 August 1847). Knox replied shortly before he gave his first lecture in Manchester and repeated his claims, while making assertions about T. T.'s race (clearly not 'Anglo-Saxon') and arguing for the importance of the intertwining of Jewish and Egyptian history. Knox referred to the dispute in his later book, commenting that his views were 'misunderstood and misrepresented by an anonymous writer in the Manchester newspapers' (Knox, 1862: 208). He claimed that he did not denounce Jewish talents and abilities by denying the Jewish people a literature, science and art of their own, but that he did perceive them to be parasitic on other civilizations.

This exchange of views is important for several reasons. It illustrates that not all people in the mid-nineteenth century subscribed to hard line racial beliefs and, moreover, were prepared to object to them. The timing of Knox's lectures and the objections is also politically significant. In 1847, the Jewish Relief Bill was being debated in Parliament at the same time as one of the Members of Parliament for the City of London, Lionel de Rothschild, was unable to take his seat in the House of Commons. Being Jewish, he could not swear the Oath of Allegiance on the Christian Bible. The Liberals, led by Lord John Russell, were attempting to change the Oath's requirements. However, bringing about such a change went against Radical beliefs in retaining a 'Saxon' democracy over a 'Norman' system of law, as well as Conservative precepts forbidding change to the Constitution settlement of 1688–9. As a Radical, Knox feared the takeover of a 'parasitical' race feasting on the achievements of a Saxon civilization (Feldman, 1994: 37). De Rothschild eventually swore on the Old Testament in 1849 but the Parliamentary Oaths Act was not passed until 1866.

David Feldman argues that this debate was, in part, about the idea of the nation and who is part of the nation. An idea that would cause more anxiety with the immigration of Jews from central Europe into the East End of London and elsewhere in the 1880s to 1900s and lead to the first immigration controls in the Aliens Act (1905).

It is clear that Knox felt that the Jews were not part of the Saxon nation of England. His lectures contributed to the general anti-Semitism visible in the illustrated and political press of the time, much of which was aimed at the formerly Jewish, but baptized Christian, Conservative politician Benjamin Disraeli. Even Henry Lonsdale, Knox's hagiographic biographer, is critical of Knox's views on Jews, observing that had he managed to travel and meet Jews in the Middle East, rather than taking his ideas from his observations of the Jewish communities in Shoreditch and Amsterdam, he might have had different ideas (Lonsdale, 1870: 304). Knox would have been well aware of the political ramifications of his ideas on Jewish people and perceptions of Jews in the debates around nationhood that were taking place; he regularly drew on current political events to justify and publicize his views. Knox's lectures were published as 24 articles in the *Medical Times* over the summer of 1848. In them, he applied his theories to the current revolutionary political situations taking place across Europe, predicting future race wars and linking race to the revolutions taking place in the Italian, French and German states. The *Medical Times* announced his articles by saying 'that history during the last six months may be considered as but one continuous advertisement of our course' and that 'the great element of [. . .] European reorganisation is race' (Desmond and Moore, 2009: 190).

Knox's views on Jews are not just extremely anti-Semitic; they are also intertwined with his views on ancient Egypt and Egyptian sculpture. Knox continuously argued in his lectures for the importance of the monumental (archaeological) record for defining race and understanding the achievements of racial groups:

> Again, monumental records, artistic remains, architectural designs, and utilitarian plans, prove beyond all question that the ancient races of men were at least equal, if not superior, to the modern. (Knox, 1862: 189)

Knox was significant not just for his racism but also for placing the plastic arts at the centre of it. Greek sculpture, architecture, Egyptian monuments and statues were all referred to in his lecture series and elsewhere in his published work.

Knox and Egypt

Two of Knox's lectures centred on ancient Egypt in the context of modern Copts and Jewish people. In these he made clear his views on the importance of reading race in the face of ancient sculpture and contemporary people. Knox argued that sculpture and material remains represented racial types in antiquity that could be used to define or interpret racial groups in contemporary Egypt. Knox used illustrations of ancient art throughout his publications and presumably in his lectures too. The published engravings were by the artist and sculptor Richard Westmacott Jr. Art was important to Knox more than simply as an illustration of a physical type; he maintained that material and literary culture was indelibly linked to race (Figure 1.3).

Ancient Greek sculpture was vital, for example, since that was all the evidence that remained of this manifestation of racial greatness, apart from 'points of resemblance between the women of classic Greece and the thorough-bred

[*Apollo; the Greek Profile contrasted with the other extreme of the fair races—the Russ.*]

Figure 1.3 Richard Westmacott Jr, 'Apollo: the Greek profile', Robert Knox, *Races of Men: A Fragment* (1862), p. 368

Saxon women of England, or Holland, or Sweden' (Knox, 1862: 408). Knox contended that examples of ancient Greek beauty could still be seen:

> It was Sir Charles Bell, I think, who said that the grand facial line or angle of the antique Greek could not now be found! Never, I think, was so great an error of observation committed, for the streets of London abound with persons having this identical facial angle; and it is in England and in other countries inhabited by the Saxon or Scandinavian race that women resembling the Niobe, and men the Hercules and Mars are chiefly to be found. (Knox, 1862: 403)

And, as we have seen, with the corpse of Mary Paterson, Knox argued that the modern races of Greece were 'Russ' not 'ancient Greek', while the modern races of Egypt were a 'mixed barbarian and savage race of slaves' (Knox, 1862: 97). Knox contended that civilizations may have developed but race did not change through the ages; there were distinct fixed types that could be seen in the sculpted and painted art of Egypt:

> On the tombs of Egypt, the most valuable of all existing records, there stands the Negro, the Jew and Copt, the Persian, the Sarmatian, nearly as we find them now; this is enough for our purpose. Herodotus says that the Egyptians of his days were black men: very possibly; but neither before nor since his period has this remark been found to be true. (Knox, 1862: 98–9)

Knox asserted that Herodotus was not even in Egypt (Figure 1.4).

He had visited the explorer Belzoni's exhibition of Egyptian statues and other material in 1822–3 and at the time noted that 'neither time nor climate seems to have had any effect on the race'. He elaborated on this idea in his lecture entitled 'Coptic, Jewish and Phoenician races'. Knox thought that of the races in Egypt today the Copt most resembles the ancient Egyptians according to 'the busts still preserved' but is not certain:

> [. . .] the physiognomy of the labourers of ancient Egypt, are represented on the tombs and temples, is not of foreigners, but evidently Coptic. Different races of men are sketched on the walls of the tomb opened by Belzoni, showing that the characteristic distinctions of races were as well marked three thousand years ago as now; the Negro and the other races existed precisely as they are at present. (Knox, 1862: 180)

[The Egyptian Sphynx.]

Figure 1.4 Richard Westmacott Jr, The Egyptian Sphynx', Robert Knox, *Races of Men: A Fragment* (1862), p. 146

Knox used monuments as 'proof' that races remained the same over thousands of years and pointed to similar monuments across the world, making parallels with pyramids in the Central Americas. He argued that they are 'vestiges of a nature not to be doubted, of a thoroughly Egyptian character reappear: hieroglyphics, monolithic temples, pyramids' (Knox, 1862: 182) (Figure 1.5).

He considered who may have erected the buildings, hypothesizing that it could scarcely be the American Indians, yet carvings seem to show Indian physiognomy. Knox is unable to answer his own question, while his comparisons and ideas of a 'travelling race' are not entirely unlike that of some pseudo-archaeological theories today or the early twentieth-century theory of diffusionism (Knox, 1862: 182; Sheppard, Afterword).

Knox also speculated about one of most 'remarkable monuments' the 'Head of the Young Memnon' that he first saw in the Belzoni exhibition and is now in the British Museum. This is now known as the Colossal Head of Ramessess II:

But the land of Egypt still abounds with its ancient monuments; the race was quite peculiar, and was I think, African, or at least allied to the African races. The mouth and lips all but prove this. Nevertheless, their identity

[*The Egyptian Pyramid.*]

Figure 1.5 Richard Westmacott Jr, 'The Egyptian Pyramid', Robert Knox, *Races of Men: A Fragment* (1862), p. 178

with a great section of the present Jewish race cannot be doubted [. . .]. (Knox, 1862: 185–6)

Yet Knox contradicts his previous argument that the Egyptians could not be 'negro'. He discounted the 'barbarous and savage Turk and Arab' from being related to ancient Egyptian but thought that the 'Fellahs or modern Egyptian labourers' may be related, referring to the recent archaeological expedition by Lepsius in the hope that he may 'solve some of these great questions, connecting at least the history of other races with the monumental history of Egypt'. (Knox, 1862: 187)

Knox returned to the 'bust of the young Memnon' when he discussed visiting the 'Jew quarter of modern Amsterdam'. He describes visiting the British Museum shortly before going to Holland and contemplating the bust when a new idea struck him: he has seen the same likeness or physiognomy in Britain among Jews (Figure 1.6).

On arriving in the Jewish quarter of Rotterdam:

Near me, almost within reach, stood a youth about sixteen, and not far from him others, the perfect likeness of the young Memnon [. . .] Thus I learned that originally the ancient Copt and a large section of the Jewish people were one and the same race, with slight differences, however, which the Egyptian sculptor knew how to caricature. (Knox, 1862: 203)

[*Bust of the young Memnon : British Museum.*]

Figure 1.6 Richard Westmacott Jr, 'Bust of the Young Memnon: British Museum', Robert Knox, *Races of Men: A Fragment* (1862), p. 185

Knox thus draws on and contributes to creating physical stereotypes of Jews at a time when Jewish people were increasingly being described as a race or separate 'nation'. He was one of the first to study the physical appearance of Jewish people and his ideas were utilized in the 1860s and 1870s (Cohen, 2002: 76). Knox is even more confused and contradictory on Egypt and the ancient Egyptian race than usual, even Lonsdale says that Knox 'offers nothing tangible or satisfactory; he has his hypothesis around which he weaves a large amount of weft, more coloured than substantial' (Lonsdale, 1870: 302). As we have seen Knox's views on Egypt and Copts were criticized by 'Toleration' in the *Manchester Time and Gazette* for being 'illogical' and having no 'historical basis' whatsoever. Despite this, the idea of a connection between Egypt and the Jews gained currency and clearly attracted interest. The *Manchester Times and Gazette* reported that Knox had written in the *Medical Times* that the 'Coptic portion of the Jewish race may be seen walking our streets, the lineal descendants and facsimile, as to features of the Egyptian busts in the British Museum' (27 June 1848). Knox's ideas foreshadowed the late nineteenth-century anti-Semitism that 'haunts Trollope's Palliser novels' for example, while his interest in Egypt and contradictory ideas about it were reflected in the work of racial scientists in the United States at the same time (Cohen, 2002: 433).

Samuel George Morton, who had worked with Combe, was interested in the collection of Egyptian skulls 'to prove his hunch that humanity had always been divided into racial groups'. In Morton's view, ancient Egypt was as close as modern man could get to the 'dawn of creation' (Fabian, 2010: 105). Thus, Morton commissioned George Gliddon, a merchant and honorary diplomat for America living in Egypt, to collect skulls for his research. Gliddon took his collection on the US lecture circuit in 1842, simultaneously working with Morton on a publication of the skulls, using them to 'bolster arguments about polygenism and the antiquity of racial hierarchy' in *Crania Aegyptiaca. Observations on Egyptian Ethnography derived from Anatomy, History and the Monuments* (1844) (Fabian, 2010: 107). These arguments were buoyed by a wave of Egyptomania in America in the 1840s. Gliddon later worked with J. C. Nott and Louis Agassiz while touring in the Southern states; Gliddon and Nott subsequently produced a 'baggy racist tome' *Types of Mankind; or Ethnographic Researches, Based upon the Ancient Monuments, Painting Sculpture and Crania of Races and upon their Natural, Geographical, Philological and Biblical History* (1855), taking Morton's theories to a new group of readers (Fabian, 2010: 111). These ideas were, of course, rooted in the justification of slavery in America, which Knox entirely opposed. However, they reflected Knox's belief that racial groups were unchanging and his perception that ancient Egypt was essential for understanding race.

Nott and Gliddon's *Types of Mankind* promoted the Greek head as an ideal and used the facial angle of the Dutch anatomist Petrus Camper as evidence for which 'type' of mankind ancient sculptures fitted. The adulation of Greece and the ancient Greek city states was also linked to defending slavery (Malamud,

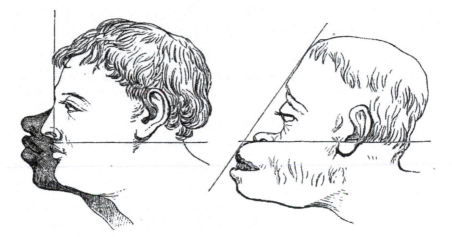

[*Profile of Negro, European, and Oran Outan.*]

Figure 1.7 Richard Westmacott Jr, 'Profile of Negro, European and Orangutan', Robert Knox, *Races of Men: A Fragment* (1862), p. 404

2009: 80). Knox used a version of this facial angle in *Races of Men*, showing the difference between an idealized European profile, based on Apollo Belvedere, 'a negro and an Oran autan' (Figure 1.7).

The most notorious use of Camper's facial angle showed the comparative profiles of the Apollo Belvedere and a Greek skull, an African and a 'skull of a Creole Negro', and a chimpanzee and chimpanzee skull to illustrate that comparative use of skull types indicated different racial types in a hierarchy of difference. This was by no means universally accepted; some British reviews of *Types of Mankind*, such as one published in the *Athenaeum,* thought this view was too extreme (Cowling, 1989: 61). In their preface to *Types of Mankind,* Nott and Gliddon acknowledged Knox's work, reworking his claim that ancient Egyptian monuments showed 'from 3,000 years ago, four distinct species as recorded by Egyptians'. Despite their acknowledgement of Knox's influence, they overthrew the idea that all men are created equal as different races were formed in early history unequally; an argument that Knox thought highly hypocritical.

The interest for racial scientists in Egyptology was due to a 'major emphasis in writing about race in this period that gets placed on the history of black civilizations (particularly, though not exclusively, Egypt)' (Young, 1995: 124).

Nott and Gliddon combined biology and Egyptology for the basis of a new 'scientific' racial theory, as Robert Young argues:

> What is significant is that the academic account of Egypt was not simply influenced and changed because of increased racism and racialism but actually provided the key to the arguments and constituted the proof of racial theory itself. (Young, 1995: 126)

There was, of course, an alternative use of ancient Egypt (and Carthage) by the African–Americans themselves in education and they made connections with ancient African civilizations as part of reclaiming their own African heritage (Malamud, 2011). Morton, Agassiz, Nott and Gliddon demolished these ideas and aspirations of the African–Americans, projecting an ideal of Egypt that reflected their own racist views.

Legacy and racial theory

In Victorian Britain, race was a powerful concept that provoked discussion. In Disraeli's 1847 novel *Tancred,* the character Sidonia, a powerful Jewish figure, exclaimed:

> But England flourishes. Is it what you call civilization that makes England flourish? [. . .] Clearly not. It is her inhabitants that have done this; it is an affair of race. A Saxon voice, protected by an insular position, has stamped its diligent and methodical character on the century. And when a superior race, with a superior race, with a superior idea to work and order, advances, its state will be progressive, and we shall perhaps follow the example. All is race: there is no other truth. (Disraeli, 1847: 169)

This statement in a novel, which is partially about how the 'Asian race' can reinvigorate the European and vice versa, reflected a growing consciousness about race in Victorian society. *Tancred* was published the same year Knox was touring the country with his lecture series. Clearly Knox and Disraeli had very different attitudes to racial construction, miscegenation and colonial politics since *Tancred* seemingly argued for a mingling of Jewish and Saxon races (and values). *Tancred* haunted Disraeli in the 1870s when he was Prime Minister and handling the so-called Eastern Question around territories in Europe, the Middle East and North Africa that were part of the Ottoman Empire. It contributed to depictions of Disraeli as a pharaoh or in Egypt. For example the illustration 'Mose in Egitto', featured in *Punch* on 11 December 1875, showed Disraeli in eastern dress standing in front of the Sphinx who is winking at him holding a key entitled the Suez Canal with a tag attached reading 'The key of India'. Disraeli could never escape his 'Jewishness' despite his assimilation into Christian England. *Tancred* was later used by Disraeli's political opponents to position him as belonging to the 'Jewish race' and protecting the interests of the Orient rather than Christian Europe (Feldman, 1994: 98–9). The cartoon is also an explicit alignment of his supposed Jewishness with Egypt.

Two societies based in London lay at the centre of intense debates about race in the mid nineteenth century. They represented different yet overlapping concepts: monogenesis, a belief that racial types came from the same genetic model, and polygenesis, a belief that the different races were different racial species. Both considered that there were different racial 'types' in a hierarchy at varying stages of progression. The English Ethnographic Society was formed in 1843 (from the Aboriginal Protection Society) and followed monogenesis; while the Anthropological Society was formed in 1863, shortly after Knox's death, as a polygenesistic splinter group from the older society. Knox had become an honorary fellow of the English Ethnographic Society in 1860 where he read a paper on human crania and early civilization. The Anthropological Society was led by Knox's follower the anthropologist James Hunt and was racially deterministic. Hunt regularly invoked Knox's work (Young, 2008: 75). The creation of the Anthropological Society meant that there was wider acceptance of racially deterministic thinking among the Victorian intellectual elite, though 'in general prejudices rather than theories prevailed' (Marsh, 2005: 16). Evelleen Richards has illustrated how the differences between the two groups came to reflect differences between Darwinian followers, the so-called Quaker clique who accepted monogenesis and evolution of one human species, and the more hard line polygenesis and political views of James Hunt. When James Hunt resigned from the Ethnological Society, for example, it was Charles Darwin's cousin Francis Galton who became Honorary Secretary in 1863, despite having only become a member in 1862, while Charles Darwin himself had only become a member in 1861. Both groups, however, 'agreed on a causal relationship between race and civilization and both factions assumed the biocultural inferiority of non-Caucasoids' (Richards, 1989: 416).

The Anthropological Society became increasingly linked to Confederate racial theorists in the United States; the American racial theorist Nott became a member (Desmond and Moore, 2009: 332). It also had an unsavoury reputation, becoming increasingly less respectable due to the behaviour of some of its members – among its detractors, it was known as the 'Cannibal Club' (Richards, 1989: 430). Knox did have 'considerable influence on later thinking' with regard to Anthropological Society and his protégé James Hunt, but ultimately the more Radical elements of his ideas, such as anti-slavery and anti-colonization, were ignored (Young, 1995: 49). Ultimately, by the end of the 1860s, there was central agreement around race between both societies and in 1871, after the death of James Hunt, they reunited as the Anthropological Institute of Great Britain and Ireland. The foundation of this institute was led by key Darwinian figures such as Professor William Flower, John Evans, Thomas Huxley and Francis Galton. Richards argues that 'We may draw a straight line from Knox's "moral anatomy" through Hunt's "anthropology" and on to "social Darwinism" and the "social surgeons" of the eugenics movement' (Richards, 1989: 435). At the heart of Knox's ideas were the use of monuments and material culture from antiquity, in particular Ancient Greece and Egypt, to understand more about race and racial achievements. Knox used these monuments and sculpture to emphasize reading race in the face, whether on sculpture, forms of portraiture and living people. These ideas were accepted within the embryonic disciplines of archaeology and anthropology during the late nineteenth century.

2

Galton and Genius

On a small piece of paper in the Galton Special Collection a shaky f r a n c i s is written between two guiding lines, with the words 'Francis did this when he was two years old' inscribed by the boy's older sister and teacher Adele (Figure 2.1). Galton's family considered him a child prodigy; he was able to write his name by the time he was two and recite Shakespeare at five years. As a child Francis Galton had a prodigious talent, though he did not excel at school, possibly due to illness and falling behind in study. He began to train as a doctor at Birmingham at the age of 16, then went to Kings College London before changing subject to mathematics and attended Trinity College Cambridge. Galton was ill through much of his later studies at Cambridge and appeared to have a nervous breakdown in his final year at university through overwork; this pattern would reoccur through his life. Traditional academic schooling of the period did not suit Galton, as it did not suit his cousin Charles Darwin, who was famously equally miserable at Shrewsbury School and Cambridge.

Today Francis Galton is often known, if known at all, for being Darwin's cousin. The two men shared the grandfather Erasmus Darwin (1731–1802), a famous physician and botanist. Galton's other grandfather was Samuel Galton. Like Erasmus Darwin, Samuel Galton was part of the Birmingham Lunar Society, which brought together scientifically minded men during the eighteenth century. Francis Galton was very interested in and proud of his family achievements and, despite his mixed success in traditional education, he had a sense of inherited ability and talent. The belief in his own inherited ability was echoed by Galton's eugenic disciple Karl Pearson, who published the 'eugenic sources of Galton's talents' as a frontispiece to his edition of

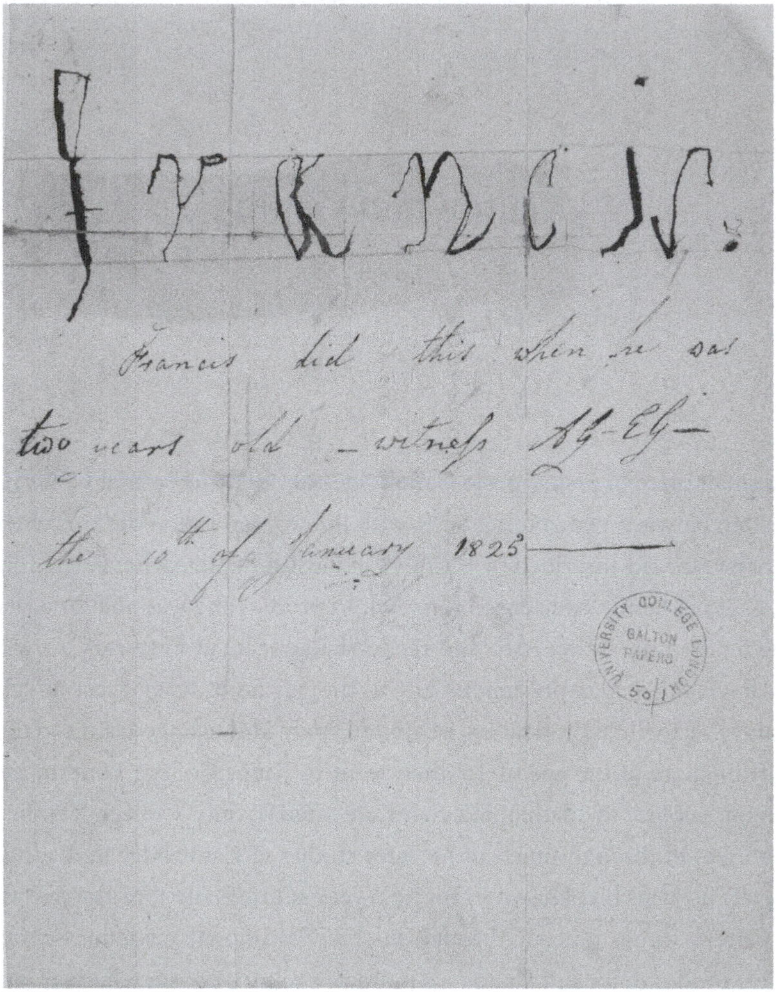

Figure 2.1 'Signature of Francis Galton, age Two', Galton Archive, UCL Special Collections: Galton 50 © UCL Special Collections

Treasury of Human Inheritance in 1912 (Porter, 2004: 276). A portrait of Galton is depicted in the centre of the page under the title 'Sir Francis Galton and some of his noteworthy ancestors' with four ancestors (two male and two female) and their portraits in the corners of the page underneath headings for the qualities they provided. Lucy Barclay (Mrs. Samuel Galton) 1757–1817 provided 'Tenacity, physical and mental' and was 'Descended from the Apologist Barclay, Cameron of Lochiel and James I of Scotland', while her husband Samuel Galton (1753–1832) provided 'Power of Organisation' and was a 'Leader of Industry and Physicist'. Erasmus Darwin provided 'Scientific Imagination' being a 'Physician, Naturalist and Poet', while the Grandmother of Erasmus' wife Catherine Sedley, Countess of Dorchester (1657–1717), a 'court beauty and wit', provided Wit and Literary Power' (Pearson, 1912, frontispiece). This sense of inherited genius no doubt influenced Galton in his studies on heredity and led to the concept of eugenics, which was akin to ancestor worship.

By the time Galton was involved with the Ethnological Society in the 1860s, he had travelled extensively. He journeyed to Egypt, Sudan and the Middle East while a young man in the 1840s, had had a few years' hunting and shooting funded by an inheritance from his father, and explored South West Africa for almost two years in 1850–52. It was this last journey and his travel book *Narrative of an Explorer in Tropical South Africa* (1853) that established Galton's reputation as an explorer and scientist and brought him to public attention. He was awarded the Gold Medal by the Royal Geographical Society (RGS) in 1852, serving on the RGS Council for years afterwards, directly influencing later 'explorations' in Africa as 'there is ample room in Africa for men inclined for adventure to carry out in them, if nowhere else, the métier of explorers' (Galton, 1853: xiii). Like Knox, Galton's interest in race, racial purity and different groups of people seems to have been influenced by his travels in southern Africa and earlier travels down the Nile Valley (Coombe, 1994: 56). However, unlike Knox, Galton wrote little on racial difference as related to ethnic identity within his studies on human heredity (Kevles, 1995: 8).

Galton's *The Art of Travel, or Shifts and Contrivances in Wild Countries* (1855) influenced the whole image of travel and the traveller in regions 'off the beaten track' during the mid-to-late nineteenth century. Compiled from other travellers' accounts, containing practical advice on what to pack, how to pack it, how to carry it (or rather who to carry it) and arcane sartorial details such as how to tuck one's shirt sleeves up, *The Art of Travel* went through eight editions in the nineteenth century with the last in 1893. The contemporary image of Henry Morton Stanley, David Livingstone and other white male travellers, as well as archaeologist explorers such as Austen Henry Layard, owe as much to Galton and his *The Art of Travel* as their own work (Challis, 2008: 6).

Galton became a man of scientific clubs and societies, and he was secretary of the British Association for the Advancement of Science (BAAS) from 1863 to 1867. From its inception in 1831, BAAS was 'keen to disseminate knowledge of science to a large audience' (Yeo, 1981, 72). Its main purpose was to publish papers and hold a large annual conference outside the capital that would bring science to the industrial and provincial towns across Britain with the idea of producing 'scientific workers' (Macleod, 1981, 29). Not needing to work for a living, Galton was able, like Darwin, to spend his time in various scientific pursuits: 'in a sense, the best kind of dilettante – interested in many things dabbling in some, pursuing others with great care, but without the discipline of a professional' (Cowan, 1972: 509). It was in the 1860s, while he was involved in the disputes of the Ethnological and Anthropological Societies and secretary for BAAS, that Galton first became more seriously interested in issues around and consequences of inherited characteristics.

Race relations in the 1860s

The 1860s is considered one of the most significant decades in defining race and racial issues in Britain (Bolt, 1971: 38). A series of events, the Indian Uprising, the American Civil War and the Morant Bay Uprising, ensured that race remained a top priority in current affairs. The aftermath of the Indian Uprising in 1856–57, when tensions between settlers, the East India Company and many Indians of all backgrounds, broke out violently, was still being felt. In the wake of the Uprising, the British government took over the lands governed by the East India Company and established a more formal rule of this vast area as an imperial colony. In doing so, they imposed more rigorous divisions between British and Indian communities. The American Civil War (1861–5), centring on the issue of slavery and the application to African Americans of the First Amendment guaranteeing individual freedom in the United States' constitution, meant that race, equality and slavery was widely discussed in Britain at the same time as it was brutally contested on battlefields across America.

The reprint of Robert Knox's *Races of Men* in 1862 fits into these contemporary events, relating to wars linked to race, land acquisition and the impact of 'Saxon' culture, as Knox defined it, globally. Knox's death shortly after this second edition caused the *Lancet* to comment that he will be 'best remembered for *Races of Men*' ('Obituary: Robert Knox', 3 January 1863). Contemporary publicity on the last remaining Tasmanian Aborigines in the 1860s, after years of murder, resettlement and kidnapping for labour by white settlers, appeared to illustrate that some races would become extinct. Knox had written:

> In Australia it can scarcely be said that an antagonistic race faces them [European races], so miserably sunk is the native population. A ready way too of extinguishing them has been discovered; the Anglo-Saxon has already cleared out Tasmania. It was a cruel, cold blooded, heartless deed. (Knox, 1862: 143)

The Morant Bay Uprising in Jamaica was severely repressed during October 1865 by Governor Edward John Eyre, who had previously earned a reputation in Australia in the 1840s for showing humanity to the plight of Aborigines. Public outrage over the killing and imprisonment of hundreds of people, mainly Black Jamaicans, and the trial and almost immediate hanging of the radical 'coloured' (mixed race) politician George William Gordon led to a Royal Commission into the rebellion and its suppression. The Commission was critical of Eyre and he was dismissed. Two groups were formed: the Jamaica Committee, which attempted to bring Eyre to trial for murder, and the Eyre Defence Committee, which defended Eyre's actions in the name of the British Empire. The Jamaica Committee was mainly composed of Radical liberals and evangelical philanthropists and from 1866 was led by John Stuart Mill with subscribers including Charles Lyell, Charles Darwin, Thomas Huxley, Henry Fawcett, Thomas Hughes and Herbert Spencer. The Eyre Defence Committee was sustained by subscriptions from the literary world, reflecting the views of Tory and Tory Socialists such as Thomas Carlyle, John Ruskin, Charles Kingsley, Charles Dickens and Alfred Tennyson (Kostal, 2004). This controversy rumbled on for several years and 'brought colonial matters to the forefront of public debate' as well as attitudes to race and the right to rule (Heuman, 2004). It also illustrated that there were no fixed ideas around colonialism or racial hierarchies, but a distinct interest in such issues among intellectuals at this time.

At the end of this decade Thomas Huxley became President of the Ethnological Society, starting a project to photograph all the races of the British Empire via different colonial offices and officials using a controlled method of photography. Colonial officials were given instructions on how to take the images, what poses were appropriate as well as what measuring devices to use. The face and the body were formally positioned as the crucial means of determining racial difference. The public spectacle of looking at different groups of people from across the globe had been popular since the mid-eighteenth century (and previously in royal and courtly circles). In the mid-nineteenth century this spectacle could be seen in 'scientific' and educational discourses through the use of displaying peoples in lectures and at exhibitions. For example, in 1853 at the newly enlarged Crystal Palace, anthropologist Robert Latham developed hand-painted wooden models of the 'varieties of mankind', situating non-European peoples according to developmental theory based on the idea of the 'Great Chain of Being' (Edwards, 2009: 174). Elizabeth Edwards has noted that there were not many photographs sent back that applied this controlled method of taking photographs, while many Colonial Governors were unhappy about taking such images that involved nudity and a process of dehumanization (Edwards, 2001: 131–57). There was clearly a difference between the expectations of London scientific society and local official attitudes across the Empire.

There is no doubt that Huxley's project was informed by the events of the 1860s. The debates on whether all groups of people were equal, in both an evolutionary sense and a political one, was also played out in the conflict between the Anthropological Institute and the Ethnological Society. The controlled use of photographs to define people and their features was an area to which Francis Galton returned shortly after Huxley's project. In 1870, Huxley published his arguments on race, defining five races: (1) Australoid; (2) Negroid; (3) Xanthchroid ('fair whites of Europe'); (4) Melanochroid ('dark whites of Europe, North Africa, Asia Minor, Irish, Spaniards and Arabs'); (5) Mongloid (people of Asia, Polynesia and the Americas'). Huxley supplied physical descriptions of these races and positioned them in a map across the world, but did not place them in a hierarchy as Galton had done in *Hereditary Genius* a year earlier (Huxley, 1870). The eighteenth-century idea that races were formed by climate and geography was still influential. However, it soon became intertwined with class and Galton's grading of different types of people according to intellectual and physical abilities (Malik, 1996: 99). Huxley was more interested in defining the physical characteristics of the various types of people, for which the photographs, measurements and anthropometric data were key evidence. Race terminology was still vague and unfixed; in many ways it reflected the fragmented and ambivalent nature of attitudes to the idea of race during the mid-nineteenth century. The undefined terminology illustrates a lack of consensus within scientific societies and the wider educated population until the 1850s (Cowling, 1989: 184). Reactions to Darwin's seminal *On the Origin of the Species* (1859) ushered in new terminology to describe race and bolstered the idea of placing people into types.

Darwin's evidence and previous ideas on evolution were reworked and applied, not only to biological change over millions of years, but also to the way in which society and political systems functioned over decades. Yet Social Darwinism existed prior to 1859. Herbert Spencer, a philosopher and social theorist who wrote on the freedom of the individual, developing forms of society and the progression of civilized human societies, coined 'survival of the fittest' and 'evolution'. Spencer was, of course, influenced by earlier social theories, particularly those of the political economist Thomas Malthus and utilitarian ideas on human behaviour and social organization. He published his first book *Social Statics* in 1850, which treated human society as 'governed by immutable natural laws', though these ideas achieved a greater popularity through his later articles for *The Economist*. Spencer's biologically determined distinctions of race and civilization, and his idea that there was an evolutionary 'stepladder of civilized and primitive peoples', were thought to be allied to Darwin's work, though Spencer described capitalist and socio-economic systems rather than biology (Harris, 2004). It is little wonder that Darwinian ideas of natural selection in biology and evolution over millions of years became connected to the idea of the 'survival of the fittest' in society.

Galton considered that the publication of the *Origin of the Species* 'made a marked epoch in my own mental development' and 'was encouraged by the new views' to pursue inquiries into 'Heredity and the possible improvement of the Human Race' (Galton, 1908: 287). Galton's idea that human society was framed by natural (or biological) laws had been circulating prior to 1859, but it was in the 1860s that social failure was more clearly equated with biological unfitness and a biological view of society 'drawn from social Darwinism' began (Mackenzie, 1976: 503). A 1911 survey of the modern eugenics movement, written in reaction to Galton's death, placed its origins in 1865 with two articles written by Galton on inheritance (Field, 1911: 3).

Inherent genius

Galton's two articles articulated his ideas about inheritance, his fears of a racially degenerating society and the civilized and racial perfection of ancient Athens, which fed key themes in nineteenth-century literature and art, as well as anxieties around race, immigration and a hardening of colonial attitudes. Galton judged social considerations and nurture in forming an individual as irrelevant; rather, he considered nature to be the key (echoing *Tancred's* 'all is race'). He had no patience with the 'idea that babies are born pretty much alike' since their biological inheritance determined their abilities, development and future (Galton, 1869: 14). Along with other conceptions and assumptions, Galton's ideas about inheritance would re-work definitions of race and the hierarchy of different groups of people. These definitions were closely bound up in ideas of social class and perceptions of the socio-economic system.

Galton's first full book on inheritance *Hereditary Genius* was published in 1869. It was in fact a longer version of two articles published in *Macmillan's Magazine* in 1865: 'On Hereditary Character and Talent'. These articles considered inherited characteristics and the possible improvement of the human race. At the time, it was still highly controversial to equate human with animal instincts and to place the primacy of nature over experience and the possibility of divine redemption (Gillham, 2001: 155). Galton's views positioned him against the Christian ideal of marriage based on love, in which love was based on the metaphysical marriage of Christ to the church and the person's individual relationship to God. Improving the human race by breeding made sex (the physical act) the most important factor in marriage, though the reproduction of healthy children was of primary concern rather than sexual pleasure. *Macmillan's Magazine* catered to an intellectually challenging audience; contributors included Herbert Spencer, Matthew Arnold, Christina Rosetti, Charles Lyell and Thomas Huxley. In the context of the magazine's content, Galton's articles were not so wildly radical (Gillham, 2001: 156). Rather, they were essentially a 'statistical analysis of biographical dictionaries' of certain families and their dominance in prestigious areas (Cowan, 1972: 510). Galton used the statistics of families and lineage as an advocacy weapon. He discounted environmental factors entirely in the hope that political solutions to social issues would, in time, be predicated entirely around inheritance. With this basis, the most talented men and women, would be matched, making the mathematics of heredity essential.

While Steve Jones has described *Hereditary Genius* as a mere 'series of selected anecdotes', Galton's recent biographer Nicholas Wright Gillham has illustrated that Galton's ideas still have a modern legacy (Jones, 1994: 225). Gillham has compared Galton's grades and intellectual grading of men to the debate in the 1990s over IQ testing and race in *The Bell Curve*. This contentious form of testing and reading results ignores the way in which such tests are predicated around assumptions about peoples' background and prior knowledge (Gillham, 2001: 168). Galton is quite clear that he believed 'man's natural abilities are derived by inheritance' not environment or cultural background; in addition, he stated that his views are in 'large contradiction to general opinion' (Galton, 1869: 2). He argued his case by compiling statistics and comparing the results of 300 families from which descend a thousand 'eminent men': judges of England, statesmen, historical greats, commanders and men of literature and of science, poets, painters and musicians, divines and modern scholars, along with, somewhat incongruously, sportsmen such as 'Wrestlers of the North Country'. Galton felt that American society, where everyone is considered equal, illustrated that social class made no difference in the number of eminent men as there are no more and perhaps even fewer eminent men under the egalitarian system in the United States (Galton, 1869: 40). This concept of 'eminent men' and geniuses was very much influenced by the work of the historian Thomas Carlyle. Carlyle's book *On Heroes, Hero-Worship, and the Heroic in History* (1841) asserted the innate greatness of individual characters, such as Oliver Cromwell or Napoleon, in history 'independent of social background' (Arendt, 1944: 68). This idea of 'great men' was influential; it enforced an idea of history-making men who had great abilities as well as terrible flaws. Related adjectival terms and their use in the mid-nineteenth century, such as 'ablest', 'eminent' and genius, owed much to Carlyle's thinking.

Although his work was mainly based on distinction in different career paths, such as law or the military, Galton also considered the ability of athletes in two short chapters on Oarsmen and Wrestlers. He argued that the family records of the competitors and victors of the Olympic Games in ancient Greece 'would have been an excellent mine to dig into for facts bearing on heredity' (Galton, 1869: 335). Physical fitness and stamina was almost as important as intellectual ability in defining a great man. The great number of 'eminent men' from relatively few families, Galton argued, proves his thesis. From this he extrapolated evidence to create a hierarchical grading of different races that leaps from 'actual data' to 'grand and sweeping generalizations whose basis derives only from personal observation and prejudice has often been a hallmark of studies on genes, intelligence, and behavior' (Gillham, 2001: 168). Interestingly, Galton appeared to echo Robert Knox in his discussion about the separation of modern European races. Like Knox, he referred to 'the information gathered from the most ancient paintings in Egypt', observing further that they give evidence for representing the modern descendants of those images in Egypt today (Galton, 1869: 347 and 366).

In one of the last chapters in the *Hereditary Genius*, 'The Comparative Worth of Different Races', Galton graded different peoples from the past and present according to his understanding of their intellectual and physical ability. The 'ablest race' of all in Galton's eyes were the Athenian Greeks. It is worth quoting Galton's reasons for this assessment fully:

> The ablest race of whom history bears record is unquestionably the ancient Greek, partly because their master-pieces in the principal departments of intellectual activity are still unsurpassed, and in many respects unequalled, and partly because the population that gave birth to the creators of those master-pieces was very small. Of the various Greek sub-races, that of Attica was the Ablest and she was no doubt largely indebted to the following cause for her superiority. Athens opened her arms to immigrants, but not indiscriminately, for her social life was such that none but very able men could take any pleasure in it; on the other hand, she offered attractions such as men of the highest ability and culture could find in no other city. Thus, by a system of partly unconscious selection, she built up a magnificent breed of human animals [. . .]. (Galton, 1869: 340–1)

Galton listed the achievements of 14 illustrious men under the categories of Statesmen and Commanders (Themistocles, Militiades, Aristeides, Cimon, Pericles), Literary and Scientific Men (Thucydides, Socrates, Xenophon, Plato), Poets (Aeschylus, Sophocles, Euripides, Aristophanes) and a Sculptor (Phidias). He used statistics to reinforce his point, working out that from a population of about 135,000 freeborn males in Ancient Greece (about half of whom would survive to be over 26), the 14 illustrious men listed would make the selection 1 'great man' in every 4,822 men; much more than the figure he worked out for his own era. Galton then used this comparison to grade the Athenian Phidias and Socrates as a top grade of I or J and Pericles and Plato to a grade of H or I and compared them to the grade of G, which denoted great men in the nineteenth century:

> It follows from all of this, that the average ability of the Athenian race is, on the lowest possible estimate, very nearly two grades higher than our own – that is, about as much as our race is above the African negro. (Galton, 1869: 342)

The anxiety about degeneration is frequently perceived as belonging to the late nineteenth century and 1900s, but it is current from the 1860s onwards. Galton's use of grading and statistics (one of the first attempts at biostatistics) give an illusion of objectivity. Galton argued that the races of Europe had degenerated through decades of mixed inter-breeding (miscegenation) with lesser racial types. It is clear that Galton was warning British readers about the dangers of miscegenation, particularly in 'a small sea boarded country, where emigration and immigration are constantly going on [. . .] the purity of the race would necessarily fail' (Galton, 1869: 342). Galton believed Athens, like Britain, to have built an empire because of generations of breeding from Greek immigrants with good stock. Therefore, he promoted the idea of the emigration of Britons of the right 'stock' to colonial centres. Conversely, his main fear was the dangers of domestic miscegenation. Galton's idealized vision of Ancient Athens and comparison of its social structure with that of Britain fitted into Victorian Hellenism and an almost universal adulation of Greece (Challis, 2010: 116).

Galton later suggested that the critical reaction to *Hereditary Genius* was negative since popular feeling 'was not then ripe to accept even the elementary truths of hereditary talent and character, upon which the possibility of Race Improvement depends' (Galton, 1909: 310). He carefully kept the reviews and reactions to it, which are now preserved in the Galton archive at University College London. The review in *The Spectator* considered Galton to be ignorant about 'ancient races' and *The Morning Post* (16 April 1870) thought Galton relied on 'partial and exceptional' facts that did not 'stand up to scrutiny'. *The Scotsman* and *Saturday Review* were also negative, while unsurprisingly the *Theological Review* (April 1870) was most damning, pronouncing that the book's ideas 'should have caused more public dismay'. *The Guardian* (23 March 1870) found that this 'earnest disciple of Darwin' did not acknowledge that the 'greatest achievements' in human nature may be those of self-sacrifice rather than the 'sacrifice of the weak to the strong'. *The Pall Mall Gazette* (18 February 1870) questioned Galton's calculations of Athenian citizens and 'illustrious men' arguing that there was less of a distinction between the Athenian race and the British race in 1869 because there were more Athenians than Galton acknowledged. Galton sent a letter to the Editor of the *Pall Mall Gazette* the next day (19 February 1870), acknowledging that he had a 'strong misgiving that my results were too high' and putting the equation at 1.5 rather than 2 grades higher.

There were, however, a number of favourable reviews. *The Graphic* (22 January 1870) found it a 'delightful book' and recommended it as 'this is the book to read' on heredity; while *The Times* (7 January 1870) considered it an 'able and instructive book' for raising the human race while pointing out that there have been other 'paths of learning and achievement since Ancient Athens'. The naturalist Alfred Russel Wallace, whose paper on evolutionary change due to natural selection was read alongside Charles Darwin's in 1858, reviewed Galton's book very favourably in *Nature* (17 March 1870); finding it 'an important and valuable addition to the science of human nature.' Wallace expressed his astonishment that the current grades of today's generation were not lower in comparison to Ancient Attic genius and agreed on the question of marriage, 'it is most essential to the wellbeing of future generations that the average standard of ability of the present time should be raised'. Darwin agreed with Wallace, writing to Galton that he had 'made a convert' of him and congratulating him on such a 'memorable work' (Galton, 1908: 290). In addition, Galton received letters from people agreeing with his findings and offering their own ancestry as proof for his findings. Margaret Mylne, whose father was a Scot and his father Huguenot (French protestant immigrants of whom Galton approved), wrote to Galton saying she looked with different eyes on the 'brilliant eyes' of her father (Mylne to Galton, 29 March 1869). The press and public reaction to *Hereditary Genius* was not as negative as Galton later claimed. His later claim may have been strategically aimed to appeal to the forward-thinking Edwardians of 1908 above the blinkered Victorians of 1869.

Galton was clearly considering ways to measure physical human differences more carefully by the time *Hereditary Genius* came to print. After visiting the Fabrica of Mosaics at the Vatican and seeing the trays of coloured mosaics, he recommended the purchase by the South Kensington Museum of such artificial glass to create a standard scale by which to measure eye and skin colour (Kenna, 1964: 87). Although this purchase was not made, the language of Social Darwinism, such as 'hygiene', 'fitness', 'stock', that Galton used to describe issues of race became more fixed and, though still nebulous, was given a scientific edge (Dubow, 1995: 9). Darwin finished his *The Descent of Man* only two years after *Hereditary Genius*, and acknowledged Galton's work:

> The advancement of the welfare of mankind is a most intricate problem: all ought to refrain from marriage who cannot avoid abject poverty for their children; for poverty is not only a great evil, but tends to its own increase by leading to recklessness in marriage. On the other hand, as Mr. Galton has remarked, if the prudent avoid marriage, whilst the reckless marry, the inferior members will tend to supplant the better members of society. [. . .] There should be open competition for all men; and the most able should not be prevented by laws or customs from succeeding best and rearing the largest number of offspring. (Darwin, 1871: 403)

Darwin's conclusion that 'less civilised peoples were also less developed intellectually and emotionally than were Europeans' had a profound effect on cultural thinking, directly influencing the burgeoning science of archaeology and analysis of ancient civilizations (Trigger, 1989: 113). Ideas about the inheritance of ability and individual characteristics pervaded cultural life and theories about race and society (Stone, 2002: 100). Galton spoke about kinship links as a new religion that should pervade all areas of human life. Moreover, he was far from alone in fearing the degeneration of British 'stock'. The fear of degeneration in nation and race grew in the mid-to-late nineteenth century, as can been seen in Galton's *Hereditary Genius* in which he warns of the dangers of further miscegenation of Britain's island race (Galton, 1869: 343). This view was not unique to Galton but was echoed in the work of radical social reformers such as Herbert Spencer and Charles Kingsley.

Muscling in

Charles Kingsley, a novelist clergyman, social campaigner and popular historian delivered a series of lectures on public health during the 1860s and 1870s that fed into and were influenced by Galton's concept of the 'Ablest Race'. Kingsley's work illustrates that Galton was not alone in theorizing that Ancient Greeks, and in particular Ancient Athenians, attained intellectual prowess. Kingsley and Galton also shared anxieties about the potential of declining racial and national standards in Britain. A number of examples, including the National Olympics Association in the 1860s to improve physical health in men and the 1880s dress reform movement combating the tight lacing of corsets to produce healthy and fertile females, demonstrate concern about bodily fitness in both men and women impacting on the quality of the population. Ultimately though, unlike Galton, these practical movements considered the environment, whether poor conditions in the city or a restricted body, to be as important as nature or heredity. However, the adulation of Ancient Greece and a belief that the civilizations of the ancient world had pertinence to the modern were common.

Galton and Kingsley's views on celibacy offer another example of their commonalities. Like Galton, Charles Kingsley opposed celibacy for the clergy. His novel *Hypatia, Or New Foes with an Old Face* (1853), about the mathematician and pagan martyr Hypatia in AD fifth-century Alexandria, bound together celibacy and religious extremism as sinister unnatural forces. A review of *Hereditary Genius* in the *Daily News* refers to 'sickly celibates' and asked the church to show 'bodily and mental vigour' on the issue of marriage. Such a pronouncement echoed Kingsley and argued further in support of Galton's theory that men who pursue intellectual pursuits are frequently also physically robust:

Certain is that the men who within living memories have been most famous in the departments of learning, literature and science have, with few exceptions, been remarkable also for muscular strength and sound physical development. ('On *Hereditary Genius*', *Daily News*, 16 December 1869, Galton Archive, UCL)

The emphasis on physical ability would have been typical of a Kingsley hero. His ideas, and those on sporting behaviour in Thomas Hughes' novel *Tom Brown's School Days* (1857), in turn gave rise to the phrase 'Muscular Christianity', which was coined in the *Saturday Review*'s review of Kingsley's novel *Two Years Ago* (1857): Kingsley at first disliked the term, preferring 'Christian Manliness'. Kingsley's Tom Thurnall, a healthy and intelligent doctor (though too worldly wise), is the flawed hero of *Two Years Ago*. Thurnall expounds on the perfect ingredients for a healthy life to the opium-addicted poet Elsley Vavasour (or John Briggs) – Thurnall's foil:

Believe me, it may be a very materialist view of things: but fact is fact – the *corpus sanum* is father to the *mens sana* – tonics and exercise make the ills of life look marvellously smaller. You have the frame of a strong and active man; and all you want to make you light-hearted and cheerful, is to develop what nature has given you. (Kingsley, 1901: 201)

Thurnall's character is a perfect example of Kingsley's hero as 'a masculine, charismatic and authoritative Englishman who stands as a representative of a resolutely Anglo-Saxon and Protestant nation empire' (Wee, 1994: 67). It is the combination of energy, physical exercise, fresh air and manliness that can invigorate the nation.

Kingsley wrote to Matthew Arnold about his idea of Hellenism and Hebraism after reading *Culture and Anarchy,* commenting that it is a 'wise book':

I have for years past an inkling that in Hellenism was our hope. I have been ashamed of myself as a clergyman, when I caught myself saying to myself that I had rather been an old Greek than an Englishman. (Kingsley, 1877: 338)

Kingsley combined intellectual adulation of the Greeks with physical adulation of their sculpture. The 'transformation of the male form along classical lines', based on the Pheidian ideal as embodied in the Parthenon sculptures, was for ideas of 'national regeneration'. The influence of these ideas on mid-nineteenth-century artists has been long understood (Leoussi, 1999). This sculpture-led imagining of the perfect healthy body also influenced perceptions of female beauty and the physical fitness of the breeders of the future nation (Challis, 2011: 151). Kingsley's Hypatia (first published in 1853) is a beautiful and intellectual heroine, yet, because of her neo-Platonic beliefs (which, as revealed in the novel, are almost as extreme as the Christians), she is shown to embrace celibacy misguidedly. This, however, does not mitigate her physical beauty:

> Her features, arms, and hands were of the severest and grandest type of old Greek beauty, at once showing everywhere the high development of the bones, and covering them with that firm, round, ripe outline, and waxy morbidezza of skin, which the old Greeks owed to their continual use not only of the bath and muscular exercise, but also of daily unguents. (Kingsley, 1899: 20)

Although Kingsley describes Hypatia as akin to a statue of Athene, the emphasis he places on her golden hair and fair looks parallels the sculptor John Gibson's controversial statue *Tinted Venus*. This sculpture outraged many as it appeared to make the nude too lifelike though it was displayed at the popular venue, the Crystal Palace, in 1862. There is now a copy in the Walker Art Gallery, part of National Museums Liverpool.

Kingsley's emphasis on the physical beauty of the Greeks was more than aesthetic. In his lecture 'The Science of Health', Kingsley addressed the question of 'Whether the British race is improving or degenerating?' and considered the poor breeding of British 'stock' in unhealthy conditions among unhealthy people. He argued that both men and women should emulate the athleticism of the Greeks:

> Therefore I would make men and women discontented, with the divine and wholesome discontent, at their own physical frame, and at that of their children. I would accustom their eyes to those precious heirlooms of the human race, the statues of the old Greeks; to their tender grandeur, their chaste healthfulness, their unconscious, because perfect might: and say – There; these are tokens to you, and to all generations yet unborn, of what man could be once; of what he can be again if he will obey those laws of nature which are the voice of God. (Kingsley, 1880: 44)

Considered radical by many, especially in the established church, at the end
of his life, Kingsley concentrated on public talks dedicated to sanitary reform,
health and physical education. He gave his lecture 'Nausicaa in London: Or,
The Lower Education of Woman' in 1873 and his interest in women's education
is intertwined with his concern about health and the breeding of a fit race.
'Nausicaa in London' epitomized anxiety about degeneration (particularly
in urban areas), adulation of the ancient Greeks and instruction for Race
Improvement; much like the last section of Galton's *Hereditary Genius*.

Kingsley began by recounting how he had left visiting the Greek sculptures
at the British Museum and walked the streets of London with his head 'still full
of fair and grand forms' whose limbs and attitudes 'betokened perfect health,
and grace and power':

> For I had been up and down the corridors of those Greek sculptures,
> which remain as a perpetual sermon to rich and poor, amid our artificial,
> unwholesome, and it may be decaying pseudo-civilisation; saying with looks
> more expressive than all words – such men and women can be; for such they
> have been; and such you may be yet, if you will use that science of which you
> too often only boast. Above all, I had been pondering over the awful and
> yet tender beauty of the maiden figures from the Parthenon and its kindred
> temples. (Kingsley, 1874: 70)

Quoting the relevant part in the *Odyssey*, in which the young woman Nausicaa
plays ball with her female companions on the beach, Kingsley argued that
Nausicaa's father Alcinous was not a king in the modern sense but a wealthy
man of property or trader. This made Nausicaa, in Kingsley's reading, middle
class rather than aristocratic, perhaps echoing the composition of the audiences
to which his lecture was directed. Kingsley dwelt on the 'healthfulness' of the
scene, particularly emphasizing physical sports in the liberal education of the
Greeks and Romans. He contrasted this with modern ideas of intellectual
education, declaring that a 'wise man would sooner see his daughter a
Nausicaa than a Sappho, an Aspasia, a Cleopatra, or even an Hypatia' (Kingsley,
1874: 77). He argued that the education of women needed to include physical
exercise:

> If, in short, they will teach girls not merely to understand the Greek tongue,
> but to copy somewhat of the Greek physical training, of that 'music and

gymnastic' which helped to make the cleverest race of the old world the ablest race likewise: then they will earn the gratitude of the patriot and the physiologist, by doing their best to stay the downward tendencies of the physique, and therefore ultimately of the morale, in the coming generation of English women. (Kingsley, 1874: 87)

Kingsley talks about and gazes at women, effectively combining hygiene with sexuality (Fasick, 1994: 92). The inference is that women need to have healthy physical appetites of all kinds in order to increase fertility and the reproduction of a healthy race. Kingsley ends his lecture by exhorting physical activity and general awareness about health to combat the threat of degeneration – in his words, 'a population full of 'so many Chinese dwarfs – or idiots' (Kingsley, 1874: 88).

Kingsley's use of 'ablest race' is arguably a reference to Galton's *Hereditary Genius* (Galton, 1869: 341–2). Galton's view of the African negro being two grades lower than Anglo-Saxons paralleled Kingsley's pronouncements. Kingsley had by this time alienated himself from many of his Christian Socialist friends, including Thomas Hughes, by backing Governor Eyre's actions over the Jamaican uprising in 1866. He frequently used racist explanations for issues in society, arguing that suffrage in England should be extended to the working classes, but that Irish Celts and Black people 'lacked the historical experience and racial endowment for self-government' (Lorimer, 1978: 155). Kingsley did not just idealize the Greeks intellectually, he attributed physical prowess to their status as the 'ablest race', using their physiognomy as depicted on sculptures to present an ideal face and body in his fiction and non-fiction.

Sport and race

The themes outlined above are further illuminated through the history of Olympic celebrations or festivals which fed the creation of the modern international Olympic movement in 1896. Kingsley's and Galton's work on race improvement tapped into an adulation of the ancient past and anxiety about the strength of the present. Fae Brauer has recently outlined the cultural convergences around the growth of eugenics and its impact in visual culture. The first convergence she identifies, is 'the measurement of man' and the

'ranking of race' against the ideal bodies of classical sculpture (Brauer, 2008: 9). Brauer illustrates how classical sculpture was used as an ideal against which to measure the bodies of Olympic athletes in the 1900 Paris Olympic Games. Modern sport was given a symbolic and practical importance in the improvement of national and racial strength through which health and the body was aestheticized. This importance in part led to the revival of the modern Olympic Games in Athens 1896.

The first National Olympic Festival in London predated the start of the modern international Olympic games by 30 years, opening in London on 1 August 1866. The principal organizers were Dr William Penny Brookes of the Wenlock Olympian Games in Shropshire, John Hulley of the Liverpool Gymnasium and E. G. Ravenstein, President of the German Gymnastic Society in London. With eight others, these three men formed the National Olympian Association (NOA) at the Gymnasium on Myrtle Street on 7 November 1865 (Toohey and Neal, 2007: 32). The first day of the Festival was a swimming contest held at Teddington Lock in the Thames. The second and third days of the Olympic Festival took place at the Crystal Palace, in Sydenham South London. The sports activities included running, leaping, climbing, putting, steeple chasing, hurdle-racing, vaulting, throwing the javelin, wrestling, boxing, fencing, sabre and sabre against the bayonet, as well as gymnastic competitions ('National Olympic Festival', 1866: 81). Entry to the competition was free but entrants needed to be a member of NOA. This event attracted around 10,000 spectators and competitors. The *Penny Illustrated Paper* published an engraving of gymnast Hugo Landsberger to show the 'high state of perfection to which the human frame may be developed by continually practising athletic exercises' (Figure 2.2). The newspaper also proclaimed:

> And an equally long life (the printers are waiting or I would say more) to the National Olympian Association, which has for its motto the appropriate Latin saying of "The strength of the citizens is the strength of the state!" ('National Olympic Festival', 1866: 81)

Health and fitness was about more than just personal wellbeing and physical condition, it was about the health of society and the nation. The games were meant to encourage physical fitness through emulating the manner of the ancient Greeks and in so doing preserve the strength of the nation. The Greeks

HUGO LANDSBERGER, THE AMATEUR CHAMPION GYMNAST.

Figure 2.2 'Hugo Landsberger, the amateur champion gymnast', *Penny Illustrated Paper*, 11 August 1866: 81

and their sports were believed to hold wholesome and rational masculine virtues (Stevenson, 1998: 199). This first Olympic festival in London concentrated on male athletic prowess, but women played an important part, not least because (as Kingsley pointed out) they would give birth to the future generation.

Unlike Kingsley, Galton wanted to remove political and social concerns from 'Race Improvement'. He worked on theories about inheritance over the next decade in a number of ways. One theory stipulated that physical characteristics could be changed by the exchange of blood in transfusion (known as pangenesis). During the 1870s Galton worked on experiments in inheritance, corresponding with Darwin, who responded to Galton's ideas in *Hereditary Genius* (Galton, 1869: 363–5). The results of his experiments were disappointing, but Galton was not deterred from continuing his research on inheritance. In 1877, he spoke on his experiments with variations in sweet pea plants at the Royal Institution. Applying the laws of probability to heredity, Galton found that planting sweet peas from parental seeds revealed that the offspring of plants with extreme variations were closer to the population mean than their parents (Cowan, 1972: 518). Galton extrapolated from the sweet pea experiments that children do not automatically inherit the physical characteristics of their parents, but rather that successive generations resemble each other more generally in general features. Yet the idea that children inherited an average of physical (and moral) qualities from both parents prevailed.

Galton's use of mathematics and his 'reversion to the mean' became essential to statistics. His research led to Karl Pearson's work in statistics, curves and biometrics; 'with numbers and graphs he believed he could detect the separation and mixing of races and varieties, and the pressures of natural selection' (Porter, 2004: 239). Galton's sweet pea work was contemporaneous with the scientist monk, Gregor Mendel (also experimenting with varieties of sweet peas), whose work on genetic difference was not widely accepted until the 1900s, after Mendel's death. Although in some ways Galton's work was an important breakthrough, particularly in applied statistics, it also led to a myth of inheritance that a child is a genetic average of both parents (Jones, 1994: 46). The controversies over inheritance would take place in the 1900s, shortly before Galton died. Over the next few decades, Galton worked on locating physical similarities and evidence for inheritance and placed increasing emphasis on collecting anthropometric data.

3

Fitting Aesthetics

The Department of Statistical Sciences at University College London holds a craniometer, used for measuring skulls, that belonged to the archaeologist William Matthew Flinders Petrie. A letter from the Egyptologist Margaret Murray to George Dancer Thane (Professor of Anatomy) dated 6 April 1911, accompanying the instrument, identifies it as Petrie's. My colleague Subhadra Das, curator of the Biomedical Collections at University College London (including the Galton Collection), showed me this device in February 2012. The craniometer is part of a measuring kit; accompanying it are various notes describing the use of the other instruments, some of which appear to be in Petrie's handwriting (Figure 3.1). These include a device for the strength of a human grip, the strength of pull and 'Galton's tape for measuring the circumference of heads'. The kit corresponds to Petrie's description of an ideal anthropometric measuring undertaken during his excavations in Naukratis in February 1885, which was detailed in a letter to Francis Galton. Petrie was responding to Galton's publication of data on the results of the measurements of the public from the Anthropometric Laboratory in the journal *Nature*. He sent Galton ideas for the perfect portable anthropometric kit, including instructions for a craniometer:

> A frame length enough to go round the head with a fixed point in front & another on one side & sliding pistons with narrow ends to pass through the hair & read off on a scale would enable breadths and length to be quickly read off. (Petrie to Galton, Galton Archive, UCL: 12 February 1885)

The instrument belonging to the Statistics Department matches this description exactly. It is in pristine condition. However, it was not just the living who were

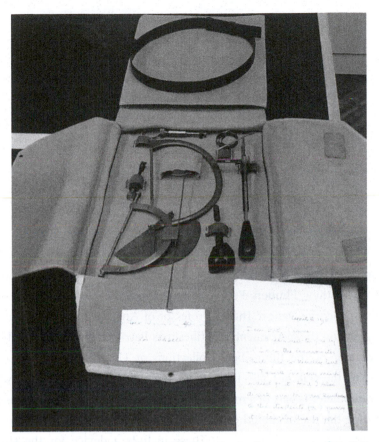

Figure 3.1 Craniometer belonging to Flinders Petrie, Department of Statistical Science, University College London. Photograph by Debbie Challis, 2012

measured for their anthropometric data but the dead as well; particularly the dead of Egypt and Palestine. Petrie measured and collected their skulls for the entirety of his working life as an archaeologist. Head spanners, craniometers and other measuring devices were key instruments in anthropometry (the comparative measurement of the human body). Measurement was connected to classification and thence to hierarchical grading; this in turn was often related to skull shape and ideas about 'brain mass and social attributes such as intelligence' (Kwint and Wingate, 2012: 41).

Data on inheritance and family lineage underpinned anthropometry. In the 1880s, Galton actively engaged with the general public to collect and collate physical and familial details in order to continue his work on inheritance. Like Galton, Petrie had a well-developed sense of his own talent, taking pride in his

family lineage. This pride is reflected in the first chapter of Petrie's autobiography *Seventy Years in Archaeology* (1939), which detailed his genealogy and his early life from birth in 1853 until 1880. Petrie commented 'looking back, I can see how much I owe to my forbears' and elaborated on how he inherited characteristics and strengths from his various ancestors, in much the same manner as Karl Pearson outlined Galton's inherited talents in his biography of Galton. From his grandfather Petrie came 'handling of men and materials' as well as drawing; from his great grandfather Mitton, business and banking; from three generations of Flinders' surgeons 'patching up the bodies'; from grandfather Matthew Flinders 'precise surveys and his firm hold on his men'. His immediate family had a part to play too: from his father Petrie obtained an interest in chemistry, engineering and draughtsmanship; and from his mother knowledge of history and minerals. This was an impressive array of talent and abilities by anyone's standards, which Petrie wholly attributes to his genetic inheritance:

> Any success in work was not due to myself but to reflecting my ancestors. To them be the praise "Poets are born and not made", and this is true, in the wildest sense of all poets; whatever anyone can originate is a faculty born with him, to which events can only give facility. (Petrie, 1931: 18)

Sixty-two years after the publication of *Hereditary Genius*, Petrie echoed Galton's premise that all is nature not nurture. It is a profound statement of Petrie's continued eugenic thinking towards the end of his life and the influence of Galton's ideas 20 years after Galton's death.

Petrie and Galton's relationship began in the late 1870s. It is likely that Petrie first corresponded with Francis Galton in the pages of the international scientific journal *Nature* in 1878 on stereoscopic vision:

> WITH reference to Mr. Galton's observation in his instructive paper in NATURE, vol. xviii. p. 98, that 'sometimes the image seen by the left eye prevails over that seen by the right, and vice versâ, I may mention that, as I had noticed some years ago, this may be best observed without a stereoscope'. (Petrie, 1878: 115–16)

Petrie continued to describe how to look at images in this way. This chapter explores Petrie's and Galton's early professional connections and their emphasis on the importance of measurement and classification. Anxiety about a degenerating present and future ran parallel with an adulation of an ancient past, which Petrie and Galton shared. In this shared anxiety and adulation, the face as well as the skull size of the past was re-conceived and sometimes imagined as the face of the present.

Face of the past

The importance of Greek art is reflected in the influx of classical art such as the sculptures from Nereid Monument in Lycia and the Mausoleum of Halicarnassus in Bodrum into Britain through the mid-nineteenth century. The increased use of the classical figural type in art works, classical history subjects and the depiction of everyday life in Greek and Roman antiquity was part of the revived classicism in art that took place in Britain from the 1860s until the end of the nineteenth century. Nineteenth-century classicism was informed 'the idealization by the life sciences of the body of the ancient Greek athlete as healthy', which became preoccupied with the physical health of the modern nation in comparison (Leoussi, 1999: 79). The anthropometric measurements of the ancient Greeks, which were taken from ancient sculpture, became the racial and physical ideal of modern Europeans in handbooks on art and physical development. For example, the athleticism and Greek-styled modelling of the nude hero in G. F. Watts' *Cecil Rhodes Memorial* in South Africa has been read as celebrating 'what was for Watts the triumph of Aryanism in the dark continent' (Hatt, 2001: 43). The depiction by artists of languorous women in Greek robes emulating classical sculpture placed greater emphasis on the female body as well as the male for the importance of the physical health of the nation.

The classicizing style of costume became more pronounced in art through the paintings of various artists in the 1860s. Elizabeth Prettejohn points to the classical influences in three paintings by James Abbott McNeil Whistler (*Symphony in White, No. III*), Albert Joseph Moore (*The Musicians*) and Frederic Leighton (*Spanish Dancing Girl*) that were all exhibited at the Royal Academy Exhibition in 1867:

> Moreover, all three include classicising elements, such as clinging, intricately folded drapery and poses reminiscent of the Parthenon marbles, but without antiquarian strictness: Leighton's 'Spanish' dancing girl wears draperies that closely imitate classical Greek sculpture, with crossing cords and a heavy

overfold at the waist; Moore's setting includes palm fans and a 'Japanese'-looking spray of flowers; and Whistler's picture combines a Japanese fan with another asymmetrical spray of foliage and curious 'Regency'-style dresses, with high waists and puffed sleeves. (Prettejohn, 2007: 110)

The transparency of the body beneath the drapery is a clear reference point to the female reclining figures from the Parthenon pediment sculptures that Charles Kingsley uses as inspiration in 'Nausicaa'. This is obvious in Albert Moore's *Beads* (1875), which depicts two young women reclining asleep in different positions on a soft fabric bench with their legs, breasts, nipples and small folds of their stomachs clearly visible beneath their white diaphanous Greek clothes. Similarly, G. F. Watts' *Ariadne in Naxos* (1875) depicts Ariadne sitting staring out to sea in rolls of draped Greek clothing showing the lines of her body but with less fleshy detail.

Kingsley's plea for the uncorsetted body was no doubt assisted by these languorous maidens in diaphanous drapery depicted in numerous paintings of the period. In his lecture 'The Two Breaths', Kingsley rails against the practice of making girls sit up straight, commenting that 'lolling around' is as graceful as 'every reposing figure in Greek bas-reliefs and vases'. His main contempt was, however, reserved for 'stays' which did not allow women to exercise and made the female figure unnatural:

> I spoke just now of the Greeks. I suppose you will all allow that the Greeks were, as far as we know, the most beautiful race which the world ever saw. Every educated man knows that they were also the cleverest of all races; and, next to his Bible, thanks, God for Greek literature.
>
> Now, these people had made physical as well as intellectual education a science as well as a study. Their women practised graceful, and in some cases even athletic exercises. They developed, by a free and healthy life, those figures which remain everlasting and unapproachable models of human beauty: but – to come to my third point – they wore no stays. (Kingsley, 1880: 27)

By the time the reaction against unhealthy female fashion became more popular among small intellectual and cultural circles in the 1870s and 1880s, there was another idealized form of Greek statuary to aspire to in addition to the Parthenon sculptures. Tanagra figurines, dating from the fourth-century BC to first-century BC, so-called because many were found at a site called

Tanagras in Boeotia Greece, though similar statuettes were found across the Hellenic world. These terracotta figurines were mainly of women and children and often were inspired by New Comedy in Greek Theatre. The figurines of women sometimes depicted them in action but always within floating drapery that revealed the female body. They were mould made and usually hollow. The heads would often be modelled separately in solid terracotta and added to the body. The discovery of these statues in great numbers at Tanagras in the early 1870s led to looting, followed by proper excavations by the Greek authorities (Higgins, 1990: 29–30). The antiquities market as a result was flooded with these figurines. Such was their popularity that a number of fakes were also widely available and both fakes and antiquities were more affordable to a greater number of the middle-class (Mathieux, 2010: 17). The figurines retained their appeal until the end of the nineteenth century because these statuettes were perceived to portray 'everyday life' rather than idealized goddesses. In 1878, the writer on fashion in clothing and furnishings Eliza Haweis included four sketches of these 'Tanagra' terracottas to illustrate how Greek women dressed using 'numberless folds to both reveal and conceal the body' in her dress reform book *The Art of Beauty*:

> How gracefully the dress followed the movements of the body, may be perceived better from the small coloured clay figures in the British Museum, than even from marble statues, for they represent their ordinary domestic manners and are not carefully posed and idealised goddesses. (Haweis, 1878: 46)

The face of the specially modelled heads of these Hellenistic figurines was usually that of an idealized female beauty, which was based on the head of the mid-fourth-century BC Aphrodite of Knidos by the sculptor Praxiteles. The physical characteristics of this 'type' can be seen in these examples in the Petrie Museum collection (Figure 3.2a and b). These idealized Praxitelean faces informed the ideal and most fashionable female facial profile in the nineteenth century. This profile was thought to be soft and feminine, as well as connected to ancient Greek lineage. The face was as important as a healthy female body. This classic Greek face was idealized in literature and painting of the period; as this description of Theodora Campian in Disraeli's novel *Lothair* (1870) encapsulates; 'pale, but perfectly Attic in outline, with the short upper lip and

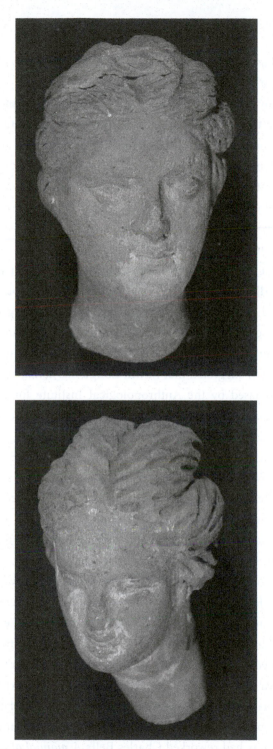

Figure 3.2a and b Terracotta heads from Memphis UC48477 and UC48476 © Petrie Museum of Egyptian Archaeology, University College London

round chin' (Disraeli, 1881: 34). As we have seen, Kingsley's description of Hypatia's profile corresponds to this perfect female face.

Physiognomy was used by a range of writers through the nineteenth century and the public that read these descriptions looked at paintings 'with much the same psychological and physiognomical expectations' (Cowling, 1989: 86). Physiognomic principles were applied to the depiction of the ancients as much as to contemporary Victorians. Character observation was combined with anthropology in the many scenes of the Greek, Roman and Egyptian civilizations by Alma Tadema and other artists. Edward Poynter's massive historical painting *The Visit of the Queen of Sheba to King Solomon* (1884–90) captures the detail of the ancient Near East and is clearly influenced by archaeological discoveries in Assyria and Palestine. It also depicts the imagined anthropological exoticism of the biblical East; in the painting, different 'types' of people are depicted along with peacocks and myriad kinds of fruit in a sumptuous court. These 'history paintings' were valued by intellectuals. The critic John Ruskin suggested that Edwin Long's *Babylonian Marriage Market* (1875) be purchased by the Anthropological Institute for its depiction of exotic racial types; it was eventually purchased by Thomas Holloway for Royal Holloway College in 1882 (Cowling, 1989: 233).

Another painting by Edwin Long, *The Chosen Five* (1885), depicts five young women with different hair and skin tones in various states of undress sitting for a Greek artist. Although the women are variously red-, blond-, dark-, brunette- and auburn-haired with skin tones from pale to a dark tan, their visible Grecian facial profiles, breasts and bodies are all very similar. The actress Lily Langtry was supposed to embody this classical beauty, she sat for John Everett Millais in *The Jersey Lilly* (1878), for Leighton in *Idyll* (1881) and for Edward Burne-Jones in *The Wheel of Fortune* (1888). Photographic postcards of Langtry became popular collector's items. The artist Lord Leighton declared in his 1884 address to students of the Royal Academy that the ideal form of beauty preserved by Pheidias can 'only be found in women of another Aryan race – your own' (Leighton, 1896: 89). Leighton echoed Robert Knox's claim in *Races of Men* that there was a resemblance between women of classical Greece, as seen on sculptures of Venus, and 'Saxon women of England' (Knox, 1862: 408). In fact Knox had reworked Charles Bell's *A manual of artistic anatomy for the use of sculptors, painters and amateurs* in 1852 and used it to argue that the facial characteristics found in antique sculpture were 'more common in Europe at this day' and this 'noble face' was transmitted 'to us [Saxons] by the Greeks' (Knox, 1852: 36). Leighton's favourite model was Dorothy Dene who, like Lily Langtry, was considered to have the perfect Attic facial profile. A photograph of Dorothy and three of her sisters show the four Denes face on to the camera, while two mirrors on either side of Dorothy's head capture her profiles. The idea that photographs of facial profiles would depict the ability and possibly character of a person were embedded in these physiognomic principles that were found throughout Victorian art and literature.

The physical ideal based on classical sculpture and the belief that a person's moral and intellectual abilities are depicted in their features fed into a larger racial corporeal discourse. Galton developed a camera which could record overall 'ideal' or 'typical' features from a number of individual portraits on the same photographic plate. The strongest facial features would come through in the short exposure time given in the development of the plate. He used these photographs to record the statistical 'normality' of facial features and measure how character 'traits' manifest themselves. He was influenced in this by Herbert Spencer, who had tried similar experiments. Both men were attempting to pin down the typical physical characteristics in a face. Galton practised composite photography on dozens of ancient coins depicting Alexander the Great or Cleopatra VII in order to identify the inheritable facial features and racial types they embodied (Gilham, 2001: 219). He was also trying to determine the features of great men from antiquity and their 'most probable likeness' on coins and medals (Galton, 1878: 100).

Galton spoke on the composite photographs in the 1877 BAAS conference and then at the Anthropological Institute. He subsequently published a paper on the results of this composite photography in 1878 in *Nature* in which he showed examples of composites made from photographs of criminals. The study of criminality as a field of scientific enquiry was influenced by the publication of *L'uomo delinquente* (The Delinquent Man) by Cesare Lombroso in 1876, which studied criminal tendencies and crime as an anthropological area (Green, 1984: 10–11). Lombroso 'revived the classical discipline of physiognomy by arguing that moral propensities were evident not only in the shape and expressions of the face but also in the dimensions of the brain that lay behind it' (Kwint, 2012: 13). Galton advocated that families across Britain should take similar photographs to isolate their shared characteristics; with this knowledge they would be able to forecast the results of marriages between families. So strong was his belief in the power of the composite photographic evidence that he published a circular letter to be sent to amateur photographers in an attempt to collect this data from families in 1882.

The idea that scientific evidence on 'normal social behaviour' could be collected through both photography and the face was an appealing one. This appeal was due in part to the development and growing popularity of social photographic portraiture (Hamilton and Hargreaves, 2001: 57). In 1878, following Galton's remarks, BAAS began a racial survey of the British Isles through photographic portraits and data collection (Edwards, 2001: 131). Like Huxley's earlier survey across the British Empire, the success of this enterprise was limited. However, it illustrates a desire within scientific circles for 'racial mapping' and a willingness among sections of the population to participate in it. The idea that characteristics made people more susceptible to criminal behaviour, for example, was linked to physiognomy. In his autobiography, Flinders Petrie recounts the story of an Egyptian worker at Abydos 'who, from his face, I much mistrusted' (Petrie, 1931: 179). He was, however, persuaded by a friend to let the man help with packing. Various objects went missing during the packing and the next winter the man was wearing some of Petrie's clothing. From this episode, it is clear that Petrie believed in his ability to read the face in order to understand character.

The chosen inch

Petrie's first journey to Egypt was motivated by a different kind of measuring. It began as a response to a book by Charles Piazzi Smyth. Petrie had purchased Piazzi Smyth's *Our Inheritance in the Great Pyramid* (1864) at the age of 13 (Petrie, 1931: 13). Piazzi Smyth, an astronomer, was an old family friend of his father William Petrie; both men had lived in the Cape of Good Hope, South Africa. William Petrie had almost proposed to Piazzi Smyth's sister and in fact met Anne Flinders, Petrie's mother, at gatherings at the Smyth family's house. Like Anne and William Petrie, Piazzi Smyth and his wife Jessica were committed Christians, though William Petrie and the Smyths were more evangelical than Anne and attended a Plymouth Brethren meeting together in Lewisham in 1869 (Brück and Brück, 1988: 136). So strong was his interest and dedication to Smyth's theories that in some ways, William Petrie was considered one of Piazzi Smyth's disciples (Drower, 1995: 29).

Smyth was intrigued by the metrology of the Great Pyramid at Giza and the idea that the 'base of the pyramid appeared to bear the same relation to its height as the circumference of a circle to its radius' (Brück and Brück, 1988: 97). He believed this meant that the pyramid builders knew of the numerical value of the number pi (3.14159265). Smyth's premise was based on the work of John Taylor, whose book *The Great Pyramid – Why was it built and Who built it?* was published in 1859. Taylor promoted the idea that the Pyramid had been built in around 2,400 BC under divine guidance by people chosen by God, rather than the Egyptians. Therefore the Great Pyramid was a deeply holy place, meaningful for Christians rather than for the pagans of antiquity. Taylor postulated that the pyramid was based on a measurement known as the pyramid inch and a 'sacred cubit akin to the Hebrew', which was made up of 25 pyramid inches, measuring precisely 1.001 of a British inch (Drower, 1995: 28). These ideas were not new to the nineteenth century. Previous mathematical studies had imbued the Egyptian Pyramids with mystical power. John Taylor drew on the work of the seventeenth-century natural philosophers John Greaves and Isaac Newton, who discovered the standard of the 'sacred and profane cubit' for his book. The British Israelite movement was another popular group influenced by Taylor's work. It was a deeply religious sect that believed that the British were one of the ten lost tribes of Israel and Taylor's theories apparently vindicated their claims. The parallels between this sacred inch and British inch contributed to their belief that the British were one of the ten chosen tribes with their origins at the dawn of biblical time in Egypt. Piazzi Smyth was cynical about Taylor's claims until he became a convert in 1864; he later had some sympathy with the British Israelites. William Petrie was not a British Israelite but he supported Piazzi Smyth's ideas and his later proposal to go to Egypt and carry out accurate measurements of the Great Pyramid.

The subject of measurement was particularly pertinent in 1864. In that year, a bill to introduce the French metric system of measuring instead of the British imperial yard came to Parliament. Many people did not like the thought of using a French system, despite the advantages it could bring to trade. J. F. W.

Herschel, scientist and astronomer, championed the imperial system in the 1860s due to his belief that 500,500,000 British inches accurately measured the length of the earth's polar axis. Pyramidologists even attracted respectful press coverage in the campaign to retain the imperial system (O'Gorman, 2003: 566). The argument in 1864 was that British units of measurement could be traced to monuments dating to the biblical age and even the dawn of time, feeding into ideas about the national and racial identity of British people. The debate appeared to influence the influential art critic John Ruskin. Ruskin's parable lesson on 'The Pyramid Builders', from his series of lectures for 'little house wives' *The Ethics of Dust* (1875), invoked the mathematical calculations of Egypt in a mystical and exotic reading while considering the lessons in science from the Egyptians for the modern world.

After the publication of his book, Piazzi Smyth and his wife visited Cairo and the Great Pyramid for four months from November 1864. With the assistance of the Egyptian khedive, Ismail Pasha, who provided Egyptian workers and equipment, they cleaned and measured the main chambers of the Pyramid in early 1865 (Boorskin, 192: 136). Piazzi Smyth had prepared for his surveying work by designing and ordering adjustable rods that could measure to a hundredth of an inch as well as a 'novel box camera to take small plates' that could be processed on site (Brück and Brück, 1988: 104). The Piazzi Smyths stayed in rock tombs near the pyramids at Giza and hired as an assistant Ali Jabri, one of the Najama bedouin who had settled in Giza and had worked as a boy for the Egyptologist Howard Vyse 30 years earlier (Quirke, 2010: 19). Piazzi Smyth was the first person to take interior photographs of the great Pyramid and he worked with some visiting British railway engineers to uncover the corner pieces of the pyramid. Although he did not complete an extensive survey, Smyth argued that his measurements show that pi was incorporated in the building through the relationship between the altitude and circumference of the Pyramid. These results were published in *Life and Work at the Great Pyramid* (1867), which had a favourable reception even among non-pyramidologists and British Israelites. However, Smyth's reputation as a scientist was severely damaged by his beliefs in pyramidology, especially when the Royal Society refused to read his paper on his measurements. Eventually, he resigned from the Society's membership.

William Petrie had intended to go to Egypt in 1872 to verify Smyth's claims but family commitments stopped him. William Petrie had been a civil

engineer before he switched to chemistry. He ensured that his son Flinders
was trained as a surveyor; under his tutelage, Flinders made accurate surveys
of large monuments, such as Stonehenge, while studying for a visit to Egypt
in the 1870s. As mentioned above, neither William nor Flinders Petrie were
British Israelites and their relationship with Smyth waned in the late 1870s.
It is unclear exactly why Flinders Petrie was interested in the Great Pyramid:
was it a puzzle to be solved? a challenge to his surveying prowess? a change to
learn more about the Egyptians in Egypt? or an early belief in divine destiny
influenced by his parents' evangelical views? The answer is probably a mixture
of all these reasons.

Flinders Petrie travelled to Egypt alone, arriving in Cairo in November
1880. He brought with him his father's measuring instruments. Smyth's
former assistant, Ali Jabri, assisted Petrie in setting up camp at Giza; his
accommodation was a tomb, near to the location of the Piazzi Smyth's camp
(Petrie, 1883: 3) (Figure 3.3). He spent two winters in Giza, accurately surveying
the Great Pyramid, drawing plans, calculating the triangulation of the interior
and photographing it through a camera using slow exposure that (like Smyth)
he made himself (Drower, 1995: 48). He found that the 'dimensions of the
pyramid were seven times forty cubits for the height and eleven times the
same quantity for the side. The simple ratio 22/7 together with the length of
the normal cubit replaced the perfect pi and the imagined sacred unit' (Brück
and Brück, 1988: 229). This disproved the theories of Piazzi Smyth and others,
though it did not stop Pyramid theories circulating (as indeed they do today).
Petrie recounts a story of an American who had believed in Pyramid theories
until he stayed with him for a few days at Giza:

> [. . .] and at our last meal together he said in a saddened tone, – 'Well, sir!
> I feel as if I had been to a funeral.' By all means let the old theories have
> a decent burial; though we should take care that in our haste none of the
> wounded ones are buried alive. (Petrie, 1883: xii)

In 1883 Petrie submitted his manuscript to the Royal Society, having heard that
they had granted £100 to the Royal Engineers to carry out the same survey.
Francis Galton was tasked with reporting on Petrie's work and was so impressed
by it that he persuaded the Royal Society to give the grant directly to Petrie
for the report's prompt publication. *The Pyramids and Temples of Giza* was

Figure 3.3 Flinders Petrie outside his 'rock tomb', Giza

published in 1883. Aside from providing an accurate and careful measurement of the Pyramid, it disproved Smyth's theory and established Petrie's reputation as a scientist and archaeologist. Another consequence of this grant was Petrie's 'friendship with Francis Galton which lasted until his death' (Petrie, 1931: 35). Galton's early involvement in Petrie's career is significant; he assisted Petrie several times over the next few years.

Defining eugenics

In 1883 Galton published *Inquiries into Human Faculty*, a collection of experiments, correspondence and data on inheritance, human ability and psychological tests. It was in this book that Galton created the word 'eugenics' to describe the science and idea of breeding human 'stock' to give 'the more suitable races or strains of blood a better chance of prevailing speedily over the less suitable' in a footnote (Galton, 1907: 70). 'Eugenics' came from the Greek words 'genus', translated as race or kin, and 'eu', meaning good or well. Examples of composite photographs were included along with a reference to Flinders Petrie. Petrie had written to Galton in 1880 enquiring about Galton's data collection for his imagery studies and visualizing numbers. Galton was attempting to investigate how scientific men used mental imagery and whether it had any bearing on their abilities. Galton sent out a questionnaire on the vividness of imagery to members of the Royal Society and other bodies. The results from the survey and his conclusions were published in *Nature*, *Mind* and the *Fortnightly Review* in 1880 and he subsequently received a great deal of correspondence from across the world (Burbridge, 1994: 462). One of these respondents was Flinders Petrie shortly before he began his ground-breaking survey of the Great Pyramid in Giza. It is interesting to speculate as to whether Galton was influenced by Petrie's survey of the Pyramid to include in his notes a reference to a young man who would be 'eminent'. This letter from Petrie to Galton is reprinted as 'Appendix C' in Margaret Drower's biography *Flinders Petrie. A Life in Archaeology*:

> Mental arithmetic I always do as on paper; though the numbers, beyond the half-dozen or so immediately operated on, are not so much remembered by the mental image, as by the mental speech; going through the will of speech just short of actually using any muscles; except perhaps a slight accenting of the breath. (Drower, 1995: 476)

It was this letter and further conversations that Galton referred to in *Inquiries into Human Faculty*, in which he described Petrie as having 'one of the most striking examples of visualizing power it is possible to imagine' (Galton, 1907: 166). Petrie and Galton established a friendly working relationship, a relationship which was central to the events and ideas detailed in this book. Their mutual interest in race and defining different racial types in antiquity was shared with a wider number of individuals working in archaeology, anthropology, geography, biblical studies and philology. It is that interest and those connections that framed Petrie's journey up the Nile in 1886–87 to collect 'racial types' from ancient monuments in Egypt and informed his collecting strategy on that expedition, as well as his later work.

The first edition of *Inquiries into Human Faculty* sold gradually. A second edition was published in 1907, by which point the book and the idea of eugenics had become more popular. After the first edition of Galton's book, he established a temporary laboratory at the International Health Exhibition in South Kensington to take anthropometric measurements of personal data. The International Health Exhibition in 1884 contained displays and lectures covering various topics such as home, food, sanitation for all social classes and dress. This greater interest in health combined with anxiety about racial degeneration in the 1870s and 1880s no doubt contributing to the exhibition's success (Pict, 1989: 130). The health exhibition was more popular than expected with large crowds attending and queuing to take part in the various data collection devices on height, weight, eye colour, strength and so on, at Galton's lab (Gillham, 2001: 210). The exhibition was extended by two months and was popularly known as the 'Healtheries'. It was during this exhibition that Galton became interested in fingerprinting, later proving that people have unique prints, as well as analysing family data for hereditary traits. Galton's Anthropometric Laboratory was later transferred to the South Kensington Museum (Figure 3.4). Although it closed in 1894, it was the prototype for the more permanent Eugenics Records Office at University College London.

The International Health Exhibition's dress displays were linked to the fascination with health and race. Edward W. Godwin, the designer and member of the Anti-Tight Lacing Society, addressed the Health Exhibition on hygiene and beauty in dress, promoting the adaptation of Greek-style dresses over woollen undergarments. In the same year, Godwin was asked to direct the new Costume Department at the Liberty department store. He adapted costumes of the past, including interpretations of ancient Greek clothing, to modern needs (Adburgham, 1975: 63). The *Official Guide* to the exhibition noted that the display had 'more reason than artistic sense' and considered that the 'prejudices of fair sex [caused] considerable difficulties to their subjects' (*International Health Exhibition*, 1884: 31). The Lancet noted Godwin's models showing deformities caused by dress, and in particular tight lacing. The interest of the medical press reveals the interest of the medical profession in 'rational dress' for women. Writers on dress and hygiene reform placed emphasis on the need for women to be fit and active in order to be future mothers of a healthy nation and race. Wearing a tightly laced corset for long periods was likely to damage the body and make pregnancy unsafe or difficult to achieve. The discourse of hygienic and sanitary reform was articulated as a form of control; it was linked to greater socio-political questions around the management of the 'social body through public medicine and discourses of health' (Gilbert, 2007: 3–4).

ANTHROPOMETRIC
LABORATORY

For the measurement in various
ways of Human Form and Faculty.

Entered from the Science Collection of the S. Kensington Museum.

This laboratory is established by Mr. Francis Galton for
the following purposes:—

1. For the use of those who desire to be accurately measured in many ways, either to obtain timely
warning of remediable faults in development, or to
learn their powers.

2. For keeping a methodical register of the principal measurements of each person, of which he
may at any future time obtain a copy under reason-
able restrictions. His initials and date of birth will
be entered in the register, but not his name. The
names are indexed in a separate book.

3. For supplying information on the methods,
practice, and uses of human measurement.

4. For anthropometric experiment and research,
and for obtaining data for statistical discussion.

Charges for making the principal measurements:
THREEPENCE each, to those who are already on the Register.
FOURPENCE each, to those who are not:— one page of the
Register will thenceforward be assigned to them, and a few extra
measurements will be made, chiefly for future identification.

The Superintendent is charged with the control of the laboratory
and with determining in each case, which, if any, of the extra measurements may be made, and under what conditions.

H. & W. Brown, Printers, 20 Fulham Road, S.W.

Figure 3.4 Anthropometric Laboratory Poster © UCL Special Collections

Rational dress was a rebellious reaction against an unhealthy orthodoxy in fashion that had a limited appeal since mainstream fashion still placed emphasis on a thin waist and a corset. It was believed that Greek dress revealed women's natural contours and shape, and enabled them to move and be physically active, as Charles Kingsley had advocated in 'Nausicaa'. J. Moyr Smith makes this explicit in his book *Ancient Greek Female Costume* (1882):

> Though more fully clad in most parts of Greece than in Sparta, the costume of the young girls and women was such as allowed the body to develop its natural beauty, and permitted a graceful freedom of motion. (Moyr Smith, 1882: 17)

The dress reform movement's use of Greek costume illustrates the practical impact of ideas on antiquity and the emphasis on the female body. It was linked to a growing concern around 'race-motherhood' and female fertility that became an important interest of the eugenics movement (Soloway, 1995: 116). Dress reform was part of a wider discourse around the control of female body and the campaign against the 1866 Contagious Diseases Act, which decreed that women suspected of prostitution to be examined for venereal disease in a bid to the spread of sexually transmitted infections. The Act was repealed around the time of the 'Healtheries' in 1885. The female body was thus desirable and dangerous, but its health was important for the future of race improvement.

Anxiety about degeneration of the race was often combined with an adulation of the ancient past and a sense that looking back on the achievements of antiquity, particularly those of the Greeks, could assist with race improvement. This belief can be seen in diverse areas from dress reform to athletics to contemporary art. Petrie's letter on the perfect craniometer and measuring devices that opened this chapter was a response to Galton's popular public laboratory and his plea for more data about families and anthropometrics. The results of the data Galton collected at the Fair and the data on families sent to him by the public was published in *Natural Inheritance* in 1889. Petrie's work with Galton needs to be framed within these larger cultural ideas and ideals of antiquity that were part of late nineteenth-century intellectual and social discourse. Measuring and data collection, whether of people or pyramids, was considered key to solving the mysteries of human development.

4

Photographing Races from Antiquity

There are few copies of Flinders Petrie's *Racial Photographs from the Ancient Egyptian Pictures and Sculptures* available, even in academic libraries. The Petrie Museum of Egyptian Archaeology does not have one, neither does the library of University College London and there does not appear to be one in the British Library or in the Egypt Exploration Society's library. It is a difficult book to catalogue since it is a report for a committee rather than a directly authored book. The copy at the Sackler Library Oxford contains Petrie's report on the photographs with analysis by Rev. Henry Tomkins, followed by thumb-nail images of the photographs. The copy at the Palestine Exploration Fund (PEF) has the two essays followed by slightly larger photographs in each of their volumes that can be folded out concertina style.

In these volumes the photographs or casts of faces are clipped away from their monuments, devoid of any spatial context, with a number and label of their ethnic type underneath. In the case of the PEF copy, Petrie's handwritten notes underneath appear to update the information or place the faces in a further category. This archaeological ethnography is not peculiar in the context of the late nineteenth century when anthropology and archaeology were intertwined and both disciplines were in their infancy. Neither is the concentration on face as an indication of race strange when considered in the light of the BAAS project to map the British population's physical characteristics during 1878–83. Or the earlier request, based on instructions made by Professor Thomas Huxley, from the Colonial Office to all colonial governors requesting specifically composed photographs of all races in their territories in 1869. The idea of 'surveying mankind' has led to many such collections of photographs and anthropometric measurements, sometimes made in the belief that such records would be important after the 'extinction' of groups of people. This belief gives related photographs and photographic collections a sinister edge (Falconer and Hide, 2009: 130).

The nineteenth-century passion for reading race in the face, whether on ancient sculpture or through photographs of living people, has been considered in the first three chapters of this book, as has the attribution of mental and moral characteristics to physical features. In *Raw Histories: Photographs, Anthropology and Museums,* Elizabeth Edwards asks a basic question 'what kind of past is inscribed in photographs?':

> Photographs are very literally raw histories in both senses of the word – the unprocessed and the painful. Their unprocessed quality, their randomness, their minute indexicality, are inherent to the medium itself. It has been suggested that anthropologists, and for that case historians, are worried by still photography because, lacking the constraining narratives of film, still images contain *too many meanings.* (Edwards, 2001: 5)

The past inscribed in *Racial Photographs* is still with us today in the collections of the Petrie Museum of Egyptian Archaeology, which displays and stores many of the objects Petrie himself thought most useful for teaching at University College London. The Petrie Museum is, to a limited extent, a repository for Petrie's typologies and ideas about Ancient Egypt. Limited because no museum collection, even if not added to, remains in aspic as the history of the collection, of the building, the space and the curators and other staff always enlarge and shift the original intention of collections. It is for this reason that rather than recoiling from the multitude of meanings captured in *Racial Photographs* and Petrie's own handwritten typologies on the PEF copy, I considered that an examination of these photographs during the Galton centenary in 2011 at UCL and the reasons how they were brought into being was crucial to the exhibition *Typecast: Flinders Petrie and Francis Galton.*

It is important to fully understand the context of Petrie's journey and the *Racial Photographs*. Margaret Drower describes Petrie as undertaking a 'commission' for Francis Galton after he had fallen out with the board of the Egypt Exploration Fund in 1886 (Drower, 1995: 106). Petrie was in fact officially working for the BAAS but their committee only awarded him £20 to take *Racial Photographs* and so Galton part funded Petrie's expedition. Petrie was accompanied for over three months by the Oxford Egyptologist Francis Llewellyn Griffith in order to split costs. Petrie undertook a commission for a committee from BAAS and, though his personal relations with Galton cemented the journey and indeed guaranteed backing of the committee. Petrie's collection of photographs was made after consultation with and support from a wide number of influential people. Both Petrie's and Galton's interest in race and defining different racial types in antiquity was shared with a wider number of individuals working or interested in archaeology, anthropology, geography, biblical studies and philology. Many of whom came together in the yearly conference of BAAS.

Scientific support

BAAS still exists as the British Science Association and was (and is) an important centre for public engagement with contemporary science and scientific debate. Its history of bringing science to a wider public and connecting scientists – amateur and professional – was established in the nineteenth century, at the heart of which was its annual meeting. The annual meeting was spread over several days and always took place outside of London in different cities and towns around Britain, and in a few cases around the British Empire. From its inception in 1831, the purpose of the British Association was to 'disseminate knowledge of science to a wider audience'. Its progressive outlook meant that it soon held meetings in industrial northern towns, such as Newcastle and Manchester, as well as opening membership to women in 1848 (Yeo, 1981: 72). By the time of Petrie's involvement with BAAS in the 1880s, the annual meeting had passed its heyday of the mid-nineteenth century, partly because science was becoming more specialized and universities were finally establishing academic departments that reflected this specialization (Macleod, 1981: 2).

However, the BAAS annual meeting was still a big public space for contemporary scientific ideas and brought people from disparate areas together. In the period from the 1880s until the early 1900s, BAAS reflected contemporary concern and political developments around the growth of imperialism and the annual meeting correspondingly had a greater international focus. A Geography section (Section E) had been founded at the annual meeting in 1869 and this was followed by Anthropology (Section H) in 1884 at the meeting in Montreal, the first annual meeting to take place abroad. Within this new section, race and racial characteristics featured strongly and, despite the increased international and colonial focus, much attention was also paid to ethnography in the United Kingdom (Worboys, 1981: 171). Anthropology at this point encompassed disciplines such as anthropology, social studies, archaeology and aspects of philology. Therefore Petrie speaking on 'The discovery of Naukratis' at his first BAAS meeting in 1885 was in keeping with the other papers.

The 1885 BAAS meeting was held in Aberdeen and the President of Section H was Francis Galton. Galton's presidential address was on hereditary physical characteristics. He had spoken on eugenics at the meeting only two years earlier and as Michael Worboys points out, BAAS was supportive of Galton and his early work on eugenics and related areas (Worboys, 1981: 171). Beginning with the skeleton of the eighteenth-century performer Charles Byrne, or the 'Irish Giant', on display in the Hunterian Museum at the Royal College of Surgeons in London, Galton lamented the fact that few comparative measurements of people had been made until recent years. He outlined why his Anthropometric Laboratory at the International Health Exhibition last year (1884) had proved so useful and allowed him to collect data over at least two and in some cases three generations. Following an outline of 'positive eugenics', Galton argued that the data collected would enable 'selective breeding by selection in mating' in order to 'reduce the preponderance of those ancestral elements that endanger recession' (Galton, 1885: 1213).

Galton's 'Address' set the tone of the Section even if papers, such as Petrie's, did not directly contribute to the theme of hereditary characteristics, anthropometric data and racial science. Petrie outlined his main findings at the ancient Greek trading colony of Naukratis in Egypt, which he only located 'through inquiries with Arab dealers' and traced the influence of the Egyptians on the Greeks through the material culture:

> In short, we see here the Greeks, with a versatile and highly plastic nature, rapidly developed their arts and manufactures upon the modes of the old civilization of Egypt. (Petrie, 1885: 1216–17)

Petrie spoke on the same day alongside Theodore Bent on 'Insular Greek Customs' and 'On Ancient Tombs in the Greek Islands', General Pitt-Rivers on 'On the Working of the Ancient Monuments Act of 1882', and Arthur Evans on 'The Flint Keepers' Art in Albania'. On the last day of the meeting Joseph Jacobs presented a paper 'A Comparative Estimate of Jewish Ability', which was described as a parallel investigation into Jewish ability alongside that of Galton's *Heredity Genius*. Jacobs found that there 'was a considerably greater chance of finding distinguished men among a million Jews than among a million Englishmen', but also noted that more Jews live in urban areas and often came from 'a long process of unnatural selection' (Jacobs, 1885: 1220). Ideas about heredity, selective breeding and transferences between civilizations dominated the proceedings at the 1885 BAAS Meeting.

The following year the annual meeting was held at Birmingham where the president was the politician Sir George Campbell whose 'Address' stressed his interest in 'guides to races', but disagreed with Galton's emphasis on anthropometric data and inheritance. He argued that the difference in races as regards intelligence may not be so fixed:

> With the superficial knowledge that we have, no one can say that Europeans, Hindus, Chinese are born with brains superior or inferior to the other, and even in regard to the negro I do not know that it is yet known that with equal advantages negro babies might not grow up nearly or quite so intelligent as Europeans. (Campbell, 1886: 830)

Yet Campbell appeared to back Galton on his ideas about 'fitting marriages' and using information about breeding 'instead of giving way to foolish ideas about love and the tastes of young people whom we can hardly trust to choose their own bonnets' (Campbell, 1886: 831). Campbell followed his address up with a paper on 'What is an Aryan?' later at the meeting, in which he argued that the features of Aryans could be seen in what 'we call Jewish features' but have been 'toned down by intermarriages in India and Europe'. (Campbell, 1886b: 842)

The 1886 BAAS meeting again clearly reflected a deep interest in race and racial origins, perhaps more so than on heredity and inheritance. This interest was illustrated by papers on ancient and modern Egypt such Sir Charles Wilson 'On the Native Tribes of the Egyptian Sudan' and Sir J. William Dawson's 'Note

on Photographs of Mummies of Ancient Egyptian Kings', which detailed
the findings of the recent 'unrolling' by Dr Schweinforth of mummies at the
Boulak Museum in Cairo. Dawson argued that the features of Seti I, Ramses
II and Ramses III:

> [. . .] are of great interest as enabling us to see the actual features of these
> ancient Egyptian Kings, and to compare them with their representations in
> monuments and with modern Egyptians. (Dawson, 1886: 845)

He found that Seti I and Ramses II had 'narrow and somewhat retreating
foreheads and strong jaws, indicating that they were men of action rather than
of thought'. A 'Committee for investigating the Prehistoric Race in the Greek
islands' also reported on Theodore Bent's excavations on early graves in the
Greek Archipelago, where he was examining the early origins of the ancient
Greeks, and renewed his grant. Given this emphasis on race and determining
characteristics through evidence from material culture, human remains and
reading the face, it is unsurprising that another committee was also set up at
the 1886 annual meeting 'for the purpose of procuring with the help of Mr
Flinders Petrie, Racial Photographs from the Ancient Egyptian Pictures and
Sculptures'.

Francis Galton was the chair of this committee, which was composed of
eminent men from across the scientific world. These included the collector and
archaeologist General Pitt-Rivers; the zoologist Professor William H. Flower,
who was at that point Director of the Natural History departments of the British
Museum in South Kensington; the surgeon and anatomist Professor Alexander
Macalister; the geologist and geographer Frederick W. Rudler, then Curator
and Librarian of the Museum of Practical Geology, London, and President of
the Anthropological Department of the British Association; Reginald Stuart-
Poole, a founding member of the Egypt Exploration Fund (EEF) and Keeper
of the Department of Coins and Medals at the British Museum; and the
secretary of BAAS, Mr Bloxam. A grant of £20 was awarded to Petrie for this
purpose. These BAAS committees supported a leading researcher with some
financial assistance, but more importantly gave them authority which could
prove helpful in carrying out research (Brook, 1981: 104). The photographic
survey across the British Empire to map and delineate 'race' and 'type' put
in motion by Thomas Huxley in 1869 was followed by a BAAS survey of the

British Isles in 1878; but both had limited and varying results (Edwards, 2009: 190). However, as this committee around 'Racial Photographs' from ancient Egypt illustrates, there was clearly a belief that such projects were scientifically useful in determining what and who racial types were, and underlining these beliefs were ideas about heredity and the human type.

Logistics and money

The authority of BAAS may have been important in establishing connections and opening doors, but the money was insufficient for what Petrie was expected to do. Galton contacted one of the BAAS committee members, Reginald Stuart Poole, for advice on which heads to take copies of. Poole had given an address to the Anthropological Institute on 25 May 1886 on 'The Egyptian Classification of the Races of Men'. Poole argued that Egyptian art from 1500–1200 BC pushed back current knowledge of different races over 3,000 years. Despite their differences at the EEF, Poole had advocated sending Flinders Petrie out to obtain correct photographs of the portraiture of different races several months before the annual BAAS meeting at which this was agreed (Poole, 1887: 376). Poole listed the most important subjects for Petrie to capture in a letter to Galton six weeks after the BAAS meeting:

A. Bulak Museum

    1. Hyksos heads

    2. People of Punt from reliefs (Asurit)

B. Beni Hasan

    3. Fresco at Shemile

C. Thebes

    4. El-Karnak

        North Wall Type of each conquered nation
        South wall
        a. one Hebrew figure from relief of Surobak
        b. Khefu king
        c. Man of Ascalon

5. Luxor

Typical figures from pylon (Khela)

6. Asasif

People of Surl

7. Ramesseum

Typical figures from pylon including mercenaries

8. Medinet Habu

Typical figures from each relief copied by Rosellini

9. Tombs of the Kings.

All extant figures of the four races.
(Poole to Galton, UCL Galton Archives, 26 October 1886)

Poole's list was mainly of ancient Egyptian depictions of their conquered enemies, neighbours and their own depiction of the 'four races' they saw in their world. This list mainly covers monuments from the time of Dynasty 19 (1292–1186 BC), during the New Kingdom, when Seti I and Ramses II were defending the large Egyptian empire from growing powers in the region, such as the Hittites. The thinking behind this list is clearly to try and capture the 'types' of people in the Middle East at that time.

It was a long list to be covered for £20 (£966.20 is the equivalent amount today calculated with 'Currency Converter' on the National Archives website). Petrie wrote to Galton on 29 October that the money was insufficient and would just cover the cost of the photographs, not the journey itself. Petrie detailed his camera to Galton who had a noted interest in photography and camera equipment:

> Details of camera. ¼ flat camera used travelling use of ½ plate belonging to a friend who goes with me. I like the ¼ plate, its sharp, and on the distance from the black to white on a plate is 1/1700 it will bear enlarging. The advantages of a ¼ plate are lightness [. . .] & suitability for the lantern slides direct without any change. (Petrie to Galton, UCL Galton Archive: 29 October 1886)

A few days later Petrie mentioned to Galton that he has sent the list to Rev. Henry G. Tomkins, a member of the Society of Biblical Archaeology, and

Amelia Edwards, founding member of the EEF and Petrie's mentor, to check whether they had anything to add. He also inquired as to whether modern subjects are needed (Petrie to Galton, UCL Galton Archives, 1 November 1886). Tomkins sent Petrie an additional list of ancient monuments, which has also been checked by the scholar of Hebrew and Assyrian language A. H. Sayce. Petrie forwarded this extended list to Galton and detailed the difficulties with taking anthropological photographs of contemporary Egyptians, since they give false names and run away. Although he found a way round taking photographs of monuments or objects surrounded by people:

> in this way one can sidle up to a group who imagine they are mere spectators, & think that you are doing something away at right angles from them. (Petrie to Galton, UCL Galton Archives, 4 November 1886)

While the lists went back and forth, Petrie had been desperately trying to arrange the practicalities of his travel and funds. Amelia Edwards had suggested organizing a trip up the Nile with Francis Llewellyn Griffith so the cost could be shared, but Griffith, possibly because he had experienced the spartan conditions in which Petrie travelled, needed persuasion (Drower, 1995: 106). Petrie decided to leave anyway, while Edwards persuaded Griffith to go to Egypt and accompany him. Days before he was due to travel on the ship from Liverpool to Alexandria on 29 November, Galton confirmed he would give a further grant of £40 more to the £100 grant he had already given Petrie from his own pocket and £300 if Petrie made a full expedition. Griffith and Petrie met in Alexandria and travelled onto Cairo to find the new Director of Antiquities and obtain the permits for their expedition.

The journey

Evidence for what Egypt looked like to contemporary English visitors can be gleaned from travel guides that were widely available at the time, such as the Murray *Handbook for Travellers in Lower and Upper Egypt*, which gives a sense of how people travelling along the Nile were connected via telegrams and post. Egypt was certainly not the exotic wilderness for Europeans that it had been; tourism at this point was hand in hand with British colonialism since Egypt had become a protectorate in 1881. The journey that Petrie and Griffith made can be traced in some detail due to the unpublished journals Petrie wrote on a weekly basis that are now preserved in the Griffith Institute, University of Oxford (Quirke, 2011). These journals, along with notebooks at the Petrie Museum, and photograph albums, also at the Griffith Institute, can be put together with Petrie's letters to Galton for a greater understanding of how Petrie went about working on the BAAS report. The itinerary below is taken from the online concordance to these photographs and journals *Petrie's Photographs of Egypt. Landscape, Monuments, People* and captures how much ground Griffith and Petrie covered:

29 Nov to 14 Dec 1886	Liverpool to Alexandria
13 to 19 Dec 1886	Alexandria, Cairo, hiring the boat, to Minya
20 to 24 Dec 1886	Life on boat, mention of Beni Hasan
23 Dec 1886 to 1 Jan 1887	el-Ashmunen, Antinoë, Bersheh, Isbayda, Tell el Amarna,
	Gebel Abulfoda, Manfalut, Beni Muhammed
10 to 18 Jan 1887	Bellianeh, Abydos, How, Chenoboskion, Keneh, Denderah, to Luxor
14 to 26 Jan 1887	Koft, Koos, Shenhur, Gurneh, Deir el Bahri, Luxor
	Erment, Gebelen, Esneh, El Kula, Hieraconpolis, El Kab
27 Jan to 7 Feb 1887	Edfu, Gebel Silsileh, Saba Rigaleh, Kom Ombo, Assuan, Elephantine, Philae
7 to 14 Feb 1887	Konosso, Philae, Bigeh 14 to 23 Feb 1887 boat Aswan to Luxor, Karnak
22 Feb to 1 March 1887	Medamot, *Griffith leaves Petrie at Karnak,* Luxor (tombs, Deir el Bahri, Drah abul Negga, Medinet Habu)
8 March 1887	Luxor (Medinet Habu)
6 to 17 March 1887	Boat Luxor to Siut, train to Wasta, by donkey on east bank Brimbal to Helwan, Atfieh, Turra quarries, to Bedrashen
18 to 26 March 1887	Bedrashen, Cairo, Sakkara, start of Dahshur work

Figure 4.1 Image of the Nile, going north from Luxor. Photograph by Debbie Challis, 2012

This was a rare occasion when Petrie did the more tourist activity of hiring a boat and travelling, for Petrie, fairly luxuriously up the Nile (Figure 4.1). However, he was not a typical tourist in Egypt; he was there to work and had no time, or indeed money, for luxury hotels, shooting trips or multi-course dinners by the pyramids. Even on this trip, Petrie recruited some of the Egyptians who had previously worked with him; including two Egyptian men – Said and Muhammed el Jabri – who were part of Ali Jabri's extended family. Ali Jabri was Petrie's Egyptian colleague whom he worked closely with during this period after their work measuring the pyramids a few years earlier. Stephen Quirke speculates that time on the boat may have enabled Petric to get to know his Egyptian colleagues better on this journey (Quirke, 2010: 68).

In the early months of 1887, Petrie was clearly scoping out various sites along the Nile and he returned to excavate at many of these over the coming years. This chapter concentrates on the times when Petrie was carrying out his mission for BAAS. Petrie could not take pictures at his first port of call in Beni Hasan as the tombs were too dirty:

> [. . .] but we mainly came here for F[rancis] to see the places, and for me to photograph the tombs at Beni Hasan; unhappily they are too much dirtied

for it to be possible to take them. The whole of the tomb want a good washing down, which might be quite safely done with sponges. (Petrie, Notebook 16/1/2 1886–7, 21 December 1886)

Petrie's main site for the photographs and squeezes he needed to make for his BAAS commission was in and around Luxor; namely the Luxor temple, the temple complex at Karnak and tombs in the Valley of the Kings. When he reached Karnak and began work in mid-February, Petrie wrote that:

> After a good deal of wondering about here, I set to work on the foreigners, beginning by taking squeezes of all the foreign heads here on the temple walls. I soon found that the squeezes were so manoeuvrable and clear that I determined to do all I could by squeezes, and only photograph where squeezes were impracticable. The result will be that I shall have a gallery of plaster casts of some 200 or 300 heads probably when I have worked them all off in England; and photographs can be taken far better from clean white casts arranged in a good light than directly from the monuments. Such a set of actual casts too will be in the collection either for Francis (as Ethnology), or for Oxford under Tylor. (Petrie, 1886–7, 14–23 February 1887)

Petrie refers here to the anthropologist Edward Burnet Tylor who was Keeper of the University Museum at Oxford. Before the trip Petrie had already outlined to Galton his preferred option of making squeezes 'where there is no paint to be injured', that is, soft paper squeezed into the relief so that an impression of the face is made which could then be turned into a mould for a cast (Petrie to Galton, UCL Galton Archives: 1 November 1886). This involved climbing up long ladders to capture heads from scenes on, for example, a pylon in Luxor. Petrie's intention was to create a cast gallery, supplemented by photographs where that was not possible, of 'racial types'. Petrie vividly describes this process in his autobiography:

> To reach many of the sculptures, it was needed to hang a rope ladder down from the top of the wall then go up with sheets of wet paper rolled round a spike-brush, full of water. Hooking the left arm through the ladder, the paper was unrolled, the wall wetted by the brush and then the paper beaten on, into all the hollows, and left to dry and the wall. (Petrie, 1931: 77)

Petrie took over 200 squeezes, which were made into casts, and 40 photographs. In most of the tombs in Thebes, Petrie took photographs of the painted scenes

Figure 4.2 Face from Tomb Seti I No. 776, Flinders Petrie, *Racial Photographs* (1887) © Palestine Exploration Fund

though this was dependent on how extant the pictures still were. For example, in the tomb of Seti I (KV17) Petrie only took one photograph, (Figure 4.2) no. 776, Book XIV *Racial Photographs,* as his notebook records that there was only one extant figure left with 'black brown hair', which could be photographed (Petrie, Notebook 123, 1887). The main different racial types were defined by the Ancient Egyptian depiction of four groups of people, usually found in tombs in paintings of the 'Book of Gates', such as the Tomb of Merenptah (Valley of the Kings KV8). In the tomb of Seti II were an extant, if unfinished, depiction of the four 'races' of Ancient Egypt. These were 'roughly done and unpainted' and Petrie made a jotted sketch of one head plus the inscriptions. The Tomb of Ramses III (KV11) had an extant set of the four races of men along the bottom of the Book of Gates, which Petrie managed to photograph (Figure 4.3).

Petrie's squeezes were taken from New Kingdom monuments (mainly Dynasty 19) in Karnak, the Ramesseum, Medinet Habu and Luxor Temple. Karnak is a vast temple complex just north of Luxor in Upper Egypt. Built over a period of 2,000 years, there are many different temples, shrines and chapels to a number of different kings and gods. The Great Hall at Karnak is

Figure 4.3 Face from Tomb Ramses III No. 777, Flinders Petrie, *Racial Photographs* (1887) © Palestine Exploration Fund

a hypostyle hall, or a pillared courtyard, in the main temple dedicated to the god Amun. Started by Seti I (c.1291–1279 BC) and completed by Ramses II (c.1279–1212 BC), the relief work on the walls and columns of the interior of the Great Hall of Karnak show a variety of festivals and offerings to the king. The outer walls are full of propagandistic war scenes to illustrate the 'awesome power of the gods and their king' and the role of the king in maintaining order (Weeks, 2005: 84). The war scenes include various depictions of peoples and Kings vanquished by the Egyptians, usually depicted at the time of submission in battle, alongside an inscription giving the name of the people concerned. The peoples depicted are mainly from the west of Egypt, such as Libyans, or the Eastern Mediterranean, such as the Hittites from the area of contemporary Syria or the Shasu of southern Palestine.

The scale of Petrie's operation can be seen when visiting Karnak and the other places he took casts from today. This scene from the north outer wall of the Great Hypostyle Hall shows Seti I driving vanquished enemies before him. The first illustration shows a wider shot of the scene (Figure 4.4); the second one shows a close up of the top line of the prisoners on which some of the heads that Petrie took squeezes of, can clearly be seen (Figure 4.5).

Figure 4.4 North outside wall of Great Hall at Karnak. Photo taken by Debbie Challis

Figure 4.5 Close up of Great Hall at Karnak

Across the Nile in the Temple of Ramses III at Medinet Habu, Petrie also took similar casts of captives dedicated to Amen from the first pylon (Figure 4.6). Inside the doorway is a procession showing captive peoples. Figure 4.7 is an overview of the scene while Figure 4.8 shows the lower line of people depicting

Figure 4.6 View of the First Pylon of Medinet Habu. Photograph taken by Debbie Challis

Figure 4.7 Inside doorway of Medinet Habu. Photo taken by Debbie Challis

Figure 4.8 Detail of above showing people on lower line

Figure 4.9 Detail of above showing people on upper line

Petrie casts 174–7 and Figure 4.9 the upper line depicting Petrie cast 178 (Figures 4.10 and 4.11).

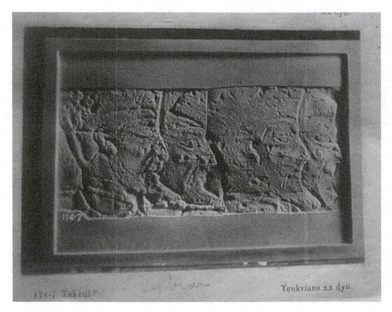

Figure 4.10 No. 174–7, Flinders Petrie, *Racial Photographs* (1887) © Palestine Exploration Fund

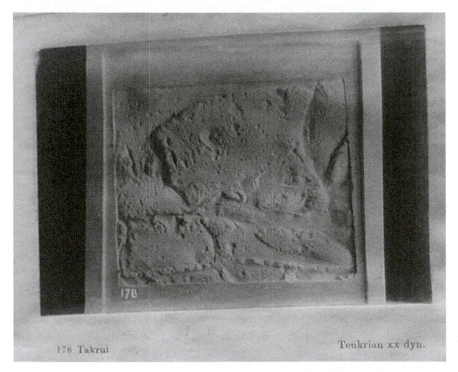

Figure 4.11 No. 178, Flinders Petrie, *Racial Photographs* (1887) © Palestine Exploration Fund

It took Petrie six weeks to take the photographs and squeezes. He wrote to Galton, after he had finished his commission for BAAS and before he started work at Dahshur on his 'old business of surveying pyramids', that he was grateful for Galton's financial assistance. Petrie proposed to take a 'series of casts and classify them racially' and needed the opinions of members at the BAAS committee as to the 'most valuable and suitable for reproducing as typical photographs, or for composite photographs' (Petrie to Galton, UCL Galton Archives: 2 April 1887). Having surveyed the pyramids at Dahshur and after visiting the museum at Cairo, Petrie got the slow boat from Alexandria on 27 May and was home in June, making the casts from the squeezes he had taken over summer 1887.

Back home

Petrie presented a report, his photographs and casts at the 1887 BAAS conference at Manchester in early September, with Rev. Henry G. Tomkins, who had advised on the original list, speaking on the findings. Numbers attending the conference were 3,838. The *Birmingham Daily Post*, for example, commented that 'attention was devoted by the majority of members to the sections dealing with geography, economies and anthropology'. The Anthropological Section was presided over by Professor A. H. Sayce. Sayce, who had also advised Petrie on the list for *Racial Photographs*, delivered an 'Address' in which he compared the study of language to the study of visual representation and linked both to distinctions of race:

> The distinctions of race must be older than the distinctions of language. On the monuments of Egypt, more than 4,000 years ago, the Libyans are represented with the same fair European complexion as that of the modern Kabyles, and the painted tomb of Rekh-ma-ra, a Theban prince who lived in the 16th century before our era, portrays the black skinned negro, the olive coloured Syrian and the red skinned Egyptian with all the physical peculiarities that distinguish their descendants today. (Sayce, 1887: 887)

Sayce's address on race, Aryan and Semitic languages and faces in antiquity and the importance of understanding invasions and migrations in locating racial groups in modern Europe set the tone for the BAAS meeting. For example, Canon Isaac Taylor gave a paper on 'The Primitive Seat of the Aryans', which argued that Northern Europe rather than Central Asia was the home of the undivided Aryan race and J. S. Stuart-Glennie gave a paper on 'The Non-Aryan and Non-Semitic White Races and their Place in the History of Civilisation'. Sayce's address around invasion, migration and racial movement in Europe and the Near East gives an indication of the thinking at the time, which would be influential on Petrie's later work.

Petrie's report was delivered and his account was later published in the BAAS Meeting proceedings and as a separate pamphlet with Tomkins' paper and the photographs. Most of the photographs in the report are of casts, which were numbered and listed alongside any inscriptions he could decipher. The results were:

(1) a series of about 150 casts, comprising 268 heads which will be presented to the British Museum;
(2) other selected sets of casts from the paper moulds, which can be obtained for museums on application to me;
(3) a series of 40 photograph negatives of paintings, and a series of photographs from all the casts excluding duplicates;
(4) prints of all these plates which can be ordered from Mr Browning Hogg, 75 High Street Bromley, Kent at cost price, the charge for printing is 2s, 3d per dozen if selected from a loose set, or 45s for the whole, mounted on printed sheets in a case. (Petrie, 1887: 439)

Petrie numbered the photographs by site and monument in his report but gathered them into racial groups in his books of photographs. The report had a small print run. Fifty copies of the report and photographs were published with a notice inserted into all likely 'Scientific and Antiquarian Journals'. Petrie wrote to Galton after the 1887 BAAS conference that he was 'sorry not to see you at Manchester' where the casts attracted a 'fair interest in them and the subject':

> The Palestine Exploration Fund have agreed to exhibit all the casts at South Kensington on their bases, because I send them to the British Museum, where but few will see the light I expect. Thus they will be available for general inspection I hope during October and November. (Petrie to Galton, UCL Galton Archives: 14 September 1887)

Petrie was worried about the accession of the casts to the British Museum and recommended that the British Museum curator Peter de Page Renouf should be contacted directly, while suggesting that they are exhibited on the Egyptian staircase (Petrie to Galton, UCL Galton Archives: 15 October 1887). The casts are today in the accession lists for the Department of the Middle East of the British Museum.

The casts from the monuments at Thebes were put on display at the South Kensington Museum as 'Syrian portraits' under the auspices of the PEF from October 1887 until early 1888. The Meeting of the General Committee of the PEF recorded this exhibition of ethnological casts:

> The characteristic tales of the Hittites, the Amorites, Arabs, the Judaeans and the inhabitants of the north of Syria could here be for contemporary portraits; and moreover from such a number of examples that the general type could be seized without the uncertainty of errors of the Sculptor. One most prominent result in Palestine was the resemblance of the Judeans to the Amorites (agreeing with the Kings of Jerusalem and Hebron being Kings of the Amorites and Ezekiel declaring to Jerusalem "My father was an Amorite"), the faces of the former being of exactly the same type of of the latter, only rather more refined and subtle of expression. (PEF General Committee Meeting, 3 July 1888)

It was this idea that the faces of the Old Testament could be seen again that captured the imagination of biblical scholars and clergymen, which in many ways was ironic given Galton's ambivalent attitude to religion and the church. The biblical scholar, Rev. Henry G. Tomkins, presented an extended version of his findings on the places or regions to which the heads belonged, which had been published in *Racial Photographs*, at the Anthropological Institute in 1888. Tomkins goes through all of the names from the inscriptions in turn, presenting the photograph along with other evidence to locate where the person depicted is from. For example, photo 788 is taken to be an Aethiopian Queen with a complexion of reddish brown 'of a kind still found in Abyssinia, as Mr Houghton remarks in the *Bible Educator*' (Tomkins, 1889: 215). Tomkins is puzzled by having a Negro type with red hair but quotes Amelia Edwards' *A Thousand Miles up the Nile* on seeing Nubians with blue eyes and 'frizzy red hair'. Most of the profile heads taken from Karnak were of towns in and around the large region of Syria, Palestine and Jordan:

> There is great reason, I think, to place these on, or near, the Euphrates. We have among our photographs several of the defenders of Ianua (78–81) against Seti I, and here are some front faces, with broad, rounded beards, to compare with the profiles. These faces [. . .] belong to the Khal-u of Syria [. . .]. (Tomkins, 1889: 223)

The discussion after Petrie's and Tomkins' papers at the BAAS conference is not recorded, but there are some notes from Tomkins' later paper at the Anthropological Institute indicating the interest in the topic. For example, Francis Griffith, Petrie's companion for his Nile trip, pointed out a recent paper by Peter de Page Renouf on Semitic languages and Petrie was described as being 'present' and 'joining in the discussion' (Tomkins, 1889: 240). Tomkins praised Galton's Galton's 'Jewish' composite photographs, pointing to their use in Dr Neubauer's paper 'Race Types of the Jews' as well as to Joseph Jacob's work on Jewish inheritance and ability. Four examples of Petrie's casts, Nos. 36–9, from Karnak were compared with Galton's 'Jewish' composites as 'it is agreed that these photographs are singularly successful in defining a race-type'. Tomkins held 'that there is a clear similarity of facial contour':

> The four examples of Rehoboam's princes exhibit a more delicate and refined profile than any other type before us, and one has even a nose slightly retroussé, like one of our boys in the frontispiece-plate of the *Journal*. This examination might well be pursued further and illustrates the great importance of collating groups of 'modern instances' with 'the antique'. (Tomkins, 1889: 238–9)

Looking at ancient faces could, in this argument, give the viewer modern identities, 'types' and personalities. It was an argument that would be influential in reading faces from the past in Petrie's next major excavation and discovery.

5

Greek Art, Greek Faces?

The collection of Roman mummy portrait panels in the Petrie Museum is one of the museum's highlights. Looking into the case that holds the best preserved images is like looking into the faces of long dead. One of these 'portrait panels' (Figure 5.1), depicting a dark-haired woman, was described by Flinders Petrie:

> It represents a young married woman of about 25; of a sweet but dignified expression, with beautiful features, and of fine complexion. She wears pearl earrings and a gold necklace. The colouring is of a bright tone, not so grey as the other, but it has gone whitish on the surface by age. (Petrie quoted in Quirke and Roberts, 2007: 85)

When this image was recently published in *Living Images: Egyptian Funerary Portraits in the Petrie Museum* emphasis was placed on what the hairstyle and jewellery told a modern viewer about the period in which the woman had lived and both indicated the Antonine ad 160–190 date. Rather than reading the woman as 'sweet but dignified' the portrait is said to be pallid and sickly with sunken cheeks, with the suggestion is that the portrait may even record the woman's final illness (Picton, Quirke and Roberts, 2007: 164). Over one hundred years, emphasis has moved from reading and characterizing the image to looking for historical evidence or medical analysis. However, the immediate impact of seeing these faces from Roman Egypt is to see them as portraits first and historical objects after. How we as museum visitors see these objects, is affected by our own close contact with portraiture, whether in galleries or photographs of our loved ones that multiply in our homes, on our phones and

Figure 5.1 Roman Mummy Portrait UC14692 © Petrie Museum of Egyptian Archaeology, UCL

in our virtual lives. Arguably, seeing representations of faces has never been so important, but portraits signify more than depicting people we know. In the nineteenth century, reading the face was an important tool, making up the descriptive narrative of literature and framing peoples' characters in art. Therefore the discovery of faces from Greco-Roman Egypt was the discovery of the people themselves, not just the art or death masks.

On finding the mummy portrait panels in February 1888, Petrie wrote that:

> [. . .] I have the notion – beside any special exhibition that we make of these – that it would be a grand joke to send in all the paintings I bring home to the winter exhibition of old masters at Burlington House. Most of them would go in readily for their art alone, apart from their history; and

for their technical interest I should think a series of a dozen or more would be most welcome there. So I cut through the wrappings and drew out all the Portraits, which can be replaced wheresoever they finally come to rest in a museum. (Petrie quoted in Quirke and Roberts, 2007: 87)

These mummy portraits illustrated the application of a Greco-Roman art form in Egyptian burial customs at the beginning of the first millennia. Their exhibition in London in the 1880s caused a sensation. The mummy portrait panels from Roman-ruled Greek-occupied Egypt were categorized as art objects transcending historical context when first exhibited. In the twentieth century, these portrait panels became re-classified as funerary objects and, on the whole, are today displayed in museums in an archaeological context alongside other artefacts from the geographical area and historical period of Roman Egypt. Despite this re-classification of them, contemporary critical responses to the mummy portraits tend to dwell on either their artistic style or on their function as portraits of people whose image they have preserved for eternity. These portraits from Roman Egypt are examples of Greek, or Greco-Roman, painting and their naturalistic style has been heavily emphasized by critics, both in the nineteenth century and more recently.

One of the great assumptions about classical art has been around its artistic quest for naturalistic verisimilitude. Jaś Elsner argues that the Greco-Roman viewer could choose from a range of responses to art, of which seeing an image as naturalistic was only one, and that viewing in a ritualistic context has been underplayed in modern reactions to classical art (Elsner, 2007). In the regimes of spectatorship that were played out in the Greco-Roman world, various non-classical influences, customs and visual attitudes had an impact, especially in the eastern part of the Roman Empire. These panel portraits would have had multiple visual meanings: whether as a portrait of the dead, an ancestral portrait, an image of the individual to preserve their identity in the afterlife or a shroud for the face after mummification. Any of these meanings could co-exist in dialogue with each other for the ancient viewer.

When the panels are exhibited in a museum of historical objects or a gallery of art, different meanings are ascribed to them and how they are displayed defines their meaning. Where the portrait panels are placed and how they are interpreted in museums tells us something about the demarcation of objects by the museum authorities. Despite such demarcations, these panel portraits do have multiple meanings for modern audiences as visitor reactions to them that I have heard can testify. The reaction to them is dependent on the wider context around reading faces and the use of portraiture. When Petrie first exhibited the mummy portrait panels in 1888, they fed into a vibrant tradition of portraiture in British visual culture. The faces on these portraits were also read for character attributes within physiognomy and considered the face as a 'field of signs' that could be used to 'determine the inner nature of the soul behind the façade' (Kemp and Wallace, 2000: 94). The ethnographic identification of the faces in these portraits was bound up with physiognomic assumptions. These identifications would have ramifications long beyond the nineteenth century.

Found and exhibited

After his report to the BAAS conference and the exhibition of casts of racial types at the South Kensington Museum in the Autumn of 1887, Flinders Petrie was back in Egypt on his next major excavation at Hawara in the Fayoum area below Cairo. Jesse Haworth, a wealthy businessman from Manchester, and another businessman Martyn Kennard, who was also a collector, sponsored Petrie's work in 1888. Hawara was the site of the lost 'Labyrinth' of Amenemhat III in Dynasty 12 in the Middle Kingdom, the intricacy of which had impressed Herodotus in the fifth-century BC. It was also a cemetery for the population of the surrounding area, particularly Arsinoe (Medinet el-Fayum), from the late Middle Kingdom (2025 to 1700 BC) to the Roman period (30 BC to AD 300). Petrie was interested in finding and mapping the Labyrinth, though his work on this was overshadowed by his other finds. Hawara had regained importance in the Roman period and Petrie uncovered dozens of portrait panels on mummies from the Roman period.

Petrie wrote to Francis Galton about Hawara on 25 April 1888, referring to the recent exhibition of mummy portrait panels by Theodor Graf, and his excitement at finding more drips from the page. He comments that 'I have been plundering a cemetery here, of Greek and Roman age. The principal results have been a series of about 60 painted panels'. In addition, Petrie had over a hundred skulls and wrote to Galton that he was not sure whether to send them to the Hunterian Museum at the Royal College of Surgeons, London, the British Museum or Natural History Museum (Petrie to Galton, UCL Galton Archive: 25 April 1888). Virchow thanks Petrie for the skulls in this letter. He mentioned the visit to his excavations by Heinrich Schliemann, 'discoverer' of Troy, and the pathologist Rudolf Virchow on 3 April. After this visit, Petrie sent Virchow a gift of about 40 skulls (Virchow to Petrie, PMA: 14 April 1888). Virchow had made important medical discoveries, mainly around cellular pathology and comparative pathology, but, as well as being a liberal reformist German politician, he had also established the Society for Anthropology, Ethnology and Prehistory in 1869. He made a rigorous examination of Ancient Greek skulls in 1879 and his treatise on it in 1893 put such examinations on a more systematic basis (Nowak-Kemple and Galanakis, 2011: 1–16). Virchow denounced Nordic mysticism in 1885, arguing that the study of skulls disproved both the idea of a 'pure' German race and a hierarchy of races. Skull collecting and craniology was not always used to vindicate perceived racial hierarchies.

Petrie decided to send the skulls to William Henry Flower at the Natural History Museum, who had been on the 'Racial Photographs' Committee, including that of the woman 'of sweet but dignified expression' (UC14692) whose portrait and description I opened this chapter with. Petrie's excavations at Hawara in 1887–8 and then in 1910–11 were the 'best-documented discovery of mummy portraits anywhere in Egypt' at that time, though his scanty records cause despair to curators and researchers today (Roberts, 2007: 13). Although Petrie intended to match the skull to the portrait panel for potential research, his intentions were thwarted in part by his own rush to disperse the objects and head back to Egypt.

The Viennese art dealer Theodor Graf first exhibited mummy portraits in various venues to great acclaim in Europe and New York in 1887–8. There is scant archaeological information about the Graf portraits. He had acquired many of these from dealers in Egypt and they are thought to come from the region surrounding the town of er-Rubayat in the Fayum (Walker and Bierbrier, 1997: 86). Graf sold many of these portraits soon after their exhibition and the collection was further dispersed on his death in 1920. Following in the wake of Graf, Flinders Petrie exhibited the portraits and other finds from his Hawara excavation at the Egyptian Hall in Piccadilly in London's West End in June and July 1888. The venue was an established popular attraction in the cultural heart of London and its choice indicates that Petrie anticipated a huge public response. The year 1888 was the perfect time in which to stage an exhibition of new finds of art from the classical period of Egypt, particularly when the art appeared to depict ordinary Greco-Romans. As we have seen, the 1880s were the height of the so-called Victorian Olympus movement in British art in which the principal artists were leading a revival of classicism in painting and sculpture. Petrie framed and mounted each picture ready for the opening on 18 June 1888 and, in order to ensure that it made an impact, he sent personal invitations to influential cultural figures. Petrie was rewarded with the attendance of painters such as Lawrence Alma-Tadema, Holman Hunt and Edward Poynter as well as the Director of the National Gallery, Sir Frederick Burton.

Petrie wrote to Amelia Edwards on 2 July that he had had 80 entries on the previous Friday and 70 on the Saturday (Petrie to Edwards, PMA: 2 July 1888). Echoing artistic interest, there was a rapturous reception of Petrie's exhibition in the press. *The Times* reported on 2 July 1888 that:

> [. . .] in the drawing room of the Egyptian Hall, Piccadilly, there will be on view one of the most curious collections of Egyptian antiquities that has ever been brought together. Many of the objects, it is true, are of the kind in which every museum abounds, but the portraits, over thirty in number, are almost absolutely new to Egyptologists. ('Mr Flinders Petrie's Egyptian Antiquities', *The Times*, 2 July 1888)

The paper further commented that these naturalistic Hellenic and Roman portraits from Egypt 'have the appearance of being no older than Tuscan portraits of the time of Giotto'. This reference to early Renaissance painting and that of Giotto and Florentine art in particular, is a recurring one in the reception of the mummy portraits. The art journal *Academy* commented that the 'lifelike character of the portraits and their variety of type and expression [. . .] attest to the fact these are portraits in the truest sense of the word' ('Egyptian Portraiture of the Roman Period', *Academy*, 7 July 1888). In the more popular *Illustrated London News*, John Forbes-Robertson wrote that 'Greek art, which is the presentment of Nature herself, was grafted on to Egyptian conventionality, and beauty was crowned with joy' (*Illustrated London News*, 30 June 1888).

The reception was all that Petrie could have hoped for and he wrote to Amelia Edwards:

> Miserable weather but attendance good at the Hall. I suspect we shall take £100 (2000 people) against £90 of expenses. [. . .] Several solid folks have been: [Arthur] Evans, [General Lane-Fox] Pitt Rivers, [Augustus] Franks, [William Blake] Richmond, Holman Hunt all more than once. We have got hold of the right vein of folks, and not had any nasty bores or 'arrys about. (Petrie to Edwards, PMA: 12 July 1888)

He and his funders Martyn Kennard and Jessie Howard agreed to split the finds between them. Martyn Kennard presented the complete mummy Artemidorus and other portraits to the British Museum, which Petrie said he had persuaded Alexander Murray, Keeper of the Department of Greek and Roman Antiquities, to take 'as fresh painting of the Greeks' (Petrie to Edwards, PMA: 10 July 1888). Petrie referred to his acrimonious dispute with Wallis Budge in 'Oriental Antiquities' as to why he preferred the portraits to go to Murray. Jesse Howarth donated portraits and other items to what became the Manchester Museum and some damaged fragments of mummy portraits and frames went to the South Kensington Museum (later entering the collection of the Victoria and Albert Museum). Much of Petrie's own collection became part of the collection of the Petrie Museum. As well as these and other museum acquisitions, Jesse Howarth also presented seven mummy portraits to the National Gallery and, perhaps more surprisingly, the National Gallery bought another four for £95 (Petrie to Burton, National Gallery: 4 August 1888). In a letter to the Director of the National Gallery, Sir Frederick Burton, Petrie apologizes:

> [. . .] not to have persuaded my friends to give more to the National Gallery in preference to other places; but I have made a special point of securing the old man's head for you. (Petrie to Burton, National Gallery: 20 July 1887)

Burton considered the old man's head as similar to the sixteenth-century artist Giovanni Battista Moroni 'in its vitality and its workmanship' (Conlin, 2006: 324). Reporting on the matter, *The Times* commented that this acquisition added to a sense of 'unbroken sequence in the history of the arts' and that a 'national museum should aim at being in the fullest sense of the word representative', speculating that more 'mature' art from Egypt, Greece and

Rome will be exhibited at the National Gallery ('The Latest Acquisitions of the National Gallery', *The Times*, 28 August 1888). Frederick Burton's acquisition of these mummy portraits was criticized by some of the National Gallery's Trustees, but Burton argued that they belonged in the gallery alongside early Italian art:

> I consider these things as appropriate and desirable for a Gallery that pretends to be historical as any early Italian fresco or other work. They belong to European Art and show the method which had already become traditional in it from the time of the Hellenic painters. (Quoted in Conlin, 2006: 324)

Burton had a history of collecting early renaissance art for the gallery, such as Hans Holbein's *The Ambassadors*, Piero della Francesca's *Nativity* and Sandro Botticelli's *Venus and Mars*, and was influenced by German art historical methodologies. Some of these mummy portraits were first exhibited as the 'lost link' in western art in the central hall next to a thirteenth-century Margarito and late fourteenth-century fresco fragments by Soinello Aretino. Petrie later commented that he had mounted them against the colour that harmonized best and framed them 'little thinking that these mounts would be retained for over forty years at the National Gallery' (Petrie, 1931: 89).

Greek in face

In 1889, John Forbes-Robertson reviewed 'Graeco-Roman Portraiture in Egypt' in the *Magazine of Art*, in which he stressed the artistic value of the portraits as giving us an 'echo of the masterpieces of Greek genius'. Commenting the portraits were 'Egyptian in form, though Greek in face', Forbes-Robertson argued that these portraits should find a 'resting place in the British Museum and the National Gallery' as they illustrate the tradition of Greco-Roman craftsmanship before the 'blow' to art of Byzantium (Forbes Robertson, 1889: 178 and 179). A few years later, the German Egyptologist Georg Ebers echoed this 'Greek in face' comment in 'the first popular book on the mummy portraits', *Hellenic Portraits of the Fayum at present in the Collection of Herr Graf*, and claimed that the mummy portraits derived from the Ptolemaic period in Egypt and were therefore unequivocally Greek (Montserrat, 1998: 176). Ebers was a friend of Lawrence Alma-Tadema, whose painting *Love's Jewelled Fetter*, showing two women looking at a ring or token of love in front of a portrait of a man based on one of the mummy portraits, was exhibited in 1895.

Dominic Montserrat has explored the nineteenth-century fascination with the portraits as both the 'funerary images as evocations of living bodies' and 'the ability of the portraits to reanimate and evoke the people of the past in a quasi-psychic way' as arguably Alma-Tadema's painting attempted to do for the classical past (Montserrat, 1998: 176). Montserrat noted that ethnic attribution of the people represented in the portraits began early and Ebers used the mummy portrait panels to 'assign carefully graded racial types to individuals in the Fayum portraits on pseudo-physiognomic principles' (Montserrat, 1998: 176). Ebers read some of the portraits as belonging to Semitic types or Ethiopian but thought that most of the portraits were of Hellenic Greeks, noting their dark complexion:

> But the sun of the South quickly tans the fair European skin, and Hellenic Greeks whose families remained in Egypt for several generations would not be likely to preserve their original fair hue. Certainly most of the pictures show us truly Greek features, and this is the case in many of rather dark complexion. (Ebers, 1893: 38)

Ebers assumed that the Greeks were 'fair' skinned along Northern European lines rather than Mediterranean. In this way the mummy portrait panels were considered to be doubly Greek – Greek in form and Greek in face.

Ebers was not alone in reading the 'Hellenic portraits' as examples of ethnographic types in a physiognomic manner. It is perhaps no coincidence that Ebers was a novelist as was Amelia Edwards who similarly drew on physiognomy in her lecture (or chapter) 'Portrait-painting in Ancient Egypt' in *Pharaohs, Fellahs and Explorers*; the collection of lectures delivered in the United States and published shortly before her death in 1892. This lecture includes a long pre-amble on the representation of races in Ancient Egypt and refers to a previously published pamphlet by Ebers on the mummy portraits. In illustrating this topic Edwards reproduces photographs taken by Petrie for the BAAS committee (Edwards, 1891: 82). For example, she uses the image photographed by Petrie of the 'Northern race' from the Tomb of Ramsess III to illustrate 'The Typical Syrian of Egyptian Art' (Figure 5.2):

> The Asiatic type is admirably caught. This man was probably a Canaanite. He has all the ethnic characteristics of the race. The eye, as usual, is falsely drawn, but it is set at the Semitic angle, and the face has a vivid look that

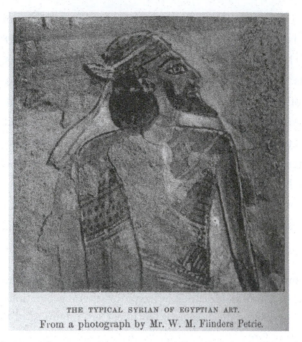

THE TYPICAL SYRIAN OF EGYPTIAN ART.
From a photograph by Mr. W. M. Flinders Petrie.

Figure 5.2 'The Typical Syrian of Egyptian Art', Edwards (1891), *Pharaohs, Fellahs and Explorers*: 82

speaks of actual portraiture. He wears a head-gear of some spotted material, bound with the Syrian fillet, yet in use. The fringed and patterned robe, the cap and fillet, are all true to the Syrian-costume of three thousand years ago. (Edwards, 1891: 82–3)

When Edwards turns to the mummy portrait panels she argues that they are so naturalistic that you can tell their identity, even when they do not have the names inscribed on their bandages or in their cases as they are 'surely identified by their racial characteristics' as 'unmistakably' Roman, Greek, Egyptian, Nubian or Semitic (Edwards, 1891: 100). For example, Edwards describes a mummy portrait of a woman (Petrie OO – now in the Egypt Museum in Berlin, Germany) (Figure 5.3) as 'a Greek lady':

This lady is clearly a Greek. The nose and forehead are in one unbroken line, the eyes are well spaced and well opened, and the mouth is prettily drawn. (Edwards, 1891: 103)

Whereas, a portrait panel of a woman (Petrie H – now in the Royal Ontario Museum in Canada) is described as 'Egyptian':

GREEK LADY.

Figure 5.3 'Greek Lady', Edwards (1891), *Pharaohs, Fellahs and Explorers*: 9

Her features are moulded in the unmistakable Egyptian type. The eyes are long and heavy lidded, the nostrils wide, the lips full and prominent. The complexion is swarthy with a dull reddish blush under the skin and the whole expression of the face is that of Oriental languor. (Edwards, 1891: 104)

Edwards described the portrait of 'Diogenes the flute-player' portrait as having 'thick and curly' hair with 'features distinctly Jewish in type' and 'that he should be a Jew would be quite in accordance with his profession for the gift of music has ever been an inheritance of the children of Israel' (Edwards, 1891: 105) (Figure 5.4).

This chapter began with a fanciful characterization of a portrait by Petrie himself (UC14692, Figure 5.1), whom Edwards described as a 'Romano-Egyptian Lady':

DIOGENES THE FLUTE-PLAYER.

Figure 5.4 'Diogenes the Flute-Player', Edwards (1891), *Pharaohs, Fellahs and Explorers*: 101

The eyebrows and eyelashes are singularly thick and dark; the eyes long, and of Oriental depth and blackness; and the swarthiness of the complexion is emphasized by the dark down on the upper lip. It is a passionate, intense-looking face – the face of a woman with a history. (Edwards, 1891: 107)

How different to the 'sweet but dignified expression' attributed to her by Petrie or the 'pallid and sickly' description of a few years ago in *Living Images*.

When looking into these faces it is hard not to see character and more depth than a simple two-dimensional image, partly because of the striking images themselves, but also because that is how we are accustomed as art audiences, and as people, to look at portraits and faces of other people. Making assumptions about ethnic identity or identifying features with characteristics is, however, misplaced and potentially dangerous. This kind of racial attribution later led to Anti-Semitic use by the German philologist Hans F. K. Günther in the 1920s and 1930s. Günther impressed the ultra-nationalist publisher Julius Lehmann with his 'eye for racial differences' and was then commissioned by Lehmann to put together a book around rassenkunde (racial kinds or racial anthropology) (Pringle, 2006: 34–6). Günther used 'portraits' from Greek and Roman art in *The Racial Elements of European History* (1925), in which he argued that there were five main races, and then seven Jewish 'type' Fayum portraits in his *Rassenkunde des Jüdische Volkes* (1930), which illustrated how you could supposedly 'identify' a Jewish 'type' as well as his contention that there were too many Jews in Europe (Fenton, 1997: 12). This is part of the wider use of racial theory in Classical and Egyptian archaeology. This ethnographic attribution of the mummy portraits is an important part of the reception and later history of them and should be remembered when we, as both audiences and academics, consider the portraits today. The danger of making assumptions based on our own pre-conceptions and prejudices around identity is always present.

From face to place

The mummy portraits' perceived link between Classical and late Medieval and early Renaissance art continued into the early twentieth century. This is illustrated in the art collection of Sir Ludwig Mond, a portion of which later entered the National Gallery as a bequest in 1924. The 1910 catalogue of the Mond Collection lists the works as belonging to Tuscan, Umbrian, German and Flemish schools as well as four mummy portraits from the Hellenistic School. The four portraits were from the Graf collection and the catalogue description primarily draws on Georg Ebers' earlier *The Hellenic Portraits of the Fayum* (1893) to describe them (Richter, 1910: 599–600). That two mummy portraits were chosen by the National Gallery Trustees in 1908 as part of Mond's bequest to the National Gallery alongside early Renaissance art (for example, Bellini's *Madonna and Child*) illustrates this belief in the link between ancient and modern forms of art. Petrie returned to Hawara in 1910–11 and his excavations resulted in a further donation to the National Gallery of four mummy portraits in 1912, this time under the auspices of Petrie's British School of Archaeology in Egypt (Mackay to Holroyd, National Gallery: 2 September 1912). There was a further bequest to the National Gallery of a mummy portrait from Algernon Brent in 1916, which had come from Petrie's excavation via Algernon's brother Cecil Brent, and, lastly, a small mummy portrait was presented to the gallery by Major R. G. Gayer Anderson in 1943. The perceived connection between the mummy portraits and early

Renaissance art was not simply an aesthetic blip of the 1880s. However, by the 1930s this perception was beginning to change.

In 1931, the Egyptologist Sir Robert Mond, a son of Ludwig Mond, bequeathed a number of mummy portraits from the second Graf collection in 1920 as well as the remaining two from his father's collection to the British Museum. Mond had been a chemist but on convalescing in Egypt after a serious illness, he developed an interest in Egyptian archaeology, working with archaeologists such as Howard Carter and Arthur Weigall, and collected antiquities, many of which he bequeathed to the British Museum (Greenaway, 2004–8). It is significant that Robert Mond, the archaeologist, bequeathed his collection of mummy portraits to the British Museum in 1931, whereas Ludwig Mond, the art collector, bequeathed his to the National Gallery in 1908. A few years after Robert Mond's gift to the British Museum, most of the mummy portraits in the National Gallery were loaned there. Notes from the Trustee's Board Minutes on 11 February 1936 noted that:

> The Director reported that the British Museum was anxious to have on indefinite loan the series of Greco-Roman portraits in the Gallery. There was no suitable place to show them at Trafalgar Square. The Board agreed to the transfer, except for the two in the Mond Collection, which by the conditions of the gift must remain [at the National Gallery].

By 1936 the mummy portraits were no longer considered important for narrating the story of European art in the National Gallery and a greater emphasis was placed upon the mummy portraits' geographical and historical context in Roman Egypt, or Egypt in late antiquity. Some of the mummy portraits were subsequently displayed in the Coptic corridor at the British Museum, and so placed later in antiquity than their supposed Ptolemaic origins championed by Ebers and others. The terms of the Mond bequest, which had a difficult legal history, meant that the two mummy portraits from the 'Hellenistic School' remained at the National Gallery. It was the mummy portraits excavated in Hawara by Petrie that went on long-term loan to the British Museum until 1994. In that year the National Gallery defined itself as housing the 'nation's European paintings from 1300 to 1900' and used the Museums and Galleries Act of 1992 to transfer:

[...] certain works of art in the National Gallery to other national institutions where they would be better cared for and better displayed and where the public would be more likely to expect them. (The National Gallery Annual Report April 1993–March 1994 (London: National Gallery Publications, 1994) Appendix C.)

This included the 17 mummy portraits (accession numbers: NG1260–1270, 2912–2915, 3159, 5399), as well as Byzantine icons. At same time a long-term loan for the Mond portraits was agreed with the descendants of the Mond family.

In 1997, the *Ancient Faces: Mummy Portraits from Ancient Egypt* exhibition at the British Museum placed the mummy portrait panels firmly in the public gaze again, though as, Dominic Montserrat points out, before *Ancient Faces,* they appeared 'as cover art for the occasional classical book' (Montserrat, 1999: 18). Morris Bierbrier, co-curator of the 1997 exhibition *Ancient Faces: Mummy Portraits from Roman Egypt*, commented in the catalogue that 'artistic interest waned' in the mummy portraits after the 1890s and they became seen by critics 'as an isolated phenomenon without due consideration of their Egyptian and Roman context' (Bierbrier, 1997: 23–4). This view has been contested. In a review of *Ancient Faces*, Jed Perl argued in *Modern Painters* that 'these portraits have tended to be the purview not of art historians but of archaeologists, who are, I think, not very interested in what contemporary artists feel' (Perl, 1997: 40) Perl contended that the interest of Henri Matisse and André Derain and others has been overlooked partly 'since these products of Roman Egypt could be fitted into neither a primitivist nor a classicist reading of the origins of modern art.' The mummy portraits have had a greater influence on European artists than recognized, but it is fair to say that there was a revival of interest in the mummy portraits in the 1990s. This is illustrated by Euphrosyne Doxiadis' *Mysterious Fayum Portraits: Faces from Ancient Egypt* in 1995, *Portraits and Masks: Burial Customs in Roman Egypt* edited by Morris Bierbrier in 1996 and the *Ancient Faces* exhibition at the British Museum 14 March–20 July 1997.

This exhibition at the British Museum was also followed by an exhibition a year later that toured Greece, *From the Fayum portraits to early Byzantine Icon painting*, which placed more emphasis on artistic technique and made connections between late classical and early Byzantine art. *Ancient Faces* was the first comprehensive display of the mummy portraits since the 1880s. The mummy portraits were displayed alongside the portraits still encased in mummies on display, plaster masks, gilded cartonnage masks, and objects found near the mummies from tombs to place them in historical and archaeological context. The portraits were grouped together as far as possible by site or geographical area with the archaeological record (or lack of it) described. However, the actual reaction to the portraits as recorded in the media of the time, emphasized the naturalism of the portraits and the impact of looking at these long dead faces.

Most critics in media considered *Ancient Faces* as an 'art show' and reviewed it as such. For example, *The Guardian's* art critic Adrian Searle went so far as to review *Ancient Faces* alongside the annual BP Contemporary Portrait exhibition at the National Portrait Gallery, arguing that the mummy portraits have 'more presence than anything in the National Portrait Gallery':

> And, as paintings, it is difficult not to see them as the products of the same artistic canon that includes the portraits of Titian and Rembrandt, Van Dyke, Sargent, even Lucien Freud. Many are painterly in a peculiarly modern way, with their modeling, their shadows and highlights, the paint often almost sculpted on against the cursory backgrounds, the clothed shoulders rendered with thick, shorthand strokes. It is as if these 2,000 year old painters had already seen Venetian painting late Rembrandt, Picasso's Classical phase. Their plainness, as images, has a directness unfiltered by sentiment, precocity or flashiness. (Searle, 1997)

Andrew Graham-Dixon in *The Independent*, commented on the earlier reception of the mummy portraits as the 'missing link' between early Renaissance art and classical art (Graham-Dixon, 1997: 4). In *Apollo*, Jas Elsner noted his only quibble about *Ancient Faces* was a lack of investigation into the reception and modern appropriation of the mummy portraits (Elsner, 1997: 49).

Despite the archaeological emphasis of the exhibition, *Ancient Faces* was reviewed in ways reminiscent of the critics in late nineteenth-century art history journals and magazines. Brian Sewell's review for the *Evening Standard* unsurprisingly embodied this approach with his Hellenocentric tone, for example, 'this portraiture does not illustrate a native Egyptian skill or sensibility, but is Greek in origin'. His emphasis on the mummy portraits' importance in European art history is similar to that of Forbes-Robertson in 1889. Sewell attacks the transfer of the mummy portraits from the National Gallery to the British Museum, arguing that they are a:

> [. . .] footnote in Egyptology, make far better sense in the National Gallery, and it is intriguing to find that not only do two of them belong in Trafalgar Square but that a further 17 once did. A room displaying 19 such portraits, most of the highest quality, could and should have been one of the glories of the National Gallery, and a permanent reminder of how much ancient art has been destroyed, breaking the link between the antiquity and the Renaissance. (Sewell, 1997: 29)

In typical *agent provocateur* mode, Sewell's comments generated controversy for both the National Gallery and the British Museum. Sewell attacked the National Gallery trustees as being 'too complacent and lazy' to recognize the 'importance of the material so frivolously de-accessioned' and claimed that after the exhibition the public would be unable to see the majority of the mummy portraits transferred to the British Museum. The National Gallery and the British Museum both issued responses that emphasized that, not only was the British Museum the best place to display the portraits in terms of historical and geographical context, it was also best for the appropriate environmental conditions in the museum's galleries with a conservation department that was one of few in the world with the appropriate experience to care for the mummy portraits. Sewell trades on being a maverick reactionary, but this controversy illustrates how the history of a way of seeing specific groups of objects can return, as farce if not tragedy. The main point is that positioning the mummy portraits as *either* art works *or* archaeological objects limits the recognition of multiple visualities at play in looking at these faces.

Reconstructing faces

An unexpected consequence of the *Ancient Faces* exhibition in 1997 were the connections made between the skulls that Petrie had taken from Hawara and sent to William M. Flower at the Natural History Museum (NHM), as discussed in his letter to Galton in 1888, and the portraits that Petrie had excavated. A letter from Flower in the Petrie Museum Archive dated 12 October 1889 records his politely expressed frustration with Petrie's scanty records. Flower thanks Petrie for the 'photographs of the face of which we have the skulls' but asks for publication and location details as otherwise 'we can't catalogue them or publish them properly' (Flower to Petrie, PMA: 12 October 1889). Petrie recorded in his Journal for 1887–8 that he was interested in preserving the skulls underneath the portraits as at some point in the future they could reconstruct them and consider whether the living appearance is preserved by the portraits. He later sent skulls from his 1910–11 Hawara excavations to Professor Alexander Macalister, Chair of Anatomy at the University of Cambridge from 1883, who like Flower was also on the 'Racial Photographs' BAAS Committee.

It was not until Paul Roberts, curator at the British Museum and then preparing the *Ancient Faces* exhibition, was giving a talk at the Petrie Museum in November 1996, that Meredith Thompson, a member of the audience and student at UCL, informed him that 'at least 20 of the skulls had in fact survived and were in the collections of the NHM. These skulls were then positively identified as being those from Petrie's excavations through the identification letters used by Petrie in his reports being written clearly in pencil on the skull. A skull of a woman (Petrie VV) and of a man (Petrie AJ) were then taken to Richard Neave and John Prag at the Manchester Museum to be reconstructed. Roberts stresses that 'at no time was the portrait linked to the skull seen by those involved in the reconstruction' (Roberts, 2007: 30–1). The remarkable results of these reconstructions were put on display towards the end of the *Ancient Faces* exhibition and the similarity between the reconstructed skulls and the portraits attracted a great deal of attention in the media:

> FATIMA gazed back as Paul Roberts ran an admiring finger along her chin. "She is wonderful, isn't she?" he said. Fatima has been dead for almost 2,000 years. Her head has just been reconstructed from her skull, and it matches, hauntingly, the portrait from her mummy. She has gained immortality, as her family intended.[…] Experts are still unsure whether they were painted while the subject was still alive, or just after death. Their discovery revolutionised ideas on the history of painting; critics have said there is nothing comparable in Western art until the Renaissance. (Kennedy, 1997: 9)

The connection between the portrait and the skull proves the naturalism of the portrait, in these instances at least, and can, as Petrie intended, tell modern experts more about the lifestyle of these Egyptians living in Greek influenced towns during the period of Roman rule. There is of course more to Petrie's collection of skulls as he was also interested in defining what the racial type of the people in these portraits was and thought that examination of the skulls would assist with this identification. The importance of the face and seeing these people from the past is still as important as it ever was, but assigning ethnic identities and categorizing them as Greek, Roman, Egyptian and so on, has happily become more complex.

In this case skulls were collected with an aim, among others, of locating a racial type. This raises an interesting ethical point in museum practice about the use of data and material collected for, what we may consider as, ideologically dubious and scientifically inaccurate theories. In this instance, the data was useful as it effectively established that it is likely that, most of the time, the mummy portrait panels were naturalistic portraits of the people whose faces they covered. Skulls can give us limited information about the medical condition of the people when they died, though not as much as the entire body. Judith Miller used 58 skulls from Petrie's 1911 excavations in Hawara, housed in the NHM, to examine crania and the dental condition of teeth in an overview of the dentition of ancient Egyptians to speculate on diet and environment (Miller, 2008). Miller's work is an example of the usefulness in palaeopathology today and would appear to vindicate the human remains gathered by earlier 'skull collectors'. Another example is the work on paleoneurology carried out by Otto Appenzeller and others in the wake of reading the mummy portraits as naturalistic images, in which several of the mummy portrait panels were carefully looked at and along with their scanned 'matching' skulls read for signs of neurological disease such as tropia in the eyes or facial hemiatrophy (Appenzeller, Stevens, Kruszynski, Walker, 2004). More work is needed on the collection of human remains from antiquity that examines the ideological and theoretic contexts in which human remains are taken and stored before comparing their scholarly and public significance today to properly address this ethical issue.

Gallery display in museums reflects the demarcation of disciplines. What is included and excluded in display both responds to and 'constructs contemporary knowledge, organising representations of the past which articulate hierarchical structures such as the artistic canon' (Whitehead, 2009:

29). The mummy portraits were at first placed within the transcendental category of art and were invested with moral agency and racial superiority by virtue of being 'Greek'. In the mid-twentieth century, the mummy portraits were redefined as artefacts in the two biggest national collections of Britain. These mummy portrait panels fall into and between several academic disciplines and categories: art/archaeology, classical archaeology/Egyptian archaeology, classical art/Byzantine art, Hellenic Studies/Roman Studies. The list could continue. In recent exhibitions and museum displays the mummy 'portrait' panels from the Fayum have been used to illustrate the early art of Byzantium; Roman life in Egypt at the time of Hadrian; the crossover between ancient Greek and Byzantine art; personal identity; and changing funerary practices in Egypt. (*Hadrian. Empire and Conflict* at the British Museum 24 July to 26 October 2008; *Byzantium 330–1453* at the Royal Academy 25 October 2008 to 22 March 2009; 'Human Image' and 'Rome 400 BC–AD 300' galleries at the Ashmolean Museum after its opening in December 2009). The narrative of the exhibition defines these panels differently each time they are displayed. They can also be identified as Greek, Roman or Egyptian, or, indeed, a combination of all three. We could potentially celebrate these panels as expressions of cultural diversity in a large empire and as an illustration of the continuing tradition of Egyptian funerary practice within a different cultural context. The danger is that such celebrations simply reflect our own socio-political concerns around identity politics.

Mummy portrait panels perform multiple functions for the modern viewer in museums (Elsner, 2007: 257): a past funerary ritual, people performing the past, examples of stylistic technique, a link to Byzantine art, a precursor of modern art, an influence on artists, examples of national identity or style and images of ourselves. The ways the mummy portraits can be viewed is far beyond either the art or archaeology dichotomy, which in any case is a false one. Their naturalism makes us believe that they are images of people from the past but assumptions about their 'identity' should be considered very carefully. Jas Elsner considers how early Christian icons were visualized as being in themselves holy and imbued with transcendental spirituality, which was a development of classical stories and beliefs about the power of images and imagery. Mummy portraits, in addition to all their other visual and cultural functions, have a ritualistic function, since arguably visiting museums and galleries is one of the most powerful social rituals in contemporary society. Looking at these faces in a museum case, wherever it is on display, arouses many powerful thoughts and feelings. The interest of these faces and the attribution of race for many viewers and scholars in the nineteenth century was connected to religious belief (and doubt). These Roman faces were sometimes considered as faces from the time of Christ, while Petrie's BAAS photographs and casts were connected to Old Testament peoples. The heady mix of religious belief combined with looking at faces created more powerful thoughts and feelings than the application of physiognomy in reading the face.

6

Peopling the Old Testament

In the Petrie Museum there is a finely modelled terracotta head on a mount and stand labelled 'Hebrew' by Flinders Petrie (Figure 6.1). This head comes from the city of Memphis in Middle Egypt, potentially from the Ptolemaic (Greek ruled) period from c. 330–30 BC. The city of Memphis had a large migration of different peoples, particularly from the time of the Persian conquest in 525 BC on, which included a distinctive Jewish population, known from papyri to have played a large role in the public life and administration of the city (Thompson, 1988: 85). The head (museum number UC33278) was published in Petrie's excavation report *Memphis I* in 1909. He compared the head to a tomb

Figure 6.1 The 'Hebrew' Head, UC33278 © Petrie Museum of Egyptian Archaeology, UCL

painting at Beni Hasan, which he had previously intended to photograph as part of his *Racial Photographs* in 1886–7 but could not as the tomb was too dirty. Petrie wrote 'The type is that of the Semite, as shown in the chief of the Amu at Benihasan (19), but sturdier and fatter owing to a settled life. It probably represents the Syrian or Jewish trader' (Petrie, 1909: 16) (Figure 6.2). The head was confused with this portrait at Beni Hasan listed in Petrie's excavation report and so was placed in the much earlier Middle Kingdom Dynasty 12 (1991–1778 BC) on the Petrie Museum catalogue. Petrie labelled this head 'Hebrew', partly because of the known mix of peoples in Memphis from the fifth-century BC on, but also because he thought that it matched a Semitic profile.

The old card cataloguing system, and until last year the online catalogue, of the Petrie Museum records UC33278 in this way:

> Terracotta head with black and red paint, showing typical Semitic profile – hooked nose, splayed nostrils, wide up-turned mouth and flat eyebrows.

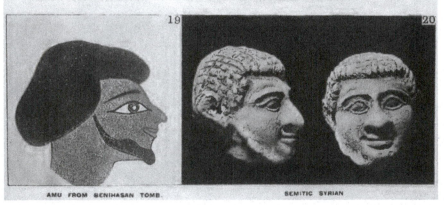

Figure 6.2 Part of Plate XXXVI, Flinders Petrie *Memphis I* (1909)

He wears his dark hair short in tight curls round the head, and a closely trimmed beard confined to the chin-line. (Petrie Museum Catalogue Card for UC33278)

This description repeats anti-Semitic conventions about appearance. After feedback from a workshop discussing this description at the Jewish Museum London in January 2011, Stephen Quirke, the Petrie Museum curator, decided we needed to change the online database to reflect concerns around the anti-Semitic description while retaining the historical integrity of the original. Stephen sent me an email saying that he had changed 'the repugnant registration on our internal "Adlib" and online catalogue. Have a look and tell me if it is any better. The difficulty is that it could depict someone quite close to the Petrie label, as there is a well attested Hebrew community in Memphis?' (Quirke to Challis, Email January 2011). The present online database derived from the Adlib museum catalogue was changed to read:

Terracotta head with black and red paint, considered by Petrie as one of a group showing different ethnic groups, reflecting the cosmopolitan population of Memphis, in accordance with early twentieth-century English views on race. In his publication Petrie wrote "the type is that of the Semite, as shewn in the chief of the Amu at Benihasan", referring to a famous Twelfth Dynasty depiction of east desert traders in the tomb-chapel of the governor Khnumhotep at Beni Hasan in Middle Egypt.

An old label on the Petrie block-mount for the head gives the narrower definition "Hebrew". Another label in the same series is "Sumerian" (UC33277); that language-name from the 4th-2nd millennia BC would not be used today as an ethnic label for images in the 1st millennium BC. However, the features of the face on UC33278 are closer to ancient Egyptian depictions of peoples in West Asia, than to ancient Egyptian depictions of Nile Valley peoples: 'hooked nose, splayed nostrils, wide up-turned mouth and flat eyebrows.' The head has black-painted short hair in tight curls round the head, and a closely trimmed beard confined to the chin-line. There is no context for the head; it may belong to the broader Hellenistic production of terracotta figures emphasizing differences between faces, of uncertain meaning and function.

(Petrie Museum of Egyptian Archaeology, UCL Catalogue, January 2011)

The description of this head as 'Hebrew' fits into the seeming obsession with defining 'Jewishness' physically and culturally in the late nineteenth and early twentieth centuries. In his address to the Anthropological Section of the BAAS Ipswich Conference in 1895, Petrie referred to the 1885 'Jewish composites', by Francis Galton and Joseph Jacobs. Petrie argued that, like the composite photographs, different types in antiquity can be recognized as 'what the camera does mechanically by mere superposition, the artist does intelligently by selection' (Petrie, 1895: 889). Petrie was not the first to make comparisons between these composites and identifying racial profiles on ancient depictions of the face. When Rev. Henry George Tomkins spoke on Petrie's *Racial Photographs* in 1888, he referred to Jacobs' same work on the Jewish composites (Tomkins, 1889: 239). The identity of groups of people in the time of the Old Testament and the identity of Jewish people were integral to ideas about race and archaeology in Egypt and the Near East. The museum history of this small object needs to be placed within the larger socio-political context around defining Jewishness and prevalent anti-Semitic description of the 'Jewish face' or 'expression'.

The 'Perfect Composite'

In 1885 Joseph Jacobs spoke on 'A Comparative Estimate of Jewish Ability' at the same BAAS Conference as Flinders Petrie spoke on Naukratis. Jacobs was an intellectual polymath who wrote on Jewish history, recorded folktales and campaigned on Jewish issues in Britain. In 1876 Jacobs was inspired by George Eliot's depiction of a man's search for his Jewish identity in the novel *Daniel Deronda* to seek evidence for a 'Jewish type' (Novak, 2008: 96). Jacobs was also influenced by Galton's *Hereditary Genius* in considering the genealogy of eminent Jewish men and families in his paper at the 1885 BAAS conference. He was one of a number of leading English Jews who were anxious about the growing number of Jewish immigrants, particularly from Central Europe, to London's East End. Boundless immigration to Britain of the 'worst stock' had been a major concern for Galton in *Hereditary Genius*. The growth of a working class and impoverished Jewish population was perceived by some as a threat to a largely integrated Anglo-Jewry. The large expansion in Jewish immigration was not just due to persecution but also to economic depression in Central Europe and a perception that London offered greater opportunities (Feldman,

1994: 152). It also placed a strain on Jewish philanthropy. In 1851 there were 20,000 Jews living in London and by 1900 there were 144,000 (Feldman, 2011: 5). Concern about this largely working-class Jewish immigration went parallel with interest in defining issues of racial difference and characteristics.

In the early 1880s Jacobs suggested to Francis Galton that he make composite photographs of boys who attended the Jews' Free School in the East End of London. At the time the Jews' Free School, in Bell Lane Shoreditch, was one of the largest schools in England with 3,000 students on the school register in 1883. Moses Angel had been headmaster there since 1842 and assisted Jacobs and Galton in obtaining photographs of the boys at the school. The composites compiled from the photographs of boys taken at the school were an attempt to prove whether there was a Jewish face or expression.

The composites were published by Galton in *The Photographic News* in April 1885. Galton thought them 'the best specimens of composites' he had 'ever produced', commenting that:

> They were children of poor parents, dirty little fellows individually, *but* wonderfully beautiful as I think, in these composites. The feature that struck me the most, as I drove through the adjacent Jewish quarter, was the cold scanning gaze of man, woman, and child, and this was no less conspicuous among the schoolboys. There was no sign of diligence in any of their looks, nor of surprise at the unwonted intrusion. I felt, rightly or wrongly, that every one of them was coolly appraising me at the market value, without the slightest interest of any other kind. (Galton, 1885: 243)

Galton's mercantile description of the 'Jewish quarter' reflects anti-Semitic clichés about Jews, money and avarice. These photographs show different groups of boys on the right (a, b, c, d) clustered together in one-lettered composite on the left (Figure 6.3). The 'Jewish face' composites are the only ones of a 'racial type' that Galton made and he defined a 'Jewish expression' or 'Jewish gaze' in their faces. Galton's anti-Semitism is imbued with class bias around the 'children of poor parents'.

These composites were exhibited at the Institute of Anthropology on 24 February 1885 alongside two papers by eminent Jewish historians: 'Notes on the Race Types of Jews' by the Oxford University librarian and historian Dr Adolf Neubauer and 'On the Racial Characteristics of Modern Jews' by Joseph Jacobs. Neubauer began with the premise that the Jews are thought to be a

Figure 6.3 Francis Galton, 'Jewish Face composite' © UCL Special Collections

'pure' race but disputed this by pointing to the number of mixed marriages mentioned in the Bible and argued that these intermarriages continued until the medieval period. He concentrated his thesis on the two main groups of Jews in Europe – the Ashkenazim (mainly in Central Europe) and Sephardim (the Spanish/Portuguese diaspora) – and their defined physical characteristics (Neubauer, 1885: 19). Neubauer contended that these different features are aligned with different habits and manners, with the 'German-Polish Jews being rough in speech and gesture'. He outlined Blumenbach's contention that the Jewish skull was peculiarly formed, but commented that there are no ancient skulls of Jewish people while the few examples Blumenbach referred to were not sufficient evidence to act as conclusive proof. He rejected the views of Robert Knox by dismissing the resemblance between Jews on Egyptian and Assyrian monuments and most Jews in Europe (Neubauer, 1885: 20). He called for a thorough anthropometric measurement of Jews throughout the world before such claims could be verified:

> Only then shall we be able to decide why the Maccabean warriors and of those who kept Titus and Hadrian thoroughly occupied for several years, are

now proportionally less fit for military service and more delicate in health than their Christian brethren. (Neubauer, 1885: 23)

Neubauer's comments reflected an idealized view of the physical fitness of Jewish ancestors and reflected a fear of physical degeneration among Jews in the present age, which was crucial for these advocates of anthropometrics. Neubauer's comments on the fitness of Jews for military service seemed to reflect an 'increasingly intense anti-Semitic critique of the Jewish body as inherently unfit for military service' (Gilman, 1992: 42). This view would be strongly argued and applied to all groups of people only a few years later by the Hungarian Zionist, Max Nordau, in his book *Degeneration* (1892).

Neubauer was followed by Joseph Jacobs' analysis of Galton's composite photographs, who argued that social conditions were primary to the creation of characteristics and inherited racial differences were secondary (Jacobs, 1885: 23). After presenting a table of where Jewish populations came from and arguing that Jewish 'blood' was more widespread in European populations due to conversions (forced and otherwise), Jacobs, like Neubauer, concentrated on the Sephardic and Ashkenazim Jews, which he argued had been socially isolated. Therefore inherited physical characteristics were a product of this isolation rather than reflecting natural differences (Jacobs, 1885: 25). Jacobs outlined a number of 'vital statistics' such as the low death rate for under-fives due to better infant care rather than racial immunity to disease, nor were Jews overally immune or more susceptible to diseases (Jacobs, 1885: 31). Jacobs considered some anthropometric measurements that had been made and pointed out that the Jews measured for height by BAAS were 'of the higher social grades, and their superiority over other Jews is undoubtedly the result of better nurture' (Jacobs, 1885: 34). In this way, Jacobs demolished the arguments that nature was all and nurture counted for nothing in the development of human beings and 'racial stock'.

Jacobs thought that the so-called Jewish expression found in the composites was indistinct. He compared one of these composites with a representation of a Jew on an Assyrian relief from about 650 BC and observed that the Jewish captives have 'very much the same sort of face as their captors' and the relief just has a 'practical identity with the ordinary Semitic type of those days' (Jacobs, 1885: 39). Like Neubauer, Jacobs discounted the idea that Jews were racially pure, pointing out the cultural and religious problems with closely connected marriages but conceded that the social isolation of many groups of Jews has led to the preservation of some 'purity'. He argued that any idea of racial purity between ancient and modern Jewry disappeared during the mass diaspora across Europe and North Africa during the Roman period (Jacobs, 1885: 52). Jacobs finished his lecture by analysing Galton's Jewish composites, arguing that the 'Jewish expression' might be defined as 'Semitic features with ghetto expression' with an intensity of gaze borne from 'isolation':

> I fail to see any of the cold calculation which Mr. Galton noticed in the boys at the school, at any rate in the composites A, B and C. There is something more like the dreamer and thinker than the merchant in A. [. . .] The cold somewhat hard look in composite D, however, is more confirmatory of Mr. Galton's impression. It is noteworthy that this is seen in composites of young fellows between seventeen and twenty, who have had to fight a hard battle of life even by that early age. [. . .] We learn, then, from those composites that the Jewish expression is considerably more complicated than is ordinarily thought. (Jacobs, 1885: 55)

Jacobs seeks a 'social reason for the "hard and calculating" glance seen by Galton, but claims to see it nevertheless' (Gilman, 1992: 68). He also stressed the appearance and adaptability of Jews (Cohen, 2002: 477). Jacobs therefore, on the one hand, pointed to the importance of social above racial factors for difference, while, on the other he utilized Galton's anthropometric techniques and ideas of inheritance. In this way, while countering the anti-Semitic comments of Galton, Jacobs advocated anthropometric practices.

These lectures took place two years before the Anglo-Jewish Exhibition at South Kensington at which 12,000 people attended between April and June 1887. This exhibition celebrated Jewish life, achievement and integration in British society and there were nine public lectures plus a private view for 1,250 people on the opening night on 4 April (Stansky, 1995: 166). This celebratory exhibition and events took place in a period during which anti-Semitism was almost unremarked upon. The deeply anti-Semitic sub-plot of Anthony Trollope's *The Prime Minister* (serialized in 1875–6) casts the unscrupulous Ferdinand Lopez as an unredeemable Jewish villain who marries a woman of an ancient English family and almost ruins her and her relations; though it is also implied that lack of knowledge about Lopez's familial inheritance is as much reason for his villainy as his Jewishness (Trollope, 1982: 118). As

John McCornick points out, as startling as this characterization is, the fact that 'no nineteenth century commentator even mentions the anti-Semitism' was because such prejudice was not considered noteworthy (McCornick, 1982: xviii). George du Maurier's bestselling novel *Trilby* (1893) depicts a dastardly and mesmerizing (literally) Jewish villain and whose name Svengali is still used to describe a sinister influence. In fact the sinister gaze of Svengali and his physical description draws on anti-Semitic assumptions about the Jewish body and the idea of the Jewish gaze, which Galton claimed to have identified in his composites, as well as an intense preoccupation with the Jew as interloper (Pict, 1994: xxi).

David Feldman has argued that Jacobs drew on Galton's anthropometric techniques and ideas around hereditary in order to distinguish which Jewish immigrants could be more easily integrated within British society than others (Feldman, 2010). Jacobs appeared to apply a form of eugenic thinking while demolishing many of Galton's principles. Within Jacobs' analysis social class rather than race was the main concern. In attempting to combat anti-Semitic assumptions, such as immunity to or from disease, Jacobs furthered practices that would later be used to define and murder Jewish people in the twentieth century. However, it was not unusual to 'read' the face in this period; as we have seen in Chapter 5, Amelia Edwards described a face on a mummy portrait as being 'Jewish in type' (Edwards, 1891: 105). These composites were 'at once a biological fact and biblical spectre, an inherited racial body and mystical ghostly inheritance' and, despite Jacobs' and Neubauer's arguments, these faces were still read in the context of the Bible and antiquity (Novak, 2008: 103). Petrie's reading of this terracotta head as 'Hebrew' was based on these investigations of the 'Jewish expression' and face.

Putting faces to the Bible

A further example of combining 'biological fact and biblical spectre' can be found in a book by Petrie's friend and colleague Archibald Henry Sayce, who utilized Petrie's *Racial Photographs* to illustrate the racial faces of the mystical past (Novak, 2008: 103). Sayce was an Assyriologist, philologist and an archaeologist as well as a clergyman since he was a Fellow at the

University of Oxford, but also raised the profile of biblical and other areas of archaeology (Gunn, rev. Gurney, 2004). He reported for *The Times* during his various travels around Europe and the Ottoman Empire during the 1870s and was their special correspondent in Greece during 1877–78. He helped found the Society for Hellenic Studies in 1879 and the Alexandria Museum in Egypt in 1880. Sayce roamed from one subject to another, which is reflected in the breadth of his autobiography *Reminiscences*. His working relationship with Petrie appears to have begun when he visited Petrie measuring the Great Pyramid in 1880 (Sayce, 1923: 210). Petrie later sailed up the Nile and copied inscriptions at various places with Sayce when it was too hot to work in Giza during 1881. Sayce, as we have seen in Chapter 4, was the President of the Anthropology Section at the BAAS conference in Manchester 1887, at which Petrie's *Racial Photographs* were presented. At the conference, he led a call for a greater understanding of the ethnology of the British people, which led to heated discussion in the pages of *The Times*. He later wrote that Thomas Huxley came to my help and 'made the "general public" understand that the substratum of the British nation goes back to the Neolithic age and belongs to the so-called Mediterranean race', rather than the Teutonic origins advocated by scholars such as E. A. Freeman (Sayce, 1923: 253).

The importance of race and racial thinking to Sayce is clear in a reading of his auto-biography, which though full of scholarly gossip and captures the table talk of prominent Victorians and Edwardians, is also punctuated by racial generalizations and descriptions. Sayce, being Welsh, consistently defined himself as a 'Kelt' and made such declarations as:

> On the one side I possessed in full the Keltic love and respect for antiquity, and on the other a belief in a form of government which should combine the democratic element of common action with its control by "the great man".
> (Sayce, 1923: 108)

In such assumptions about being 'Keltic' Sayce echoes the views of Robert Knox. Sayce re-used Petrie's *Racial Photographs* in his book *The Races of Old Testament* in 1891 and attempted to locate the antiquity of the Hebrew race and Jewish expression that was being debated at the same time (Figure 6.4). Sayce used archaeological evidence to validate the Old Testament in both

Figure 6.4 Cover of A. H. Sayce, *The Races of the Old Testament* (1891)

scholarly and popular circles. Sayce mentions his 'little book' *The Races of the Old Testament* in his autobiography, commenting that the 'basis of which was Professor Petrie's examination of the Egyptian monuments' (Sayce, 1923: 273). This 'little book' was published by The Religious Tract Society of London in the popular imprint 'By Paths of Bible Knowledge', which were compact inexpensive books that could be used as teaching aids in Sunday Schools. A year earlier, *Modern Discoveries on the Site of Ancient Ephesus* by J. T. Wood had been published in the series, which made use of Wood's excavations to provide evidence and visualize St Paul's time at Ephesus and the New Testament more generally (Challis, 2008: 137–8). In this way, the Bible was materialized for late Victorian readers and school children.

Figure 6.5 Frontispiece in A. H. Sayce, *The Races of the Old Testament* (1891)

Sayce used Petrie's photographs of casts from monuments to put a face to many of the different peoples mentioned in the Old Testament, essentially providing portraits of people in the Bible (Figure 6.5). Sayce argued for the fidelity in which Egyptian artists pictured the faces of the prisoners led into Egypt, comparing them to that scientific absolute, the photograph:

> The pictures and sculptures bequeathed to us by the Egyptians have, however, an ethnological value far exceeding that of other similar relics of Oriental antiquity. The Egyptian artist had an innate gift for portraiture; he seized at once the salient traits in an individual face, and reproduced them with almost photographic fidelity. Doubtless at times he may have exaggerated some striking feature in the head of a foreigner [...]. But such exaggerations only bring into stronger relief a racial peculiarity, and it may after all be questioned whether the exaggeration is as great as it seems. (Sayce, 1925: 4)

The Races of the Old Testament was first published in 1891 and republished in 1925. It is still available on the internet, embedded in an unpleasant rightwing website based in the United States and is used there as an illustration of the superiority of Christian white races. *The Races of the Old Testament* illustrates the perceived importance of reading race in the face and the use of Petrie's *Racial Photographs* as didactic tools with a wider public.

Sayce began with the 'fact that mankind is divided into races' and how this is familiar in modern literature', but pointed out that race is used in a very loose sense with no real definition. He differentiated race from nation or community and argued that language 'is no test of race', using the Jews as an example since wherever the   y go they learn the local language and sometimes even forget Hebrew but are a distinct race (Sayce, 1925: 10). In essence, Sayce defined race as about different physical characteristics of which skull size and shape is among one of the important 'characteristics that distinguish races from one another' (Sayce, 1925: 14). Sayce placed humanity into two essential groups dolichocephalic (or long-headed), while others are brachycephalic (or round-headed). Interestingly, Sayce provided a glossary of scientific or biological terms describing physical differences at the end of the book. He detailed the various physical differences between different races – hair (colour and texture), teeth, eye colour, skin colour and the facial angle. Sayce disputed the notion that specific moral and intellectual abilities could be attributed to different races:

> We talk about "the impulsive Kelt", "the dogged Anglo-Saxon", "the brilliant but unstable Greek". But anything like a scientific determination of the psychological character of race is at present exceedingly difficult, if not impossible; the materials for making it are still wanting. We cannot even

gauge the intellectual capacity of a race. It is generally asserted, for instance, that the intellectual growth of a negro ceases after the age of thirteen; and yet there have been negroes like a Toussaint or a recent ambassador from Liberia who have shown themselves the equals in intellectual power of the most cultivated Europeans. (Sayce, 1925: 25)

Shortly after writing this Sayce also had contact with a 'negro' of 'intellectual power' since he corresponded with the African–American philological scholar William Sanders Scarborough in 1893 (Ronnick, 2005: 123). Scarborough was a high achieving classicist and an eloquent advocate of 'negro rights' and was by no means the only African–American classicist in this period. A touring exhibition of early African–American Scholars in the Classics curated by Michele V. Ronnick is subtitled 'A Photographic Essay' and viewers are invited to 'look into their faces and salute them' (Ronnick, 2004: 101). The emphasis in this exhibition was still on the face and who is seen rather than who is doing the seeing, though in this case celebrating racial achievement rather than looking for racial difference.

Sayce was not a whole-hearted disciple of Francis Galton, partly because of his deep religious faith. Yet, as with Joseph Jacobs, he followed many of Galton's and other racial scientists' techniques and thoughts. After a chapter on race and language, Sayce uses race typologies to find evidence for the different peoples described in Chapter 10 of the book of Genesis. Petrie's *Racial Photographs* were not utilized until 'Chapter IV: The Semitic Race', in which Sayce defined the various Semitic races and languages and considered how the modern Jewish type has changed since antiquity. He turned to the depiction of tribute bearers on an Assyrian obelisk from 842 BC that is in the British Museum:

Among them are the servants of Jehu, King of Samaria. Each is portrayed with features which mark the typical Jew of to-day. No modern draughtsman could have designed them more characteristically. The Israelite of the northern kingdom possessed all the outward traits by which we distinguish the pureblooded Jew among his fellow men. (Sayce, 1925: 77)

Sayce argued that the modern Jews were so mixed that these sorts of assumptions should not be made today; yet continued with a lengthy description of how to spot contemporary Jewish people who have the purest race, playing a part with the seeming obsessive search for defining Jewishness (Cohen, 2002).

There was no ambiguity about Sayce's thoughts on the race of the Egyptians who he thought were white and similar to northern Europeans but with a

IANUA (MITANNI).

Figure 6.6 'Mitanni', A. H. Sayce, *The Races of the Old Testament* (1891), p. 123.

red-skin due to sun-burn and black or red hair (Sayce, 1925: 83). Evidence for this point of view is taken from mummies, such as Ramses II, as well as the depiction of Egyptians on statues and monuments. Sayce mentioned that Petrie had found evidence for a different race in the early period of Egypt at Meydum who have different burial practices, which was an early indication of Petrie's 'New Race' theory (Sayce, 1925: 87). Petrie's *Racial Photographs* were used in the latter half of the book to illustrate the different racial groups that Sayce described (Figure 6.6). Sayce speculated that the face of 'a remarkably high and refined character on a racial type from Ianua, a city under Mitanni control, belonged to a Semitic people rather than a native Mitanni. This was the same face that Petrie would use to compare with the face of the Pharaoh Akhenaten.

Despite Sayce's earlier warnings on generalizing about intellectual ability and physical characteristics, while commenting on depictions of Nubians, Sayce described 'the Negro' as 'simple' and in character 'indolent, superstitious, affectionate and faithful' (Sayce, 1925: 145). He contended that the 'Greek' profile from Karnak 'might be of the statue of some Greek goddess in the classical days of Greek art. The nose, lips, and chin to which Greek has accustomed us are already present' (Sayce, 1925: 137). Sayce commented that this profile may be of Aryan or mixed Aryan stock 'whose purest representatives are now to be found in the Scandinavian Peninsula' but is certainly of a white race but one that is of another 'stock' to the modern Greek. He thus repeated the idea

that the ancient Greeks were a different race to the modern Greeks that had
been most forcefully put forward in the 1830s by the Austrian theorist Jacob
von Fallmerayer (Peckham, 2001: 35). Sayce finished *The Races of the Old
Testament* with an emphasis on the importance of these findings since, despite
his hesitation in the opening chapter, racial traits 'include not only physical
characteristics but mental and moral qualities as well'. This, Sayce argued, is
why the study of ethnology was fundamental to understanding the influence 'of
education and inheritance upon a race':

> More especially does it concern us to know what were the affinities and
> characteristics, the natural tendencies and mental qualifications of the people
> to whom were committed the oracles of the Old Testament. Theirs was the
> race from which the Messiah sprang, and in whose midst the Christian
> Church was first established. (Sayce, 1925: 173)

The importance of the Hebrew face or Jewish race was, for Sayce, connected to
the identity of Jesus Christ and the formation of Christianity.

In 1931 Sayce gave the Huxley lecture on anthropology in which he
stressed the importance of archaeology, while critiquing what people
believed in the nineteenth century; commenting that many people believed
in the traditional dates of the Old Testament and that some of the books
'were written by Moses himself' (Sayce, 1931: 272). He did not, however,
critique his own beliefs and held deeply racist views, later writing on visiting
Chicago in *Reminiscences*:

> The foreigner is even more in evidence at Chicago than he is in New York.
> And by the foreigner I mean Jews, Slavs, especially low-class Russians and
> the scum of Central Europe. More than 80 per cent of the population is not
> American in the true sense of the word. (Sayce, 1923: 425).

Sayce's views are here as much about social class prejudice as anti-Semitism
and his prejudice against working class Jews from Central Europe was held
by many, as we have seen. This does not mitigate such views. The fact that *The
Races of the Old Testament* (and so Petrie's *Racial Photographs*) is currently
used by an extreme rightwing organization to propagate racial hatred and anti-
Semitism underlines the importance of understanding the original context of
these publications, as well as providing more reason to be wary of reading race
or anything metaphysical in the face.

Faces of Israel and Egypt

A golden haired young woman with a Grecian profile holding an anxious looking and pale fair-haired child sit on a donkey, alongside which walks a darker skinned and bearded man. They pass traders selling shabtis and Egyptians using amulets to heal a sick child. In the background is a procession of worshippers carrying a statue of the goddess Isis suckling the infant Horus. In the distance, is an Egyptian pylon and temple, looking like Karnak, and behind that incongruously the shapes of the three pyramids can be distinguished. *Anno Domini* (1883) by Edwin Long depicts the holy infant and the Virgin Mary alongside her husband Joseph, who is clearly not the father of the child, on their flight into Egypt to escape the persecution of King Herod. This work vividly illustrates the nature of religious interest in Egypt as well as the assignment of a white European racial identity to the Virgin Mary and her child. Now on display in the Russell-Cotes Art Gallery and Museum in Bournemouth, it is not only a work of epic proportions and content but also a work that captures the interest in the historical and racial origins of the holy family.

The idea that Britain was spiritually connected to Israel was not just held by extreme groups such as the British Israelites, but was pervasive among nineteenth-century cultural figures and influenced the view of the lands of Palestine, its antiquity and its people as well as its relationship to Egypt. Religious belief went hand in hand with archaeological discovery (Mosrop, 1999). In 1867–70 Charles Warren, who was in the Royal Engineers and established the Palestine Exploration Fund, first investigated James Fergusson's theories that the original Church of the Holy Sepulchre was on Temple Mount. Relocating the church to the site of the Jewish Temple 'had great attraction for evangelical Christians, keen on prophecy and global historical patterns' and 'thus tidily signifying Christ's fulfilment of the Old Testament' (Tromans, 2008: 165). Warren found these theories to be unfounded by the archaeological evidence. In 1911, Petrie published *Egypt and Israel*, his first full account of archaeology and connections with the Bible. He had been brought up within an evangelical household where no doubt many of the above ideas were discussed. However, Petrie placed archaeological evidence above religious ideals and for this reason wrote

Figure 6.7 'Heads of Hittites from Armenia, Amorites from Syria, Philistines from Crete', facing p. 56, Flinders Petrie, *Egypt and Israel* (1911)

Egypt and Israel after his father's death, since it dealt with the archaeological evidence not religious belief (Petrie, 1931: 12). Petrie used some of his *Racial Photographs* as evidence for peoples mentioned in the bible, such as Amorites, Philistines and Hittites much like Sayce had (Figure 6.7). Petrie followed the conclusions of Neubauer and Jacobs that the Jewish populations were fairly unmixed until Roman times, but echoed Sayce in considering the portraiture of Jewish towns used on the triumphal reliefs of Shishak in Karnak to depict the 'Syrian and Amorite type' as well as that of the 'Hebrew type' (Petrie, 1911: 101). The afterlife of Petrie's *Racial Photographs* was most used with illustrating aspects of biblical archaeology.

Petrie returned to these photographs and the terracotta head from Memphis in his lecture to the Jewish Historical Society in 1922 'The Status of the Jews in Egypt'. In this lecture Petrie detailed Semitic influences in Egypt from the Middle Kingdom with some emphasis on the special status granted to the Jews under the Ptolemies (Petrie, 1922). An undated pamphlet 'Hidden Treasures in Bible Lands' by Ann Lidderdale in the Petrie Museum Archives, probably produced in 1923–4, reused these same 1886–7 photographs of Hittites, Amorites and Philistines. Lidderdale's appeal was clearly to try and attract money from religious organizations in America since the stress was on evidence gathered through archaeology that sheds 'light on the bible' and enriches the 'whole Christian world':

> It is not a mere accident that an English-speaking nation, that nation from whom came the supreme gift of a Bible that could be "understanded of the people", should now to a large extent control those Bible lands whose soil guards the records we need. (Lidderdale, PMA/WFP1 115/2/1(1))

Here the heads of Amorites, Philistines and Hittites were used as archaeological evidence for biblical knowledge in a manner that also justifies the colonial administration of those lands by the British. Petrie predominantly excavated in the British colony of Palestine in the 1920s and 1930s and settled in Jerusalem for the remainder of his life (Ucko, Sparks and Laidlaw, 2007).

Returning to the main period covered by this book, in July 1910 Francis Galton was interviewed in the *Jewish Chronicle* for an article entitled 'Eugenics and the Jew' to gather 'his views concerning the bearing of eugenics on the Jewish race and the life of the Jewish people' (*Jewish Chronicle*, 20 July 1910: 16). Galton praised the Jewish religion for 'advancing the multiplication of the human species', but cautioned that 'it is still more important that children should be born from the fit and not the unfit'. Galton declared that persecution of different racial groups was not immoral but unmoral and in any case did not always produce 'good results'. He fondly recalled the composite photographs he made with Joseph Jacobs of Jewish children and the presentation of papers referred to in the beginning of this chapter. Neither Galton nor Jacobs foresaw where their advocacy of statistic gathering around race and Jewish anthropometrics would lead. Indeed, Galton considered that eugenics would assist race culture in 'a more scientific and kindly way' than persecution. The search for the 'Jewish type' and defining the 'Jewish expression', which provided the context for the labelling of a terracotta head in the Petrie Museum as 'Hebrew', would have far-reaching consequences for people that were neither scientific or kind.

7

Akhenaten's Bloodline

The 250 casts of heads from sculpted reliefs that Flinders Petrie made from the squeezes he had taken in 1887 all went to the British Museum. The Petrie Museum has all of these casts and photographs on glass negatives but none of the originals, or that is what we thought until early 2011. While he was working at Amarna in 1894, Petrie took casts of the faces of the Pharaoh Akhenaten and Queen Nefertiti from relief sculpture and published them in his excavation report *Tell el Amarna* (1894) alongside a cast of 'the man from Mitanni' (Figure 7.1):

> [. . .] and in a figure of a man from Mitanni from the town of Ianua conquered by Ramsessu II, we see exactly the same physiognomy as in Thyi and Akhenaten (I 2). The precise parts which have just been noted as being characteristic of mother and son are all seen here in this man, who might be almost supposed to have been drawn from Akhenaten himself (see I 2; 9; 10). The source of this peculiar face is the Mitannian blood of his mother Thyi. (Petrie, 1894: 40)

These casts are kept together in a drawer in one of the cupboards of the Petrie Museum and I was curious about one of them because it (UC24322) looked like those that Petrie had made in 1887 (Figure 7.2). It was labelled in our card and online database as being found at Amarna. However, in January 2011 when we looked at the cast and read the excavation catalogue, the Petrie Museum's curator Stephen Quirke pointed out that Petrie had written that 'the man from Mitanni' was 'from the town of Iannu conquered by Ramesses II'. Ramesses II reigned in 1293–1212 BC, 30 years after Amarna was last occupied, so this cast could not possibly come from the city of Akhenaten. A few years later

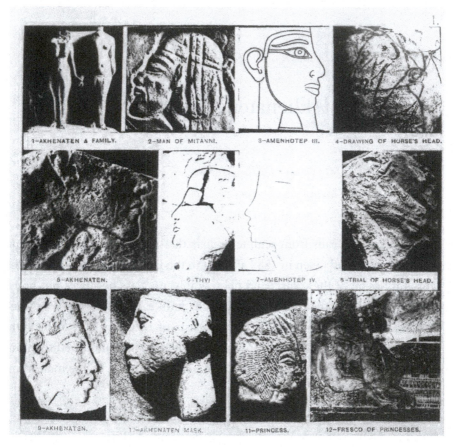

Figure 7.1 Plate 1, Flinders Petrie, *Tell el-Amarna* (1894)

Petrie referred to the cast in *A History of Egypt Vol. II The Seventeenth and Eighteenth Dynasties* (1896), a book he wrote for teaching students at University College London, in which he recorded that this cast was of a head 'among the captives on the north wall of the Great Hall at Karnak' (Petrie, 1896: 182). Petrie used this cast to argue that the physiognomy of Queen Tiye, the mother of Akhenaten, was Syrian and differed from 'any type seen before in Egypt', though her physiognomy had similarities with Nefertiti (Petrie, 1896: 183).

Four casts of heads from 'Iannu' (or Ynua/Ynuamu/Yenoam) in the Great Hall at Karnak are recorded in Petrie's *Racial Photographs* and the cast in the Petrie Museum matched photograph number 81a (Figure 7.3). Peter Brand, Director of the Karnak Great Hypostyle Hall Project, confirmed that the head

Figure 7.2 Cast of 'Man from Mitanni' UC24322 © Petrie Museum of Egyptian Archaeology, UCL

Figure 7.3 No. 81a, Flinders Petrie, *Racial Photographs* (1887) © Petrie Museum of Egyptian Archaeology, UCL

comes from the Seti I reliefs, not Ramses II, that commemorated Seti's victory over the town of Yenoam in Canaan on the exterior of the Great Hall. Brand kindly provided a picture showing the head belonging to a man falling from the top of the relief. Therefore this is a cast taken from a face on a sculpted relief on the north wall of the Great Hall of Karnak from the city of Yenoam, as Petrie had originally attributed. It appears, therefore, that the Petrie Museum does, after all, have one of Petrie's 'racial' casts in its collection.

Stephen Quirke suggested that Petrie's misattribution was potentially due to A. H. Sayce's reading of one of the Amarna tablets in 1888 about a marriage alliance between Amenhotep III, the Pharaoh Akhenaten's father, and a princess from Mitanni and from that concluded that Akhenaten's mother was from Mitanni. Petrie used the cast of the man from Mitanni to illustrate that Akhenaten, his mother Queen Tiye and possibly Akhenaten's wife Nefertiti were all facially similar to the 'man from Mitanni'. Mitanni or Mittanni was an ancient kingdom in modern Kurdistan, northern Iraq, and Syria, and was one of the most powerful states in the Near East in the fifteenth and fourteenth centuries BC. Little is known about its civilization due to scant archaeological and other evidence, but Mitanni did not exist as a major power by the time of Dynasty 19, when this relief was made. Petrie argued that the resemblance of physical features between this cast and Akhenaten illustrates that the hereditary of Akhenaten and his family was from West Asia rather than Egypt. We have seen how important a sense of hereditary and bloodlines were to Petrie personally in the way he made connections to inherited attributes from his ancestral family members in his own autobiography. These connections were almost a form of ancestor worship, which in some ways is exactly what eugenic thinking reflects. Eugenic thinking is about validating where you are from through bloodlines and natural laws, all of which could, it was believed, be reflected in the face.

Akhenaten and the Bible

Akhenaten was the so-called heretic pharaoh and his reign was perceived to usher in an artistic and religious reformation with the worship of one deity. As Dominic Montserrat points out, the epithets 'heretic' and 'reformation' belong to the historical traditions of writing European history rather than any accurate account of the complex interplay between politics, kingship and religion that occurred in Ancient Egypt (Montserrat, 2000: 36). However, Akhenaten had a special status due to his perceived monotheism and the dazzling artistry of the material remains found at his city in Tell el-Amarna. Akhenaten and Amarna had been promoted through various pious publications in the mid-nineteenth century as a ruler and place analogous with protestant Christianity in England (Montserrat, 2000: 64). Given Akhenaten was presented as a forerunner of Christ with connections to the people and places of the Old Testament it is unsurprising that his ancestral bloodline was considered so important. Petrie contended that Akhenaten's bloodline and his ethical character traits could be seen in his face through the medium of portraiture.

Akhenaten reigned during Dynasty 18 of the New Kingdom in about 1351–1334 BC and was the son of Amenhotep III and Queen Tiye. He was called Amenhotep IV at birth, but changed his name to Akhenaten in the sixth year of his reign. In the same year he created a new city as a royal residence, dedicating it to the sun-god Aten. He called the city Akhet-Aten, today it is known as Amarna or Tell el-Amarna. In the surviving record, the Aten seems to have been the exclusive focus of interest for Akhenaten hence the application of monotheistic to describe his religious practices. ('Akhenaten (Amenhotep IV)', Quirke, 2000–3, Digital Egypt website). In 1887 there was a discovery by local people of large cache of diplomatic and other correspondence on clay tablets in Tell el-Amarna dating from the period of Akhenaten and shortly before his reign. Many of these tablets may have been lost but soon about 300 were circulating on the antiquities market. Eventually, over 200 became part of the collections of the Vorderasiatisches Museum (Near East Museum) in Berlin with other fragments entering the collections of the Cairo Museum, British Museum and the Louvre (Moran, 1992: xiii). The archive mainly consists of 'letters received' from vassal states, though diplomatic correspondence with other major powers from kingdoms in present-day Turkey, Syria and Israel were also recorded in the original language. Most of the letters were in a Babylonian form of cuneiform (Moran, 1992: xviii). These letters included references to a number of rulers mentioned in the Old Testament.

These tablets were all translated and published in German in 1896, though papers on them were produced in learned societies and in the popular press in Britain and Germany almost as soon as they were first discovered and in this A. H. Sayce played a leading role. Sayce had been in Egypt when these tablets were first discovered by the antiquities authorities and verified their authenticity in 1887 (Sayce, 1923: 258). These tablets were, for example, discussed at the Society of Biblical Archaeology in London, which was founded in 1870 by Samuel Birch, Keeper of Oriental Antiquities at the British Museum. It was a scholarly rather than a religious society, which was closely connected to the British Museum and its members were a mixture of philologists working in the languages of the Bible, antiquarians, historians and clergymen. Rev. Henry G. Tomkins, who wrote the commentary for Petrie's *Racial Photographs*, was an early member. There were connections in membership and scope to the Palestine Exploration Fund, which had been founded in 1865, though the scope of the Society was more philological. The discovery of the Tell el-Amarna letters was a major topic in the 1880s and placed a greater emphasis on the connections between Egyptology and biblical archaeology (Legge, 1919: 29). Sayce was president of the Society in 1898 until it amalgamated with the Royal Asiatic Society in 1919.

In *The Races of the Old Testament*, Sayce described the importance of this 'remarkable discovery' for understanding the court of the kings of Dynasty 18 in Egypt, who had conquered the area known as Canaan and come into contact with kingdoms in western Asia. Sayce argued that these letters showed marriage into the royal family of Mitanni and the appointment of 'Semites from Palestine and Syria' into high office in Egypt:

> Amenophis [Amenhotep] IV, the son of an Asiatic mother, abjured the faith of his fathers, and endeavoured to force a new religion upon his unwilling subjects, that of the Asiatic Baal as adored in the solar disk. (Sayce, 1925: 100)

The letter that Sayce seemed to have based these assumptions on is still known as the 'Mitanni letter' and appears to be about a marriage alliance between Amenhotep III of Egypt and King Tushratta of Mitanni. It is the only letter written in the Hurrian language, which is 'inadequately understood' (Moran, 1992: 71). At the time of their discovery these letters or tablets were given importance due to their connections with the history of the Old Testament and Sayce was not alone in presenting Akhenaten as a monotheistic ruler with similarities to Judaeo-Christian practices. These ideas were informed by the 'fact' that he was of the same racial stock as the Semites from whom the Old Testament derived and his court was heavily influenced by people from Syria and Palestine.

The face of Akhenaten

Petrie used the interest in the discovery of the Amarna Letters and the biblical connections, to give his own excavations that began at Tell el-Amarna in 1891 'an increased public profile' and reported on them directly to *The Times* newspaper (Montserrat, 2000: 66). Petrie found another 22 fragments of tablets at Amarna in his excavations, all of which went to the Ashmolean Museum in Oxford. Like Sayce, Petrie exploited the biblical context of Amarna by providing an essay on the site for the 1897 edition of the popular Sunday School reader and prize *The Land of the Pharaohs Drawn with Pen and Pencil* (Montserrat, 2000: 68). However, the connections of Amarna and the reign of Akhenaten to the Old Testament were not the only tropes stressed by Petrie in his reports from the excavation. The artistry of the remains that were found at the site and the decorative arts were also given special importance. As Dominic Montserrat points out, this combination of 'beaux-arts' and 'biblical-tinged archaeology' in the 1890s and 1900s, made Amarna fit current taste and so assisted with constructing its popularity (Montserrat, 2000: 70). Petrie's excavation journal, which included a translation by Sayce of the newly discovered tablets, constructed a city and an Akhenaten based on archaeological evidence, combined with his reading of the Pharaoh as a great ruler and thinker.

Petrie's excavation journal for Tell el-Amarna as usual listed the places excavated, where objects were found, gave a background on the history of the site, had a section on inscriptions that were translated by Francis Griffith and included the translation by Sayce of the newly found cuneiform tablets. In the last section 'Historical Results', Petrie analysed the identity of Akhenaten, the new style found at Amarna and artistic production, the revolution in religion and ethics as well as the domestic arrangements of the royal family. Petrie began by demolishing some myths about Akhenaten; that he was a eunuch or that he died young and was replaced by a woman. He pointed out that some glimpses of the new style of Amarna were seen in Amenhotep III's reign. However, the key factor for Petrie in defining the identity of Akhenaten was the resemblance of his facial profile to his parents Tiye and Amenhotep III, as seen in portraiture. He discounted the contention of some scholars that Akhenaten looked nothing like his father:

> Children are often observed to resemble one parent, and yet to grow up more like the other. To suppose that Akhenaten was like his father when a boy, and that the likeness was exaggerated as being the fashionable face – yet that as his mind and body took shape between twelve and sixteen, under the vigorous and determined tutelage of his imperious mother Thyi, he should have grown into a nearer resemblance to her (Pl. I, 6), seems not at all an unlikely state of the case. Moreover, the cast of his head is of an expression betwixt that of the two portraits I, 7, 9, and links them together. (Petrie, 1894: 129)

Petrie thought that Akhenaten can somehow grow to look like one parent due to increased dominance by them and so drew on the scientifically inaccurate, but still popularly predominant, idea that a child inherits a mixture of features and characteristics from each parent. Even in the fashionable stylization of Akhenaten found on sculpture, which stressed his 'dreamy eye', resemblance can be seen to both parents:

> These [portraits] must evidently be of Thyi, as the face is too old and too dissimilar to be that of Nefertiti. Here the resemblance to Akhenaten is obvious (see I, 10); the same forehead almost in line with the nose, the same dreamy eye, the same delicate nose, the same expression of lips, the same long chin, the same slanting neck. That the boy inherited his face from his father (see I, 3, 7) cannot be doubted; and that he grew up like his mother seems equally clear. (Petrie, 1894: 134–5)

Petrie placed a great deal of emphasis on the value of portraiture in reading the face and so the discovery of Akhenaten's 'death mask' was of immense importance (Figure 7.4). He had its function as a death mask and cast for making sculpture verified by an independent expert, the sculptor and exponent of the New Sculpture movement Alfred Gilbert (whose most famous work

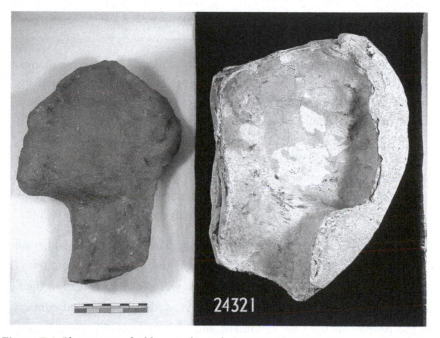

Figure 7.4 Plaster cast of Akhenaten's mask, UC24321 © Petrie Museum of Egyptian Archaeology, UCL

is Anteros or Eros at Piccadilly Circus in London). Petrie was by no means the first archaeologist to place such emphasis on a 'death mask'. Heinrich Schliemann had grandly declared that he had found the 'mask of Agamemnon' in the tombs at Mycenae in November 1876; the mask 'represents the human face of Homeric epic' but one which also fitted the 'very image of a fashionable European prince of Schliemann's time' (Gere, 2007: 2 and 78).

Petrie was similarly interested in the personality and face of Nefertiti, whom he read as having a 'marked personality' and 'one fragment of nose and lips preserves to us a brilliant portrait (I, 15)' (Petrie, 1894: 136). Petrie admired the 'artistic revolution' which he argued was matched to a revolution in religion and ethics with the worship of one god, the sun disk Aten, and the domestic monogamous relationship between Akhenaten and Nefertiti. Akhenaten was described by Petrie as an original thinker whose revolutionary philosophy was due to his familial link with the peoples of West Asia through the influence of his mother Tiye. Giving an overview of what happened to Amarna after the death of Akhenaten and the remains he found there naming Tutankhamen as sucessor, Petrie finished his excavation report with a laudatory account of Akhenaten as a visionary idealist:

> Even his royal position might not have enabled him to make such a change, had he not possessed a character of boldness and extreme tenacity – perhaps a dreamy obstinacy – with much delicacy of feeling, kindness of manner, a sense of humour, and a pleasure in popular enjoyments. All this may be seen in his face – his very own face that we have preserved in the death-mask, apart from all transcription. In his remarkable position, the greatness of his changes, the modernity of his thoughts, the wreck of his ideas, this strange humanist is one of the most fascinating characters of history; and into his face we can now look, as if we had seen him in the flesh. (Petrie, 1894: 148)

There can be no clearer account of the importance of the face and reading character traits through facial features in the nineteenth century. The importance of inheritance and racial origins were, for Petrie, read in the face of Akhenaten. The face of Akhenaten was viewed as Semitic and connected to the peoples of the Old Testament and ultimately, if this view is carried to an extreme, to Jesus Christ. According to this mode of thought, defining Akhenaten's parentage was important for understanding such a profound visionary since it was believed that certain races had a predilection towards higher thinking and the civilized arts.

Archaeological fantasy

The idea that different racial groups had a predilection for certain behaviours, with the 'higher' races developing civilization conformed to a racial hierarchy, which was found in popular literature of the period. The adventure novels of Henry Rider Haggard were vivid expressions of this belief. Haggard collected antiquities and three rings from Amarna made up part of his Egyptian collection, which he had inherited from his collaborator and friend the writer Andrew Lang (Blackman, 1917). In 1916 Aylward Blackman inspected Haggard's small collection of antiquities and asked Flinders Petrie to assist in verifying their provenance. Haggard told Blackman that the antiquarian William J. Loftie had bought these items from some Egyptians who had discovered them in a tomb at Amarna along with other gold jewellery inscribed with the name of Tiye and

Nefertiti in 1883. Loftie bought this material on one of this winter vacations to Egypt and sold much of it to Talbot Ready, the dealer for the Royal Scottish Museum, but kept these rings aside for Lang. Blackman verified the fact that the Royal Scottish Museum had a signet ring inscribed with the name of Nefertiti. Petrie, who had worked with Loftie on his collection of scarabs about the time of his acquisition of the rings, commented that the supposed tomb of Akhenaten had been looted in the early 1880s. The Amarna royals feature in Haggard's short story *Smith and the Pharaohs*, which depicted Akhenaten as an effeminate bore rather than a great pharaoh (Montserrat, 2000: 148–50). Akhenaten may not have fitted Haggard's expectations of manhood but the connection between the pharaoh and items in his collections was still important enough to boast of in his autobiography *The Days of my Life* (1926).

Haggard gave the ring inscribed with the name of Akhenaten to his fellow writer and friend Rudyard Kipling in 1925, which is now in a private collection (Montserrat, 2000: 6–7). One of the other two rings depicted a lion jumping with a tambourine and this is currently in the collections of the World Museum in Liverpool. It is displayed in the entrance to the Egyptian galleries at the World Museum in Liverpool and acts as an introduction to how people viewed Ancient Egypt and how they acquired objects in the late nineteenth century. Also on display is a gilt mummy of a man named Neskin from the Ptolemaic period; described by the museum as contributing to the inspiration for Haggard's novel *She* (1886) in which the Greco-Egyptian civilization of 'She' still turn their dead into mummies. Like the rings, the mummy was formerly in the collection of Andrew Lang, to whom Haggard dedicated *She*. *She* is one of Haggard's best-known novels and details the journey of Leo, a young man of Grecian athletic beauty, in search of his ancestral origins with his guardian Holly, a physically ugly Cambridge Don, and their pessimistic servant Job. Leo traces his ancestry back thousands of years through old documents and a ring left in Holly's trust by Leo's father shortly before his untimely death. Leo decides to go to the area in northern Africa where his family appeared to originate; there the group are taken captive by a native tribe of African/Arab people called the Amahaggar, before being delivered to their terrifying but beautiful mistress Ayesha, 'She Who Must be Obeyed'. Ayesha appears to be forever young and immortal. It becomes clear that Leo is the incarnation and descendant of Ayesha's former lover Kallikrates and must now stay with her to assist her plans to take over the world. Ayesha has a socially Darwinist vision about the survival of the fittest, as she makes clear to Holly:

> [. . .] in this world none save the strongest can endure. Those who are weak must perish; the earth is to the strong, and the fruits thereof. For every tree that grows a score shall wither, that the strong one may take their share. We run to place and power over the dead bodies of those who fail and fall; ay, we win the food we eat from out of the mouths of starving babes. It is the scheme of things. Thou sayest, too, that a crime breeds evil, but therein thou dost lack experience; for out of crimes come many good things, and out of good grows much evil. (Haggard, 2001: 205)

In the end Ayesha fails in her goal dramatically. Social Darwinist visions and the horrors and achievements that might accompany them were clearly part of popular culture at this time; Ayesha's description of the amorality of strength is not unlike that of Galton's in response to the questions put by the *Jewish Chronicle* 27 years later.

Haggard utilized forms of scholarship in the reading of ancient manuscripts and material objects in a way that must also have been recognizable from the popular accounts of archaeology (Mazlish, 1993: 734). Relics evoke a fantasy ancient world; arguably Haggard's ring and mummy are still used in this way in the World Museum in Liverpool. The novel fits into an adventure fantasy genre that combined geographic travel with travel through time and civilizations and depicted racial conflicts and subjugation in the process; another earlier example in this genre is Edward Bulwer-Lytton's *The Coming Race* (1871) and a later example is H. G. Wells' *The Time Machine* (1895). Haggard was an 'imperial pessimist' who believed that the British Empire was doomed to fall but that there was a 'sacred duty' to hold the 'lantern of civilisation aloft, before passing it to the Americans. Imperialism, racism, ethnology and archaeology, when welded in a well-told yarn, could be a potent instrument of persuasion' (Murray, 1993: 180–1). *She* was immensely popular and sold over a million copies in Haggard's lifetime (Tangri, 1990: 295). This and Haggard's *King Solomon's Mines* (1885) were influenced by his experiences in South Africa while a young man with the discovery of Great Zimbabwe by the German explorer Karl Mauch in 1872, which Haggard later visited. Mauch thought that the immense architectural remains were too complicated to have been made by the people local to the area and concluded that the monuments were the result of Mediterranean colonists, potentially linked to the Old Testament King Solomon. Haggard fused the material remains of the ancient past with such readings based on contemporary archaeological ideas and finds to create adventure fantasies around race and civilization.

Trading race

Petrie's search for the ancestry of Akhenaten through his face and his conclusion that the Pharaoh owed his visionary ideals to his natural inheritance illustrated the practice of attributing civilized achievements to race. Petrie was by no means alone in this. The Great Zimbabwe in southern Africa is a notorious example of a group of monuments and artefacts that were considered too 'civilized' in construction to have been made by the native populations surrounding them. This idea also happened to benefit colonial acquisition of land and exploitation of material resources. Cultural racism went hand in hand with imperial appropriation. Cecil Rhodes justified the land acquisition by his British South Africa Company, in what is now the modern state of Zimbabwe, through reference to these monuments that were perceived as the products of an ancient colonization before being overrun by local African tribes. Rhodes sponsored J. Theodore Bent to excavate Great Zimbabwe and to report on his finds (Tangri, 1990: 296). Bent had previously excavated prehistoric tombs on Greek islands in the 1880s and had spoken alongside Petrie at the BAAS conference in 1885. He also received funding from BAAS and was granted a further award for investigating the Prehistoric Race in the Greek Islands during the same year that Petrie was commissioned for his *Racial Photographs* project. In 1891 Bent, assisted by his wife and a group of local people, recorded and mapped the stone structures at Great Zimbabwe and made some attempt at excavating material finds from the site. All of these efforts were published in his book *Ruined Cities of Mashonaland* in 1892, which went through three editions by 1895 (Baigent, 2004).

Bent reported on his findings in a paper given at the RGS in the same year. He described the evidence he found for the destruction of the monuments and the local African tribes in the area and assumed, without particularly explaining why, that the monuments had been built by a race specialized in trading, whom he thought were Phoenician. He quoted ancient classical and Old Testament sources as evidence verifying his finds, despite the fact that the round tower was thousands of miles from the structures described on the coasts of the Mediterranean basin:

> [...] the ruins and the things in them are not in any way connected with any known African race; the objects of art and the special cult are foreign to the country altogether, where the only recognised form of religion is [...] that of ancestor worship. (Bent, 1892: 288)

He described the gold-work that he had found in the context of the mines of ancient Egypt and their use of slaves and ceramics from Arabia and China as evidence of an occupation by a commercial trading race from outside of Africa.

Bent gave a shorter paper at the Anthropological Institute, at which Francis Galton was in the chair as president. He introduced Bent after he had spoken about the anthropometric measurements of school boys that had been made by Dr Almond, headmaster of a school in Musselburgh, thus illustrating how much anthropometrics was an integral part of the Institute. Bent repeated much of what he had spoken about at the RGS, but detailed why he thought the builders of the monuments were Arabian or Phoenician; his title for the meeting was 'On the Finds at the Great Zimbabwe Ruins (with a View to Elucidating the Origin of the Race that Built Them)'. Bent referred to the glass and ceramic ware he had found that clearly came from China and other trade routes; declaring that 'It is impossible that a collection of things such as there could be brought together here by any but a highly commercial race like the Arabians were, or their kinsmen of Phoenicia' (Bent, 1893: 130). Not all people agreed with Bent's arguments as was indicated in the discussion after his talk; Sir John Evans was concerned about the lack of coins found if the traders belonged to the Ptolemaic period or later. However, Mr Read said he had previously thought that local Africans may have themselves created such soapstone objects and gold work but had changed his mind on hearing Bent's arguments. Bent further explained that native people learnt iron and gold working from a higher civilization that had been living and educating them in their midst. The findings that a trading people, a higher race from elsewhere, had occupied these lands and taught the local people new skills supported the colonial occupation by Cecil Rhodes' company. Great Zimbabwe 'became a symbol of the justice of European colonisation, which was portrayed as the white race returning to a land that it had formerly ruled' (Trigger, 1989: 131). Rider Haggard depicted this view of a trading race, albeit a doomed one, building and occupying Great Zimbabwe a few years later in his novel *Elissa. The Doom of Zimbabwe* (1899), and so fantasy fact and fiction became almost inseparable.

Bent's findings were soon challenged and the sloppiness of his excavations were criticized at the time, but supposed archaeological evidence continued to feed imperial justification and racial discrimination. Gertrude Caton-Thompson excavated Great Zimbabwe in 1928 and conclusively proved that it was African in origin, making connections between the finds there and the local Shona people (Caton-Thompson, 1929). However, this evidence was censored by the white settler government in Rhodesia until late into the twentieth century. The archaeologist Glyn Daniel (popularly famous for hosting the BBC TV shows *Animal, Vegetable, Mineral* and *Chronicle*) objected to this smothering of evidence for political and racial propaganda in an article in *Antiquity* in 1971 (Tangri, 1990: 296). In this way, assumptions supposedly based on objective archaeological evidence but in reality informed by assumptions based on racial hierarchies and racial thinking, had serious political and economic repercussions for African people in southern Africa (Kuklick, 1991: 135). The fictional fantasy that supported the colonists' assumptions and material gains became fused with the archaeological evidence.

Queen Tiye and empowerment

Petrie's excavations and analysis of Tell el-Amarna do not match the fantasy excesses of Haggard or the prejudiced conclusions of Bent. There is, for example, some evidence that Akhenaten's mother Tiye, was not closely related to the royal family at Thebes, which would have made her marriage to Amenhotep III unusual. There was greater intermarriage with kingdoms around the Mediterranean and Asia as well as a changing population in Egypt during the New Kingdom. Excavations of sites dating back to Dynasty 18 report finds reflecting greater trade with Mediterranean and Near Eastern countries as well as Nubia that may also reflect the changing ethnic make up of the population in Egypt. For example, a stirrup vase from the Mycenaean period IIIB1, found at the Gurob palace site (UC16631), dating from late Dynasty 18 (1400–1295 BC), illustrates trade with Bronze Age Greeks, as well as the possibility that one of the higher class inhabitants of the palace was from Mycenae.

Another unusual factor about Tiye is that Amenhotep III identified her with him in his rule on a set of commemorative scarabs naming her as senior wife (Montserrat, 2000: 30–1). These factors have given rise to a certain romance around Tiye; either she was an exceptional foreign princess who introduced reforms and a whole new way of thinking to Egypt, or she was from a lower class and became a formidable queen through strength of will. More recently, different origins have been claimed for Tiye. Tiye and Akhenaten's wife Nefertiti have played important roles within Afrocentric reclamations of Egyptian history. These reclamations have not been taken very seriously by the scholarly establishment, though they play a part in understanding the racism and colonial legacy of such racism in scholarship and archaeology over the last 200 years (Fluehr-Lobban and Rhodes, 2004: xv and xxii). The fact that Sayce's *The Races of the Old Testament* is still used today by an extreme right wing group to 'illustrate' the superiority of white European people, makes the perceived need to reclaim Egypt as a black African civilization obvious.

Egypt was an African civilization, whether you define it by the people, land, artefacts, monuments or culture. Geographically it sits in Africa, while also being linked to the Near East and Mediterranean cultures. In the relatively recent refurbishment of its Egyptian galleries (2009), the World Museum at Liverpool sets Egypt within an African context in a large map as you enter the gallery and repeats this emphasis throughout the displays. Work led by Sally-Ann Ashton at the Fitzwilliam Museum, Cambridge around craft and comparative histories of bespoke objects in African cultures, illustrates neglected fields of research and applies different approaches to the history of objects. A good example of this is the recent exhibition *Triumph, Protection and Dreams. East African Headrests in Context* which explores the use and design of the head rest across ancient Egyptian history and in other African societies (Massing and Ashton, 2011). A team of historians and experts on African hair are working together to curate an exhibition on 5,000 years of the Afrocomb at the Fitzwilliam Museum in 2013, with the Petrie Museum as a partner, which applies this comparative research approach to African hair and tools from ancient Egypt through different African cultures and diaspora until the present day.

I am stating my support of this work strongly, as I do not want the criticism that I make of one Afrocentric reading of Nefertiti and Tiye to indicate my disapproval, whether scholarly or culturally, of this approach to Egyptian history. Dominic Montserrat has outlined the importance of Akhenaten, Nefertiti and Tiye to Afrocentric histories of Egypt. The portrait of Akhenaten as a powerful Black leader next to Muhammed that Montserrat described in 2000 is still on the mural in Reading 12 years later (Montserrat, 2000: 119). In addition Nefertiti and Tiye have been considered as examples of powerful black queens, illustrating the strength of African women and the greater equality for women in ancient Egypt than subsequent or parallel ancient cultures. These views are presented strongly in *Black Women in Antiquity* (1987), which contains two chapters on Nefertiti and Tiye respectively. Sonia Sanchez contended in her chapter on Nefertiti that women were full partners in 'civilization-building' and 'indicated a widespread belief that women also housed the Divine' in Egypt (Sanchez, 1987: 49). Sanchez's Nefertiti was beautiful and admired and had equal status in the building of the religious and artistic movement of Amarna. Sanchez finished with a celebration of the portraits that have been found of Nefertiti:

> It is not by chance that centuries later her face appeared out of the ruins of Amarna. A face of beauty and intellect. A face of destiny.
>
> Nefertiti. The beautiful one has come again for us all to see. (Sanchez, 1987: 55)

This emphasis on the face and what it tells us about the person it represents has parallels with Petrie's reading of the death mask of Akhenaten. Similarly, Virginia Spottswood Simon defines Nefertiti's mother-in-law Tiye as a beautiful black woman from Nubia who was 'intelligent and strong-minded, as well as beautiful' (Simon, 1987: 62). Both these readings are reliant on the face and assume intellectual and ethical traits from physical characteristics in much the same way Galton, Petrie or Sayce would have done. Clearly there are important political reasons for Tiye and Nefertiti to be read in this way but, much like the readings of Sayce and Petrie, they describe the context and issues of the period in which they were written rather than Nefertiti or Tiye in antiquity. Utilizing similar techniques of physiognomy and anthropometrics to Sayce, Petrie, Galton and others, means that those methods of analysis and the assumptions inherent within in them are still given credibility. It is easy to understand why Tiye and Nefertiti are reclaimed as empowering examples of strong African queens. Part of the emphasis placed on Tiye coming from western Asia was due to biblical connections and the idea that certain races brought with them a predilection to higher forms of civilization, which for Sayce and Petrie would be found in western Asia rather than Africa. Speculation on racial origins and achievements could soon move into novelistic fantasy in the search for the appropriate racist teleology.

excavated. Petrie split the pottery into nine types to which he assigned numbers and gave them paper slips. He then applied this method to other material, such as slate palettes, and recorded the information on material found in a tomb on separate cards, known as 'tomb-cards'. From these cards and slips, he analysed how different groups of materials were found together. He then sequentially numbered these cluster groups from the most simple to the most complex and worked out his system of 'sequence dating':

> By employing this, an excavator could now take a given object, compare it to Petrie's "corpus" or list of types and immediately assign it a number that indicated its age relative to the First Dynasty. Objects with designations in the 70's were latest and those in the 30's earliest. (Hoffman, 1980: 118)

This tremendous achievement was due to Petrie's immense ability at statistics and mathematical thinking, which included seeing patterns in collected numbers. It was no doubt influenced by his intellectual relationship with Francis Galton and Galton's protégé, the statistician, Karl Pearson. Petrie's ability to think in this way and see types in numbers and collated information is much like the programming for a computer spreadsheet. Petrie's emphasis on typologies and patterns were key to his analysis of the material that he excavated, whether of people or pots. A vase that Petrie had labelled as New Race was put on display at the Manchester Museum in an exhibition *Revealing Histories: Myths about Race* (2007–9), which examined the construction of race, racism and racial identities (Lynch and Alberti, 2010: 24). Petrie's ideas about a New Race are relatively well known, yet there is still amazement that such an exacting archaeologist could get his analysis of the data so wrong.

Petrie was interested in finding evidence for the origins of ancient Egyptian civilization and so it is intriguing that when he excavated at Naqada and found the material that gave him that evidence, Petrie thought it belonged to a different race. Margaret Drower comments on the oddness of both Petrie's analysis of the evidence and the fact that he clung to his theory for two years in spite of other evidence (Drower, 1985: 215). It is not so odd when Petrie's thinking is positioned in the racial theorizing of the period that certain racial groups are predisposed for certain kinds of activity and manufacture. Along with this emphasis on racial predisposition, was the idea of migration, with the belief that racial groups migrate from place to place then degenerate and die out. Petrie's theory that the cemeteries of Naqada showed a New Race that had

8

The New Ancient Race

Two full-length portraits by society artist Philip de László were painted to mark Flinders Petrie's retirement from UCL in 1933. One in the art collection of UCL, shows Petrie holding a small bronze figurine in his professor's robes, incongruously looking like a connoisseur–collector. The other, which was given to Stephen Glanville who was Petrie's successor at UCL, shows Petrie in academic robes holding a black-topped red-ware vase (Figure 8.1). It would be hard to locate the exact black-topped vase that Petrie holds in the collections of the Petrie Museum, since there are many from the predynastic Naqada I period (c.3900–3700 BC). Petrie was deeply interested in this early period of civilization in Egypt and he was one of the first to excavate this material and recognize it as predynastic. It has been a point of some debate among staff at the Petrie Museum as to why UCL received the more traditional 'connoisseur' portrait while the portrait showing Petrie with one of his major discoveries went to Glanville and from him to the National Portrait Gallery. The pot Petrie is holding is not only one of the types that made up his famous sequential dating system but also one which Petrie briefly thought belonged to a 'New Race' that had migrated into Egypt between the Old and Middle Kingdoms of Egypt.

A long black-top red-ware pot (UC5713), type B 22a from Naqada Tomb 1554, sits in the middle of the Pottery Case 4 in the 'Pottery Room' at the Petrie Museum (Figure 8.2). It is one of the larger of the black-topped pots and gets its distinctive look from the oxidization process while firing different parts of the pots at different temperatures. It looks in size and shape similar to the one Petrie holds in the above portrait. This pot would be one of many buried

Figure 8.1 Sir William Matthew Flinders Petrie by Philip Alexis de László (1934). © National Portrait Gallery, NPG 4007

with people as part of funerary equipment that included food, jewellery and cosmetics in cemeteries at Naqada, Hierakonpolis and Abadiya for example. Concurrently, these people may have created rock art in the desert and settled in the low desert along the flood plain 6,000 years ago (Patch, 2011: 212). While excavating at Naqada in 1894–5, Petrie thought that the graves containing this material belonged to invaders from the Red Sea area who entered Egypt in a period of instability during the First Intermediate Period (2180–2040 BC). He described this pot in his excavation report, *Naqada and Ballas*, written with James Quibbell, as being 'most characteristic of the New Race' (Petrie, 1896: 36–7). Petrie's careful note-taking, combined with drawings, enabled him to develop a chronological system for dating pottery from tombs and buildings. This system later meant that he accepted, albeit ungraciously, that the material

Figure 8.2 Black-top red-ware vase, Naqada. UC5713. © Petrie Museum of Egyptian Archaeology, UCL

belonged to the Egyptian peoples but from a much earlier period of Egyptian history (Patch, 2011: 4). An exhibition at the Metropolitan Museum in New York in 2012, *The Dawn of Egyptian Art*, explored this period in ancient Egyptian history illustrating fully the connections in style, belief and custom between material found at early dynastic sites and the predynastic period. The exhibition also highlighted the importance of Petrie's system of dating pottery and other material.

It took Petrie a few years to fully develop seriation, the system of classifying pottery around 'various combinations of ware, form and decoration' which he based on material found at Naqada (Patch, 2011: 18). It wasn't until 1901 that he announced that he had constructed sequences of stylistic change that could be used to assign approximate dates to the graves he and his teams had migrated into Egypt, vanquished the local population and settled there for a few hundred years before dying out, is absolutely in tune with the racial thinking that was widespread in the 1890s. Ultimately, however, Petrie acknowledged the analysis of Jacques de Morgan, who excavated a year after him at Naqada, which found that the material belonged to predynastic groups of people in Egypt. He published a correction slip for *Naqada and Ballas* accepting that the remains described were predynastic (Spencer, 2011: 19). This was probably also due to the evidence before his own eyes while he was putting together the seriation systems. It was not the first time that Petrie accepted convincing archaeological evidence above the theories of those around him, as we have seen in the cases of the Great Pyramid and Egypt's relationship with the Old Testament. Petrie's former mistaken analysis sprang from his deep-rooted racial thinking.

Naqada I

Petrie's Naqada excavation report covered a fraction of what he excavated in 1894–5 and mentioned his system of ordering the pottery, but his conclusions stressed the New Race discovery (Hoffman, 1980: 121). James Quibble wrote up the Ballas site finds and overview for *Naqada and Ballas*, while Petrie wrote up his excavation in Naqada and brought the two sites together in his descriptions of the plates at the back of the book and historical conclusions. Petrie's 1901 correction accepted that the objects described as belonging to the New Race 'are similar to those of the early dynasties' and pushed back dates for stone vases and realigned Dynasty 7 and 8 to 'predynastic'. Otherwise, he made no re-arrangement to the book as the facts were stated with 'as little theory as possible' (Petrie, 1901). Petrie was disingenuous, since his argument that the objects belonged to a New Race, occurred throughout the report and most particularly, in his summary and conclusions. He began by stating that the New Race or N. R. 'mean those which belong exclusively to certain invaders of Egypt of the type here described, which is entirely different to any known native Egyptians' (Petrie, 1896: vii). In this Quibble concurred and similarly described predynastic finds and graves at Ballas as belonging to the New Race.

Petrie based his argument first on the graves, arguing that the foetal position of most of the skeletons found, differed from any burials found before in Egypt. The human remains themselves were measured, particularly the skulls.

Petrie thought the skulls to have a 'marked type with massive brows, deep-cut bridge to the nose and a short but very prominent nose' (Petrie, 1896: 35). He compared some of the skulls, 'selected to illustrate the profiles' of the face, to a cast he had taken in 1887 of the facial profile of a Libyan chief (*Racial Photographs* no. 157) shown on the front of the temple of Medinet Habu (Figure 8.3). Petrie stated that the diagrams of the skulls series were based on measurements by friends and showed that the capacity was 'less than that of European, Mongol or Egyptian' people and compared them to the skulls from Hindu Indians he had seen (Petrie, 1896: 51). Petrie commented that Professor Thane at UCL, the same academic who received Petrie's craniometer, was still analysing and observing the differences.

It is highly likely that the friend Petrie referred to, was the statistician and eugenicist Karl Pearson. Pearson considered that skulls were most useful in researching racial differences and corresponded with the anthropologist Franz Boas on the differences between the 'civilized' white race skulls and the

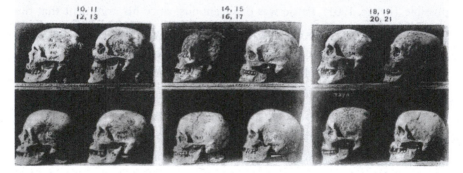

Figure 8.3 Section of *Naqada and Ballas* (1896), Plate VI

'uncivilized' American Indian skulls that Boas had collected (Porter, 2004: 263). Petrie and Pearson became colleagues at UCL as well as neighbours in Hampstead early in the 1890s. Correspondence between the men in 1895 shows that Pearson was studying a collection of skulls that Petrie had brought back from his excavations in Naqada as well as Petrie's measurements and statistical analysis of the human remains that he had made on site. Cautioning that the 'smallness of the variability' may not indicate a New Race, as Petrie had implied, Pearson nevertheless thought the numbers correlated with skull measurements of modern Parisians, German Bavarian peasants and Libyans (Pearson to Petrie, PMA: undated). Pearson only considered skulls for 'comparative purposes' and, though he would have liked to keep the skull collection at UCL, he thought it would be better if the full skeletons and skulls stayed together. He suggested the Royal College of Surgeons in London or the Natural History Museum as potential homes, since the latter had the 'beginnings of a collection of negroes and others', for value to anthropological study (Pearson to Petrie, PMA: 17 June 1895).

While Petrie searched for a home for the human remains from Naqada, Pearson arranged for Thane to temporarily look after them in the gallery of the anatomical museum at UCL while Mr Thompson completed measurements. He despaired of finding a sufficient collection of Egyptian skulls to compare with the New Race (Pearson to Petrie PMA: 11 August 1895). Pearson ultimately accepted Petrie's small variability in measurements and calculated the cephalic indices of the skulls and compared them on his scale of civilization and skull size:

> This list shows your Libyans very near the bottom in both cases. I do not lay much stress on position of ancient British, Gauls, Scandinavians and Swiss (Pitt dwellers) as I have only been able to get the measurements of a very few skulls, but the general result seems to indicate a fairly close relationship to the Egyptians and singularly low place on a scale which appears to conform somewhat to the scale of civilisation of modern race, i.e. German near the top and aboriginal near the bottom. (Pearson to Petrie, PMA: 12 August 1895)

Petrie followed Pearson's methodology by plotting the size of the skulls on curve graphs in order to graphically compare the measurements against other races (Petrie, 1896: Plate LXXXIV). Petrie argued that the depiction of the human form on pottery and elsewhere showed a different race to that of the native Egyptians, which supplemented the evidence found in the human remains. He thought that the New Race observed different races, such as 'steatopygous' races the 'bushmen' and 'hottentots' (Petrie, 1896: 34). He also considered that the products found in the tombs, such as slate palettes were too different to native Egyptian forms and so also indicated racial difference. Petrie outlined the differences in style, production, technique and decoration of the different pottery types and in so doing, positioned them in roughly accurate (predynastic) chronological order; observing that the New Race must have been present in Egypt for several generations. The later pottery of the New Race, Petrie thought rougher and more akin to the Egyptian style, thus illustrating that the New Race settler was 'declining in power, losing connection with the rest of their race' (Petrie, 1896: 42). The similar flint knives found at Abydos and elsewhere in Egypt to those at Naqada, showed that the migration of the New Race was not isolated but spread across Upper Egypt. Throughout his excavation report, Petrie stressed the differences between Egyptian remains and those of the New Race; a table was used to show the differences between 'Egyptian and New Race Characteristics'.

Petrie thus concluded that the New Race entered Egypt between the Old and Middle Kingdoms and completely subdued or cleared the areas where they lived of native Egyptians as there was no indication of influence on comparable chronological material (Petrie, 1896: 61). He found Amorite influences in some of the types of the pottery, observing that the wavy handle pottery type was similar to that which he had found in excavations in Tell el-Hesi in Palestine, which pointed to Syria as a source for the New Race (Petrie, 1896: 62). While there were western connections in the form of the burials used by the New Race, Petrie compared the square pit graves to those in Mycenae and Cyprus. The skull shape and face type Petrie thought were similar to ancient Libyans and had parallels with modern Algerians. A. H. Sayce had proposed that the Amorites from Palestine and Syria were the same race as the ancient Libyans, as suggested in their depiction on Egyptian monuments. Following Sayce, Petrie argued that the New Race were of the same stock and had invaded from the East with connections to the Red Sea and Mediterranean and possibly to Phoenician traders (Petrie, 1896: 54). It is easy to see some similarities between Petrie's New Race argument and that of Bent's Phoenician traders having built

The New Ancient Race

Two full-length portraits by society artist Philip de László were painted to mark Flinders Petrie's retirement from UCL in 1933. One in the art collection of UCL, shows Petrie holding a small bronze figurine in his professor's robes, incongruously looking like a connoisseur–collector. The other, which was given to Stephen Glanville who was Petrie's successor at UCL, shows Petrie in academic robes holding a black-topped red-ware vase (Figure 8.1). It would be hard to locate the exact black-topped vase that Petrie holds in the collections of the Petrie Museum, since there are many from the predynastic Naqada I period (c.3900–3700 BC). Petrie was deeply interested in this early period of civilization in Egypt and he was one of the first to excavate this material and recognize it as predynastic. It has been a point of some debate among staff at the Petrie Museum as to why UCL received the more traditional 'connoisseur' portrait while the portrait showing Petrie with one of his major discoveries went to Glanville and from him to the National Portrait Gallery. The pot Petrie is holding is not only one of the types that made up his famous sequential dating system but also one which Petrie briefly thought belonged to a 'New Race' that had migrated into Egypt between the Old and Middle Kingdoms of Egypt.

A long black-top red-ware pot (UC5713), type B 22a from Naqada Tomb 1554, sits in the middle of the Pottery Case 4 in the 'Pottery Room' at the Petrie Museum (Figure 8.2). It is one of the larger of the black-topped pots and gets its distinctive look from the oxidization process while firing different parts of the pots at different temperatures. It looks in size and shape similar to the one Petrie holds in the above portrait. This pot would be one of many buried

Figure 8.1 Sir William Matthew Flinders Petrie by Philip Alexis de László (1934). © National Portrait Gallery, NPG 4007

with people as part of funerary equipment that included food, jewellery and cosmetics in cemeteries at Naqada, Hierakonpolis and Abadiya for example. Concurrently, these people may have created rock art in the desert and settled in the low desert along the flood plain 6,000 years ago (Patch, 2011: 212). While excavating at Naqada in 1894–5, Petrie thought that the graves containing this material belonged to invaders from the Red Sea area who entered Egypt in a period of instability during the First Intermediate Period (2180–2040 BC). He described this pot in his excavation report, *Naqada and Ballas*, written with James Quibbell, as being 'most characteristic of the New Race' (Petrie, 1896: 36–7). Petrie's careful note-taking, combined with drawings, enabled him to develop a chronological system for dating pottery from tombs and buildings. This system later meant that he accepted, albeit ungraciously, that the material

Figure 8.2 Black-top red-ware vase, Naqada. UC5713. © Petrie Museum of Egyptian Archaeology, UCL

belonged to the Egyptian peoples but from a much earlier period of Egyptian history (Patch, 2011: 4). An exhibition at the Metropolitan Museum in New York in 2012, *The Dawn of Egyptian Art*, explored this period in ancient Egyptian history illustrating fully the connections in style, belief and custom between material found at early dynastic sites and the predynastic period. The exhibition also highlighted the importance of Petrie's system of dating pottery and other material.

It took Petrie a few years to fully develop seriation, the system of classifying pottery around 'various combinations of ware, form and decoration' which he based on material found at Naqada (Patch, 2011: 18). It wasn't until 1901 that he announced that he had constructed sequences of stylistic change that could be used to assign approximate dates to the graves he and his teams had excavated. Petrie split the pottery into nine types to which he assigned numbers and gave them paper slips. He then applied this method to other material, such as slate palettes, and recorded the information on material found in a tomb on separate cards, known as 'tomb-cards'. From these cards and slips, he analysed how different groups of materials were found together. He then sequentially numbered these cluster groups from the most simple to the most complex and worked out his system of 'sequence dating':

> By employing this, an excavator could now take a given object, compare it to Petrie's "corpus" or list of types and immediately assign it a number that indicated its age relative to the First Dynasty. Objects with designations in the 70's were latest and those in the 30's earliest. (Hoffman, 1980: 118)

This tremendous achievement was due to Petrie's immense ability at statistics and mathematical thinking, which included seeing patterns in collected numbers. It was no doubt influenced by his intellectual relationship with Francis Galton and Galton's protégé, the statistician, Karl Pearson. Petrie's ability to think in this way and see types in numbers and collated information is much like the programming for a computer spreadsheet. Petrie's emphasis on typologies and patterns were key to his analysis of the material that he excavated, whether of people or pots. A vase that Petrie had labelled as New Race was put on display at the Manchester Museum in an exhibition *Revealing Histories: Myths about Race* (2007–9), which examined the construction of race, racism and racial identities (Lynch and Alberti, 2010: 24). Petrie's ideas about a New Race are relatively well known, yet there is still amazement that such an exacting archaeologist could get his analysis of the data so wrong.

Petrie was interested in finding evidence for the origins of ancient Egyptian civilization and so it is intriguing that when he excavated at Naqada and found the material that gave him that evidence, Petrie thought it belonged to a different race. Margaret Drower comments on the oddness of both Petrie's analysis of the evidence and the fact that he clung to his theory for two years in spite of other evidence (Drower, 1985: 215). It is not so odd when Petrie's thinking is positioned in the racial theorizing of the period that certain racial groups are predisposed for certain kinds of activity and manufacture. Along with this emphasis on racial predisposition, was the idea of migration, with the belief that racial groups migrate from place to place then degenerate and die out. Petrie's theory that the cemeteries of Naqada showed a New Race that had migrated into Egypt, vanquished the local population and settled there for a few hundred years before dying out, is absolutely in tune with the racial thinking that was widespread in the 1890s. Ultimately, however, Petrie acknowledged the analysis of Jacques de Morgan, who excavated a year after him at Naqada, which found that the material belonged to predynastic groups of people in Egypt. He published a correction slip for *Naqada and Ballas* accepting that the remains described were predynastic (Spencer, 2011: 19). This was probably also due to the evidence before his own eyes while he was putting together the seriation systems. It was not the first time that Petrie accepted convincing archaeological evidence above the theories of those around him, as we have seen in the cases of the Great Pyramid and Egypt's relationship with the Old Testament. Petrie's former mistaken analysis sprang from his deep-rooted racial thinking.

Naqada I

Petrie's Naqada excavation report covered a fraction of what he excavated in 1894–5 and mentioned his system of ordering the pottery, but his conclusions stressed the New Race discovery (Hoffman, 1980: 121). James Quibble wrote up the Ballas site finds and overview for *Naqada and Ballas*, while Petrie wrote up his excavation in Naqada and brought the two sites together in his descriptions of the plates at the back of the book and historical conclusions. Petrie's 1901 correction accepted that the objects described as belonging to the New Race 'are similar to those of the early dynasties' and pushed back dates for stone vases and realigned Dynasty 7 and 8 to 'predynastic'. Otherwise, he made no re-arrangement to the book as the facts were stated with 'as little theory as possible' (Petrie, 1901). Petrie was disingenuous, since his argument that the objects belonged to a New Race, occurred throughout the report and most particularly, in his summary and conclusions. He began by stating that the New Race or N. R. 'mean those which belong exclusively to certain invaders of Egypt of the type here described, which is entirely different to any known native Egyptians' (Petrie, 1896: vii). In this Quibble concurred and similarly described predynastic finds and graves at Ballas as belonging to the New Race.

Petrie based his argument first on the graves, arguing that the foetal position of most of the skeletons found, differed from any burials found before in Egypt. The human remains themselves were measured, particularly the skulls.

Petrie thought the skulls to have a 'marked type with massive brows, deep-cut bridge to the nose and a short but very prominent nose' (Petrie, 1896: 35). He compared some of the skulls, 'selected to illustrate the profiles' of the face, to a cast he had taken in 1887 of the facial profile of a Libyan chief (*Racial Photographs* no. 157) shown on the front of the temple of Medinet Habu (Figure 8.3). Petrie stated that the diagrams of the skulls series were based on measurements by friends and showed that the capacity was 'less than that of European, Mongol or Egyptian' people and compared them to the skulls from Hindu Indians he had seen (Petrie, 1896: 51). Petrie commented that Professor Thane at UCL, the same academic who received Petrie's craniometer, was still analysing and observing the differences.

It is highly likely that the friend Petrie referred to, was the statistician and eugenicist Karl Pearson. Pearson considered that skulls were most useful in researching racial differences and corresponded with the anthropologist Franz Boas on the differences between the 'civilized' white race skulls and the

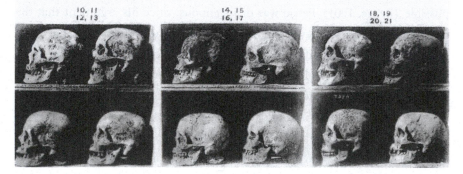

Figure 8.3 Section of *Naqada and Ballas* (1896), Plate VI

and occupied Great Zimbabwe. Petrie's racial thinking was parallel to that of other archaeologists and anthropologists at the time. Fortunately, Petrie was a more exacting archaeologist than Bent and one who would eventually put the observation of archaeological evidence above his own theories.

Jacques de Morgan, who originally trained as an engineer and worked as a mining prospector, excavated at Naqada after Petrie left in 1897 and discovered the royal tomb of Queen Neithhotep from Dynasty 1. This tomb showed the magnificence of the architecture of the early dynastic period and how closely linked the predynastic tombs were to early dynastic building. De Morgan had also found material similar to Petrie's Naqada New Race objects while excavating in Abydos in 1896 and immediately recognized them to be pre-historic (Hoffman, 1980: 107). Petrie considered de Morgan to be a sloppy archaeologist, who was untrained and had begun his career as a businessman. His derogatory tone in his autobiography undermined de Morgan's discovery while admitting the accuracy of it:

> De Morgan, who found similar graves, put them to predynastic times, though by a happy guess without any evidence. By the evidence of the royal tomb at Naqada, later cleared by De Morgan, it was proved that the latest of our new pottery linked with the earliest dynasty, and so the prehistoric age of Naqada was fixed. (Petrie, 1931: 156)

Petrie excavated at Abadiyeh and Hu in 1898 and 1899 and finds in these predynastic cemetery sites appeared to convince Petrie that de Morgan was right. In an address 'On our present knowledge of the Early Egyptians' to the Anthropological Institute in 1899, Petrie spoke on and exhibited material that had 'at first been temporarily assigned to a New Race, but further research' had shown that the objects dated from pre-dynastic stock to about 5000 BC (Petrie, 1899: 202). Petrie considered the objects to show a wide difference between the people of 5000 BC and 4000 BC due to the entry of a different race. De Morgan may have been right because he did not come from the field of archaeology and so did not let widespread assumptions about race and migration affect his judgement. The engineer's accuracy over the theories of the archaeologist echoes the case of the Royal Engineer Robert Murdoch Smith finding the actual site of the Mausoleum of Halicarnassus rather than the archaeologist Charles Newton a generation earlier (Challis, 2008: 62–3). At least here, de Morgan was credited with accurate analysis in terms of date and Petrie with exacting observation and excavation techniques.

Measuring skulls

Ernest Warren, assistant professor of Zoology at UCL, presented his findings from examining the skeletons from the 'Naqada race' at the Royal Society on 3 June 1897, interestingly after Francis Galton presented on a paper on heredity (on the 'contribution of each ancestor to the total heritage of the offspring'). The presentation of these two papers together again illustrates the overlapping interest in ancient and modern race and heredity. Warren continued using Petrie's statistical method as evidence for variation in human species and based his results on 400 skeletons of the New Race found at Naqada. Warren made 14 key observations around his measurements, mainly in comparison to European skeletons; noting, for example, that on the whole the bones tended to be longer and the 'angle of torso of the femur is much greater than in Europeans'. In all points the mean of the European skeleton is taken as a point of comparison and so physical differences become 'race characters'. Overall, Warren found a correlation in limb length between the New Race to Negro skeletons but noted 'that the sacral and scapular indices were nearly identical with Europeans' (Warren, 1897: 401). Warren just examined the bones of the skeletons; evidently leaving the skulls to Thane and Pearson.

Skulls were collected as important indicators of human difference throughout the nineteenth and early twentieth centuries. The collection of skulls was at times a kind of trophy-taking. Shortly after Petrie was excavating in Naqada in Upper Egypt, an Anglo-Egyptian army was assembled and sent to Sudan to exact long-delayed revenge for the Sudanese, led by the Madhi, defeat of a British garrison in Khartoum. After this Sudanese victory the head of the British Commander, General Gordon, was decapitated and put on public display by the Mahdi. Following their victory over the Mahdists at the Battle of Omdurmann in 1898, General Kitchener blew up the tomb of the Mahdi and had his head severed, which 'was purloined by Kitchener as a trophy of war' (Harrison, 2008: 290). Kitchener was clearly taking revenge for the treatment of his former commander and hero. He is thought to have considered using the skull as a drinking cup or, following well-established practice, to send it to the Royal College of Surgeons in London for examination. Medical museums were usual repositories for skulls, whether ancient or modern, in the nineteenth century (Alberti, 2011: 59). Kitchener's revenge was a notorious use of trophy-taking and caused a public scandal, shocking Queen Victoria. The Mahdi's head was eventually buried in a Muslim cemetery at Wadi Halfa, but, as Simon Harrison argues, the incident shows a curious disconnect between public repugnance to the mutilation of human remains in war and actual practice by British soldiers at this time. The trophy-taking of skulls 'originated in the ideologies of racial superiority' and seemed to grow after the 1820s due to the emergence of phrenology and craniology, with no apparent precursors for such activities since the medieval period (Harrison, 2008: 295). Skulls and bodies from across the world were often collected by people in the military for scientists and 'hunting' metaphors were used to describe the collection practice in this field. This language and practice blurred the distinction between war trophy and scientific specimen.

The emphasis on the skull was connected to the emphasis on reading the face. At this point, no serious scientists were reading bumps on the head to determine difference in characteristics, as had been happening in the phrenology of Gall and Coombe at the beginning of the nineteenth century. However, the brain capacity of the skull and features that determined facial characteristics were considered essential for defining human difference. The anthropologist Paul Broca had published a guide for craniologists for measuring skulls in 1875, for which he measured 1,500 skulls and gave guidelines on what skulls to take and how to describe them (Fabian, 2010: 191). Physical differences in skulls and skeletons do illustrate facets of human physical difference but this difference was, as we have seen, given additional value in terms of defining moral, social and racial characteristics. Galton's composite photographs of criminals, asylum patients and so on, were an attempt to, like Broca with his skull measurements, obtain a graphic representation of the mean, the maxima and the minima of variation in the face. These physical characteristics were then mapped to behaviour and 'evolutionary development of different population groups' (Kwint and Windgate, 2012: 42). Galton also took measurements of human heads as part of his anthropometry and head measuring took place within Britain and across the empire as part of anthropometric and ethnographic surveys.

The influence of phrenology and theories of Gall, as well as the racial theories and use of skulls by Blumenbach (among others), meant that there was a universal scramble for ancient skulls in scientific institutions and museums from the 1820s. Various skull directories were published, such as Samuel Moron's *Crania Aegyptica* (1844), and by the 1860s craniological studies was established in Britain (Nowak-Kemp and Galanakis, 2012). Trade networks were set up to buy skulls to feed this study. George Rolleston, for example, began forming the human skulls collection at the University Museum Oxford from the mid-nineteenth century and undertook exact measurements of skulls that he excavated from local graveyards in Abingdon, which led to his search for skulls from ancient Greece. Skulls from ancient Greece were soon in demand due to the adulation given to that civilization and people, as epitomized in Galton's *Hereditary Genius*. Some modern Greeks, as well as sometimes illicitly supplying the trade in ancient skulls, were also collecting skulls and human remains themselves in order to contest the predominant belief in Northern Europe that modern and ancient Greeks were different races. The 1859 circular sent by the Greek Ministry of Education stressed the importance of human remains in studying the ancient past of Greece and directed any finds to be sent to the Athens' Medical Society. This directive seems to have been one of the 'earliest measures taken in this direction by any country' (Galanakis and Nowak-Kemp, 2011: 7). It was perfectly normal during this period to place so much emphasis on the size and shape of skulls. Skulls, with their indication of brain size as well as facial profile, were primary in determining racial difference for archaeologists and anthropologists.

Petrie was far from alone in emphasizing racial difference in the formation of civilization and considering changes in cultural behaviour to have been determined by migrating races, and then collecting human remains as proof of his theories. Ironically an anthropologist and anatomist, whom Petrie disliked and disagreed with fundamentally, also argued for a similar pattern in the early twentieth century. Grafton Elliot Smith had an on-going feud with Petrie by the time they were both colleagues at UCL in the 1920s over Elliot Smith's diffusionism (see Afterword). Grafton Smith's theories on diffusionism, though in some ways no more false than Petrie's New Race ideas, were derided by many and have tarnished his reputation since. This is more fully covered by Kathleen Sheppard in the 'Afterword' to this book. However, it is worth briefly reflecting on Elliot Smith's use of human remains for understanding racial difference to more thoroughly place Petrie's New Race theories in context.

Grafton Smith first became involved with Egyptology in 1901 when he was consultant anatomist on the University of California's Hearst Egyptological expedition. In 1907, he examined 20,000 burials in the Nubia Survey alongside Gaston Maspero, George Reiner and Frederic Wood Jones; the survey was organized to record archaeological evidence due to the raising of the Aswan Dam. In his report on Nubia, Grafton Smith's overriding interest was in the racial origins of the ancient people of Nubia and, like Petrie and others, he recorded racial difference. This survey, Grafton Smith's records and the human remains uncovered from it, have been seen as laying the foundations of palaeopathology and is the subject of a major research project at the KNH Centre for Biomedical Egyptology at the University of Manchester, though Grafton Smith's 'driving interest' in it was race (Waldron, 2000: 387). He later defended Arthur Smith Woodward's reconstruction of the fragments of the Piltdown Skull, which had been announced in December 1912 as providing a missing link in the chain of human evolution. The skull was proven to be a fake after rigorous scientific tests in 1953. The mystery of the hoax is partially explained by the beliefs of the various leading scientists who were involved and supported the evidence for the 'missing link' found on British soil: they wanted it to be true; just as Petrie wanted his migrating New Race to be true.

Ipswich 1895

After returning from his work at Naqada, Petrie was President of Section H – Anthropology for the British Association for the Advancement of Science annual conference that took place in Ipswich during September 1895. In his autobiography, Petrie wrote on his motivations in chairing the section over the conference week:

> At that time harm was being done by the views of people who were ignorant of the real condition of less civilised races. The subject for my address therefore was our relations with races whom we controlled, and I invited some colonial administrators to come and state their knowledge. Several amateurs of policy were bursting to join in at the meeting, so I said we

should welcome all accounts of experience, only that a speaker must hand
up his name and state in what country his experience had been gained.
This put a stop to all the theorists. As Cromer said to me one day "I do not
know which is the greatest nuisance, the man-and-a-brother or the damned
nigger". (Petrie, 1931: 158)

Lord Cromer was, of course, Consul-General of Egypt from the time of
British occupation in 1881 until 1907 and the reference is to the anti-slave
trade campaign of the late eighteenth and early nineteenth centuries. By
this point, it referred to the interracial group and, frequently anti-imperial,
Society for the Recognition of the Brotherhood of Man (SRBM). Cromer was
well known for shutting down or minimizing educational establishments and
opportunities for Egyptians and restricting their political freedom (Reid,
2002). It is interesting that Petrie considered that assumptions about racial
superiority and the right of the white man to rule in the style of Cromer, was
being challenged to such an extent that he felt it necessary to take the actions
described above.

Petrie's address to the Anthropological Section began with the 'elastic
words' race and civilization and he spoke on the great mix of races across the
globe and man's antiquity. He attempted to define racial characteristics and
pointed to the Jews and Copts as being examples of 'purer' races due to their
social isolation, persecution and intermarriage, using Galton's composite
photographs of Jewish boys as evidence for this. Petrie spoke on 'racial taste'
and outlined that this would not be understood fully until there was a proper
anthropological museum. Civilization was dependent on race and character
as well as on climate and trade; he argued that the systems developed in cold
European countries should not be enforced on entirely different peoples in
different climates and geographies and so drew on Huxley's map of people
and regions. Petrie felt that this applied to educating colonial peoples and
used examples from within Egypt where 'Europeanized' Egyptians who
could read and write have had their 'intellect and health' undermined
(Petrie, 1895: 822). Colonial administration should therefore keep a country
stable and guide the inhabitants rather than trying to teach them or force
people into alien systems of education and self-governance. Petrie's address
in essence defined his vision of empire as a mechanism of control that does
not try to impose the systems of the higher races on the lower races, as what

works well for one race, does not necessarily work for another. His deep-set racist thinking is clear. Different races are all human but so different from each other to be almost like separate species and, beyond geographical and temporal climate. Petrie made little reference to social conditions or environment.

Petrie's address was followed by an account of the human remains of aboriginal inhabitants of Jamaica, given by his museum colleague Professor William Flower from the Natural History Museum, and then by Petrie himself on the skulls of the Neolithic invaders of Egypt. The discovery of the New Race at Naqada was the subject of a paper 'On the Skulls of the New Race in Egypt' by Dr J. G. Garson. Garson was a craniology specialist who knew Broca and Bertillon and became an adviser to the Home Office on criminal identity and facial profiling. Otherwise, the 1895 BAAS conference focused on archaeological discoveries in ancient production techniques on Friday including a paper by the soldier and game hunter (and later member of the Eugenics Society) H. W. Seton-Kerr on his finds in Somalia and another by Petrie on flints. Monday appeared to be dedicated to folklore and ethnographic studies from within Britain. Papers included one on dance by Lilly Grove (later Frazer after marrying James Frazer, the author of *The Golden Bough*); an overview of race difference in East Aberdeenshire by J. Gray; a paper on folklore by Edward Clodd, who became President of the Folklore Society that year; and a paper on illustrations of folklore by the Cambridge anthropologist A. C. Haddon. Haddon later published *The Races of Men and their Distribution* (1909) and was instrumental in building up the collection of the Horniman Museum in South London during the 1900s (Coombes, 2004). Tuesday was a day for anthropological studies of either skeletons or living people, such as 'On the Andamenese' by Maurice Portman, who was the officer in charge of the Andamanese from 1879–1899. Portman measured and photographed these people as examples of a dying race (Sen, 2009: 379). Archaeology was represented on Wednesday with, among others, a paper by Arthur Evans on primitive European idols in which he outlined his ideas on religion and primitivism in prehistoric Greece, placing the idols in an evolutionary context, much like his work on British prehistory around megalithic monuments (Harlan, 2011). The wide range of people involved and their backgrounds corresponded to Petrie's later statement that he invited colonial officials to speak as well as illustrating the interest in defining racial difference at this time.

The Saturday of the 1895 BAAS conference was reserved for reports, two of which are useful for understanding the context for the growth of interest in eugenics and how racist thinking was applied to people in Britain as well as in the colonies. After a report on 'Anthropometric Measurements in Schools', a report on the 'Mental and Physical Defects of Children' was considered. Sir Douglas Galton, an engineer and cousin to Francis Galton, chaired this committee. He had campaigned for greater care for children with disabilities and founded the Childhood Society. Alongside Galton, was Dr Francis Warner, an expert in clinical observations of children, and the craniologist Dr J. G. Garson. The report consisted of an examination and report on 100,000 children across all social classes on their physical and mental health and intellectual potential. The board hoped that 'the scientific classification of children and enumeration of conditions existing among them will lead to the adoption of means of social improvement' (BAAS, 1895: 505). The table attached to the discussion included anthropometric measurements as well as information on nerve signs, nutrition and learning difficulties. It is in many ways a precursor for the health reports and check on young children made by health visitors that we today take for granted. It is interesting to speculate whether this report later influenced Petrie in his writing about children's health in his eugenic tract *Janus* ten years later.

The final report is the most pertinent to this book since it is on an 'Ethnographic Survey of the United Kingdom'. It listed places in the United Kingdom that it was particularly pertinent to study for ethnographic purposes with five main points the committee wanted to know: (1) physical types of the inhabitants, (2) current traditions and beliefs, (3) peculiarities of dialect, (4) monuments and other remains of ancient culture and (5) historical evidence as to the continuity of race. The committee was formed of Francis Galton; the craniologist Dr J. G. Garson; the anthropologist Professor A. C. Haddon; the anatomist Professor D. J. Cunningham; the expert in Celtic art and archaeology J. Romilly Allen; the physician and anatomist Dr J. Beddoe; the geologist Professor W. Boyd Dawkins; the archaeologist Arthur Evans; the Conservative M. P. Sir H. Howorth; the chemist Sir Raphael Meldola, the archaeologist General Pitt-Rivers and the cartographer Ernest Ravenstein (who had also been partly responsible for the 1866 London Olympics). Attached to the report were letters to parish councils, doctors and local societies asking for assistance with collating the above information. It was another attempt to collect ethnographic data for scientific purposes and like previous attempts met with mixed results. However, the range of people involved with both reports illustrates the interest across a wide range of disciplines and how seriously race science and information about hereditary was being taken. It is unsurprising that Petrie clung to his New Race theory for so long as it was in line with his racist thinking and that of the scientific establishment at the time. A hierarchy of races and customs was assumed by all the speakers at the BAAS 1895 conference and it is clear that more interest was being paid to the idea of 'primitivism' and 'early man'.

Galton in Egypt

Petrie worked on the early dynastic cemeteries at Abydos in 1899, after the French archaeologist Emile Amelineau had spent three seasons there (Figure 8.4). Amelineau was reckless and did not carry out painstaking work and worse, smashed finds that he did not want to take with him (Drower, 1995: 257). Petrie, on the other hand, recorded the cemetery's layout and finds at Abydos, which increased understanding of the early dynasties and made the connections between the predynastic material at Naqada and elsewhere. While Petrie was working at Abydos, his colleagues David Randall MacIver and Arthur Mace were also excavating alongside him at a cemetery nearby that had prehistoric and late predynastic graves, later publishing *The earliest Inhabitants of Abydos: A Craniological Study* (1901). The EEF funded Petrie's work at Abydos which continued for four seasons and he had numerous visitors once the news of his discovery of the earliest royal tombs became known. A. H. Sayce, who was vice president of the EEF at the time, visited and also had lunch with Francis Galton who was visiting Egypt with his niece Eva.

Galton had visited the Middle East and North Africa as a young man when he took a year's tour across Egypt, North Sudan, Syria and Palestine in 1845–6. In 1885, his interest was evidently rekindled as he attempted to write an account from memory, recording what he had seen and where he went.

Figure 8.4 Photograph of Flinders Petrie in Abydos 1899/1900. Photographer unknown. Photograph album belonged to Margaret Murray

At the age of 77, Galton returned to Egypt in 1899 accompanied by his niece and visited Flinders Petrie on his excavations in Abydos. Petrie warned Galton not to bring any servants from Luxor as he was afraid of 'spies' and arranged to meet Galton at Baliana train station on 5 January 1900. Petrie had been carrying out anthropometric experiments with the Egyptian workforce and Galton refers to them hoping to carry out his own 'for I want opportunity of experimenting according to a new theory of mine, with eyesight, strength and the like' (Galton to Petrie, PMA: 17 December 1899). Galton was already impressed by what he had seen in Egypt, writing that 'I have been delighted throughout with Egypt: the excavators of recent years have added so much interest. It is 54 years since I last saw it.' Petrie later recalled the 'delightful visit of a week was that of Francis Galton and his niece' (Petrie, 1931: 173).

Petrie addressed the EEF on the results of the excavations in 1899–1900 and described the importance of being able to chronicle the early dynasties of Egypt. He also outlined his theory that palaeolithic man was subsumed by the

Hottentot, who in turn were taken over by the Caucasian, who were superseded by a Semitic dynastic race from the Red Sea, who gradually invaded Egypt and led to 'rapidly increasing civilisation' (Petrie, 1900: 22). Petrie contended to the end of his life that Egyptian civilization was the result of a Semitic race despite other evidence (Spencer, 2011: 21). Petrie changed his mind about the New Race but not about the effect and importance of race migration in Egyptian history as his racial thinking was fundamental to his views on historical and personal development.

9

Flinders Petrie and Edwardian Politics

In a scrap book of photographs held in the Petrie Museum Archives of Flinders Petrie, his family and some other archaeologists, is a very small blurry photograph entitled 'Flinders Petrie and John, 1909' (Figure 9.1). Petrie is shown holding and smiling into the face of an infant, whose dress and hair, as was common at the time, gives no indication of gender. It is a touching photograph of an archaeologist who has a somewhat austere public image. At the age of 54, Flinders Petrie became a father for the first time when his son John was born in April 1907. Petrie had married Hilda Urlin, who was 22 years younger than him, in November 1897, having courted her for two years. Hilda had been painted by Henry Holiday in his painting *Aspasia on the Pnyx* due to her 'wide heart-shaped face, clear blue eyes and fair hair', which was the 'type of beauty' very much in fashion for artists at that time (Drower, 1995: 232). Hilda enthusiastically took to the life of excavation and from 1897 the Petries worked as a team until Flinders Petrie's death. Hilda had expressed a fear of pregnancy and childbirth, but had two children; John in 1907 and Ann in 1909 (Drower, 1995: 304). Despite spending much time away excavating, Petrie enjoyed being a father and while at home he played with his children and took them on excursions.

In 1907, the same year as John was born, Petrie published *Janus in Modern Life*. The title refers to the Roman double-headed god Janus, who has one face looking to the past and the other looking to the future. In *Janus*, Petrie argued for the value of looking at past heredity in order to improve race and for the healthy well-being of people in the future; it was essentially an eugenic manifesto. He looked at past history and past social reforms to predict the

Figure 9.1 Flinders Petrie and his son John, 1909. Petrie Museum Archives

outcome of present ones. He used *Janus* to articulate many issues he had with the modern state and to criticize the political reforms being carried out by the newly elected Liberal government, including the new child welfare reforms. He does not explain exactly what they are; at the time, his readers would have known what Petrie was referring to in general terms, if not the exact details. In 1906, local education authorities were given the power to provide meals for the poorest children (it was not compulsory until 1914); in 1907, medical examinations had to be made of children at schools and education authorities were required to provide free treatment (though many didn't); in 1908, a separate juvenile court was established for children who were tried for crimes; and in 1907, secondary schools had to keep a quarter of their places with no fees for children from elementary schools. These measures were known as the 'Children's Charter' and the medical measures, in particular, resonate with the recommendations from the 1895 BAAS report on the 'Mental and Physical Defects of Children' that was briefly considered in the previous chapter. The legislation was influenced by the Report of the Inter-Department Committee on Physical Deterioration 1904, which investigated the physical health of thousands of children across the United Kingdom. This report questioned the value of ideas about heredity and racial degeneration. Instead, it found that poor nutrition and physical health stemmed from neglect, ignorance and inadequate medical care in both cities and rural areas (Soloway, 1995: 45). In addition, the studies of poverty by Charles Booth and Seebohm Rowntree attempted to negate the idea that being poor was the result of a character defect. At the same time, as eugenic pressure groups and publicity about eugenics grew among the professional middle classes, a major report on child health rejected the ideas about inheritance and racial degeneration that underpinned eugenic thinking.

These welfare reforms, and others, were the most substantial case of the state becoming involved in the way ordinary people lived and directing how they should be assisted. Petrie considered that such reforms would stop natural wastage and prevent natural ability of preserving the best children and thus endangered the future of the 'fit' races. He objected to reforms around the welfare of children, 'which seems most desirable and humane at first sight', on eugenic grounds:

> England produces over 300,000 excess of births over deaths yearly, and perhaps a tenth more might be added to that by care of infant life. But would that tenth be of the best stock or the worst? We must agree that it would be of the lower, or lowest type of careless, thriftless, dirty, and incapable families that the increase of population by 10 per cent, more of the most inferior kind? Will England be the stronger for having one thirtieth more, and that of the worst stock, added to the population every year? This movement is doing away with one of the few remains of natural weeding out of the unfit that our civilisation has left to us. And it will certainly cause more misery than happiness in the course of a century. (Petrie, 1907: 60)

On first reading this passage, I found Petrie's views hard to equate with the kindly man holding his son in the blurry photograph. Evidently he and Hilda were of the 'right stock' and so the care of infant life was necessary for their own children, which they, of course, provided without assistance from the state. Petrie's views need to be read in the context of their time, amid a fear of socialism, political change and a general acceptance, if not an endorsement, of eugenic ideas among much of the political classes. Britain did not have universal suffrage until 1928. After the Reform Act of 1884, householders had the vote (around 6 million people) but all men did not get the vote until

The Representation of the People Act in June 1918 and so political power was firmly out of the hands of the families Petrie referred to. Petrie evidently equated poverty with moral fault, arguing in *Janus* that state support weakens natural ability and talent. Letters in the Petrie Museum archives show that people supported Petrie's views and he was far from alone in his opinions. Placing Petrie's views in context and better understanding them, is not to condone them. Personally I find them repugnant, but others may (and do) disagree. However, it is not the purpose of this chapter, or indeed this book, to condemn Petrie. As stated in the introduction, a fuller understanding of Petrie's eugenic thinking assists a more nuanced portrait of Petrie, the man and the archaeologist, as well as giving an insight into the effects of eugenic thinking on science and society at the time. In the publications and lectures of Petrie that were explicitly informed by his eugenic thinking, we can see the results of some of the ideas he had been applying in his analysis of archaeological finds, such as reading moral character in the face or invading races.

Edwardian eugenics

Francis Galton defined eugenics and coined the term in 1883 (as we saw in Chapter 3). In 1911, James Field considered that the story of eugenics was essentially the story of Galton's own life, influenced as both he and the eugenics movement were by the new biological doctrines of the 1850s and 1860s (Field, 1911: 2). Despite the popularity of the anthropometrics laboratory in the International Health Fair in 1884 and the continuing emphasis on race and heredity in the annual BAAS conferences, it wasn't until the mid-to-late 1890s that eugenics appeared to gather wider intellectual and popular attention. Throughout the 1880s and 1890s concern coupled with anxiety about the urban poor and their conditions of life and work grew. Such anxiety was reflected in the House of Lords' Commission on Sweated Industries in 1888 and the Commission on Labour in 1892. The brutal murders by the so-called Jack the Ripper did not only repulse the newspaper reading public in 1888–91, they also drew attention to the terrible and impoverished conditions in London's East End, where a million people lived. *The Jack the Ripper and the East End* exhibition at the Museum of Docklands in 2008 built up a picture of the wretched conditions in which most people lived and illustrated how part of the interest in the murders was motivated by the morbid insight in the squalor of the victims' circumstances, as well as the gruesome manner of their deaths. The exhibition drew on Charles Booth's famous map of London (his first one dating from 1889–90), that showed the relative prosperity of streets and inhabitants. The map graphically illustrated the poverty of the East End; many of the streets in Whitechapel and surrounds were marked black for the lowest class 'vicious and semi-criminal' and dark blue for poor and in 'chronic want'. While Booth used the map to campaign for better conditions for the poor, others choose to view the map as evidence that an 'irreducible fraction were doomed to remain impoverished' (Kevles, 1995: 71).

Philanthropists had been at work in this impoverished part of London, and elsewhere, for decades and a glimpse of both this philanthropy and a small insight into the conditions of the period can be seen in the Ragged School Museum in Mile End, London. The museum preserves a classroom in a converted warehouse dating from the late 1890s and above this classroom, a 'typical' family room of the time has been created. The Ragged School was the result of Dr Thomas John Barnardo's campaigns. He had first founded a ragged school in the East End in 1867 (Ridge, 1993). As national and local government gradually took over the running and maintenance of schools in the 1900s, the ragged schools closed down. The gradual growth of trade unions and the Independent Labour Party (ILP), as well as other socialist movements, during the mid-to-late nineteenth century led to some political impact and influenced limited changes to welfare assistance and education. However, there was also a reaction among the upper and middle classes that stressed the inherent faults of degeneration and deterioration; especially among the urban poor who were seen almost as a separate race (Soloway, 1982b: 138–9). There were different responses to this urban deterioration. On one side were the middleclass socialists and Fabians, to which Karl Pearson belonged, who considered birth control and state intervention as a means of improving the conditions in which people lived; while on the other, there were the more conservative groups and Social Darwinists who believed in a mixture of 'survival of the fitness' and/or wanted no social reforms and no increased taxation. It was to this latter group that Petrie belonged.

The Boer War (1899–1902) further increased anxiety about deterioration, fertility and the fitness of the urban working classes to fight in a war. Problems for the British in fighting the largely Afrikaans White South Africans were considered by pessimistic social Darwinists to illustrate the 'racial inefficiency' of the nation (Soloway, 1982b: 140). A lecture by Pearson on 'National Life from the Standpoint of Science' at Newcastle in 1900, which detailed how the welfare of the nation was dependent on the increase of the best and strong elements of the nation, used the reverses against the British in South Africa as evidence. This lecture and Pearson's biometric calculations caused a more favourable reaction towards eugenics and heredity (Field, 1911: 17). There grew to be a feeling that Galton had predicted this a generation earlier in *Heredity Genius*, particularly in his section on the effects of urban living, and Galton became perceived as a lost prophet on race improvement (Soloway, 1982b: 156). Many supporters of Galton's brand of 'positive eugenics', which championed the rights of those who were fit intellectually and physically to reproduce, were social conservatives, but not all, as Karl Pearson who was a socialist illustrated. Support for eugenic theories and policies could be found across all political creeds of the upper- and middle-class political elite; the main objections came from some church people and religious groups. Much of eugenic thinking in this period was influenced by ideas and fears about social class and the eugenic movement represented the interests of the professional middle-classes, but it was also informed by race. The centrality of race to eugenics and heredity ideas is illustrated by the obsessive interest in Jewishness, fears of miscegenation and the assumption of 'a racial hierarchy with the White European at the top and the African at the bottom' (Stone, 2002: 95), It is, perhaps, no accident that while eugenic thinking was growing among a wider group of people, the first pan-African Congress took place in London in 1900. At this Congress, Black Britons, African Americans and Africans from colonized countries spoke articulately against imperialism and colour prejudice and this was reported in newspapers such as *The Times* and the *Graphic* (Schneer, 1999: 223). W. E. B. Du Bois wrote the opening lines to the Congress's proclamation 'To the Nations of the World', which stated that 'the problem of the twentieth century is the problem of the colour line'. It was also the same year that W. E. B. Du Bois compiled 363 photographs of mainly middle-class African Americans, made by unidentified photographers in *Types of American Negroes, Georgia, U.S.A.* and *Negro Life in Georgia* for the 1900 Paris Exposition. Du Bois did this to disrupt the constructed binary between the middle-class white American and the criminalized African–American in order to challenge the prejudiced and hierarchical way of looking at race and class that was being further enshrined by the eugenics movement in the United States (Smith, 2000). The people supposedly towards the bottom of the racial hierarchy were fighting back.

In October 1901, Galton gave the Huxley Lecture of the Anthropological Institute of Great Britain and Ireland and it was entitled 'The possible Improvement of the Human Breed under the Existing Conditions of Law and Sentiment'. Galton stressed the positive programme of eugenics – assisting the 'fit' people to breed – and presented his evidence for this through mathematical charts and statistics gained from anthropometric measurements and studies. He also finished his lecture with an observation on the reluctance with which race improvement had previously been considered and seen as impractical (Field, 1911: 19). After this 1901 lecture, Galton delivered a number of lectures to societies and the public, continuing the theme of those he had given on eugenics at South Kensington Museum many years earlier in 1887. At the Sociological Society, hosted by the now London School of Economics, Galton gave a lecture 'Eugenics: Its Definition, Scope and Aims', which outlined his programme of gathering information on heredity, educating the public on heredity, the promotion of marriage of the fit and the effect this would have on race improvement. After 1905 and another address on eugenics to the Sociological Society, Galton rarely spoke in public. However, his disciple Karl Pearson energetically delivered lectures on eugenics across the country at public and academic institutions and societies until World War One (Porter, 2004: 279). All of this made an impact. Kinship links and heredity became akin to a new religion; both Galton and Pearson spoke of eugenics in reverential terms and acted as prophets on outcomes for the future (Mackenzie, 1976: 507).

In 1907, the Eugenics Education Society was formed as a pressure group and was relatively small with 1,600 members before World War One, but very active with constant letters to the press and lobbying in parliament (Soloway, 1982b: 121). The group did not have the support of Karl Pearson, who condemned them for having limited evidence in support of their social agenda which often stressed negative eugenics, that is stopping 'unfit' people having children. Many others saw them as maverick 'hobby horse' activists (Field, 1911: 39). There is no evidence that Petrie was a member of this organization though he, like the society, emphasized the utility of negative eugenics. Karl Pearson, on the other hand, has been described as a 'socialist Darwinist' who allied eugenics with improved education and economic conditions for the working classes and thought it could guide people towards 'efficiency and racial progress. His views, typify, or perhaps caricature, the role of eugenics in the birth of the welfare state' (Porter, 2004: 282). Another socialist outlined the benefits and dangers of a eugenics programme in an imagined New Republic to the Fabian Society in 1901. Playing with the idea of Plato's Republic, H. G. Wells spoke on a future system of governance that would be eugenic in principle, for example:

> Procreation is an avoidable thing for sane persons of even the most furious passions, and the men of the New Republic will hold that the procreation of children who, by the circumstances of their parentage, must be diseased bodily or mentally – I do not think it will be difficult for the medical science of the coming time to define such circumstances – is absolutely the most loathsome of all conceivable sins. They will hold, I anticipate, that a certain portion of the population – the small minority, for example, afflicted with indisputably transmissible diseases, with transmissible mental disorders, with such hideous incurable habits of mind as the craving for intoxication – exists only on sufferance, out of pity and patience, and on the understanding that they do not propagate; and I do not foresee any reason to suppose that they will hesitate to kill when that sufferance is abused. And I imagine also the plea and proof that a grave criminal is also insane will be regarded by them not as a reason for mercy, but as an added reason for death. I do not see how they can think otherwise on the principles they will profess. (Wells, 1902: 324)

Wells' series of lectures was published as the bestselling *Anticipations* and in fact his vision of the future, which he did not necessarily agree with, shares much in common in terms of ideas with Galton's unpublished science fiction novel *The Eugenic College of Kantsaywhere*. Wells' vision, even if satirical, fits uncomfortably with the image of him as a radical science-fiction writer and social prophet, as David Lodge points out in his novelized biography (Lodge, 2012: 60–1). Wells was on the opposing political side to Petrie but it is chastening to reflect on the similarity of some of their statements around eugenics and the difficulty for many of their admirers in understanding such ideas today.

Migrations

In 1906 Flinders Petrie delivered the annual Huxley lecture for the Anthropological Institute of Great Britain and Ireland. The Huxley lecture had been established in memory of Thomas Huxley in 1900 and began with Lord Avebury delivering a lecture on 'Huxley: the Man and His Work'. Recipients of the Huxley lecture were voted for by the Institute's board for their services in the area of anthropology and they received the Huxley medal as well as having their lecture published. Galton was the second recipient of the Huxley medal and had been a colleague of Huxley at the Institute. His lecture in 1901 on improving the human race by means of positive eugenics was followed by Karl Pearson's Huxley Lecture in 1903 'On the Inheritance of Mental and Moral Character'. In 1905, the ethnologist John Beddoe, who like Galton used hair and eye colour to determine race, spoke on 'Colour and Race'. The Huxley medal and lecture was a huge honour for Petrie and illustrates the value placed upon his archaeological work for anthropology; it shows how much the two disciplines were intertwined.

Petrie spoke on 'Migrations', by which he meant racial migrations across Europe and western Asia. Kate Sheppard's 'Afterword' to this book places this lecture in context of ideas of diffusionism and its legacy within the history of archaeology. Petrie drew on the measurements that had been made of crania and skeletons throughout his lecture and referred to portraits or faces on monuments and other places as evidence for migration and racial mixing. He provided cranial measurements against a diagram of 'low' and 'high' racial groups as evidence; the racial hierarchy of Aborigines and Black Africans at the lower end and the 'white' races of the Libyans or Amorites at the upper end were assumed. An appendix to the lecture considered 'The Interpretation of Curves' of graphs of skull measurements from across Egyptian history, in which he concentrated on patterns and variability of curves, echoing Karl Pearson's work on the irregularities of curves as outlined in his 1893 Gresham lecture (Porter, 2004: 238). Pearson thought that when there was an irregular curve, a break from the normal measurement, that it showed signs of evolutionary development. Like Pearson, Petrie stressed the need for masses of data and that the statistical study of race was 'visual and graphical' (Porter, 2004: 239).

Petrie's lecture was in three parts. In the first part, Petrie concentrated on racial changes in Egypt over 10,000 years. He argued that early man or

'Bushmen', whose portraits were seen in cave paintings, were exterminated by an invading race that was connected to Libyans and Amorites. This race mixed with others before being taken over by an incoming race that became the dynastic race of Egypt, whose face is 'wholly different from all the other types' (Petrie, 1906a: 12). In essence, Petrie argued that the 10,000 years of Egyptian history were marked by invading races who subjugated other races followed by racial mixing, which Petrie considered useful as long as the right elements were fused. Unlike many fellow social conservatives, Petrie was not against immigration, as defined in the 1905 Aliens Act (the legislation that placed the first restrictions on modern immigration into Britain), as long as the migrants were industrious and of the right 'type', which could be defined by race and face.

The second part of Petrie's lecture detailed racial movement across Europe from the time of the Roman Empire, which Petrie argued would not have declined if the Romans had mixed racially with the invading Goths, and finished his overview in the ninth-century AD. He again concentrated on head types and size as evidence. He provided 28 maps showing routes of migration of racial groups such as 'Frank', 'Goth' and 'Lombard' across Europe and Western Asia. Petrie defined the anthropological tools at hand for defining race; bones, skin colour (though unstable), physiognomy and general expression (though vague and composite photography is needed for greater definition), language, culture (arts and laws) and history, which was of the greatest weight (Petrie, 1906a: 31–2). He finished the main part of his lecture with a look at the 'meaning of migrations' and the problems caused by them, which he summed up with one word: 'Weeding' (Petrie, 1906a: 32). Petrie argued, as he would do in more detail in *Janus,* that state subsidy of the poor led to the downfall of Rome since it ended natural weeding. His Huxley lecture ended with a reaction to contemporary political events:

> The most recent panaceas of political ignorance, equality of wages and the right to maintenance are the surest high road to racial extinction. The higher the walls of artificial restrictions, – the exclusion of more industrious races, the limitation of free labour, the penalizing of the capable in order to artificially maintain the incapable, – the more certain and more sweeping will be the migration of a stronger and better race into the misused land. The one great lesson of all this world-agony of

migrations is the necessity of weeding; and the statesman's duty is to see that this is done with the least disturbance, the least pain, and the most whole hearted effect. (Petrie, 1906: 32a)

It is, seemingly, a strange ending for the Huxley lecture, yet Galton and Pearson had also used the occasion to also outline their vision for future race improvement and eugenic thinking. Anthropology was here used as a tool to attempt to influence modern governance and systems of living.

Janus

The 1906 Liberal Government with Sir Henry Campbell-Bannerman as Prime Minister, H. H. Asquith as Chancellor of the Exchequer (later becoming Prime Minister after Campbell-Bannerman's death in 1908) and David Lloyd George as President of the Board of Trade (later Chancellor in 1908) legislated for a fledgling welfare state. As well as the 'Children's Charter', the Liberal Government passed The Trade Unions Act (1906), which was actually a piece of legislation put together by the Labour Party and protected trade union funds in the event of strikes and allowed for peaceful picketing. The same year, Lloyd George introduced Old Age Pensions at 5 shillings a week at the age of 70 and enabled compensation for injury to workers caused by industrial working conditions. A subsequent Liberal government, after two elections in 1910 and the dispute with the House of Lords, brought in National Insurance and payment for Members of Parliament in 1911. All these measures were designed to protect the livelihoods of working people and increase participation in social and public life for a broader range of social classes. Many people, particularly on the political right, objected to these reforms and Petrie was among them.

It is against the backdrop of these reforms that *Janus in Modern Life* (1907) needs to be read. If *Janus* reads much like 'disgusted' letters to newspapers, that is because that is essentially what it is and Petrie frequently wrote on matters to *The Times* (Drower, 1995: 342). Petrie outlined everything that he felt was wrong with the political reforms and modern life. He advocated a way of living that was essentially based around how he worked and lived his own life. Petrie made it clear at the beginning of *Janus* that it is about eugenic principles and argued that the 'quality of the race determines the future' (Petrie, 1907: 3). He drew on the statistical examples in Galton's *Hereditary Genius* to contend that these principles have been known about for over a generation. Petrie believed in self-help for the lower classes (and above) to stop atrophy and stimulate mental growth, since competition is necessary to improve mental variation (Petrie, 1907: 8). He argued that immigration is beneficial to Britain as long as it is not made up of the 'low type of immigrant from Russia and Poland' and all migrants are checked at entry into the country by vigorous mental and physical tests (Petrie, 1907: 15).

Petrie elaborated on his contention, outlined in *Migrations*, that the downfall of the Roman Empire was due to subsidizing cheap corn for the lower classes and the growth in influence of unions. He argued against taxation of work and for taxing only ostentation and luxury products; Petrie was infamous for his frugal conditions of work and abstemious nature. Compensation for accidents would, Petrie argued, only make workers more careless and cut down on competition, while poor relief would be spent extravagantly and so the ostentatious financier is a lesser curse than the poor on welfare. Smaller families bring benefits and children of the lower classes should not be saved since they would soon outnumber those of the better class (Petrie, 1907: 61). Petrie believed in the 'drastic treatment of the unfit' following and quoting from Dr Robert Rentoul's recommendations in his 1906 book *Race Culture Or Race Suicide*, which outlined the need for negative eugenics, namely sterilization, so the 'unfit' would not have to be inspected for marriage (Petrie, 1907: 87–9). Petrie concluded with the observation that the equatorial races have less vigour than those of colder climates and so the 'tropics will be the seat of the keenest competition and extinction of race' (Petrie, 1907: 103). Having outlined the economical virtues of the Chinese in America, Petrie finished with the question whether the future will belong to the races of the east or west?

Petrie's Social Darwinism was not new nor, as we have seen, unique. Many of the arguments that Petrie opined had their roots in the nineteenth century, going back to Malthusian ideas, the 1834 Poor Law and beyond. Petrie clearly thought that he lived in the manner in which all people should do; frugally, having a small family, marrying late, having healthy pursuits (but not playing sports for the sake of sports' sake) and so on. Anachronistic and egotistic as *Janus* is and despite the limited notice that appeared to be taken in the media (there was a cool review in the *Saturday Review*), letters to Petrie give an indication that readers agreed with many of his sentiments (Sheppard, 2010:

27). One from Thomas Godfrey on 31 July 1907, whom Petrie evidently knew since he had 'laughingly said I don't know that you will agree with it', congratulated Petrie and said 'I agree with almost every word of it' (Godfrey to Petrie, PMA: 31 July 1907). Arthur John Hubbard thanked Petrie for writing Janus as he agreed with it 'whole heartedly', having 'felt sick whenever I have thought of the selfishness, effeminacy and stupidity which I have seen coming' (Hubbard to Petrie, PMA: 14 August 1907). Another correspondent from Hitching concentrated on the issue of migration:

> The question of admission of yellow and dark races to compete with our western tradition is a problem not yet thought out by either political party. It will be mad to leave its solution till instead of trickling in until they come upon us in a flood from a burst dam. You do well to force these unpleasant problems upon us and as I have said I sympathise with the main line of your solution. (The Heritage, Hitching, PMA: 14 July 1907)

Yet, there is one letter in the Petrie Museum Archive which outlines, very strongly, with pages of statistical notes, the writer's disagreements with Petrie. It is from Karl Pearson, who condemned a manuscript that Petrie sent to him in early 1907 in the strongest possible terms (for Pearson) as being wrong on 'the mathematical side. Mathematics sets a standard and avoids controversy' (Pearson to Petrie, PMA: 13 March 1907). It is clear from the letter that Pearson referred to unpublished pages of *Janus*. It would have been highly unlikely that Pearson and Petrie would agree given their differing politics and Pearson's emphasis on positive eugenics for race improvement rather than sterilization.

Petrie gave a tour of 14 lectures around the country on the subject in the autumn of 1907 (Petrie, 1931: 211). His work brought him some political attention and he became a member of the Anti-Socialist Union, which was a group set up to combat socialism and collectivism after the election to parliament of socialist Labour Party MPs in 1906 (Brown, 1976: 238). The Union was, of course, largely unsuccessful in its objectives, particularly after the extension of the franchise to all men in 1918, but it gives an indication of the deep-rooted antipathy among some of the political classes to socialism and social reforms. Other members included Lord Cromer, whom Petrie knew from his time governing Egypt. Petrie also joined the right-wing British

Constitution Association and became President of it in 1914. A pamphlet in the Petrie Museum Archives outlined the aim of the British Constitution Association: 'To resist socialism: to uphold the fundamental principles of the British Constitution – personal liberty and personal responsibility; and limit the functions of governing bodies accordingly'. All of these principles were outlined in *Janus* and Petrie, despite his working life taking him away from Britain for substantial parts of the year, was clearly involved and engaged with politics during the Edwardian period. His politics, furthermore, were under-scored by ideas about race and eugenic thinking, just as much of his archaeological work had been.

Revolutions

Petrie returned to his eugenic manifesto in 1911, after several seasons excavating at Memphis, with *Revolutions of Civilisation,* which was the product of a lecture at the Royal Institution:

> The volume on civilisation I had long been planning, but waited till I had the opportunity of a Royal Institution evening to bring the subject forward, April 28 1911. Twenty years afterward that book is still in constant demand, and has been reprinted several times. It has brought me the friends of various nationalities. (Petrie, 1931: 218)

It was, in fact, reprinted in America ten years after Petrie wrote the above in his autobiography. *Revolutions* is a comparative analysis of different art and architectural forms in the ancient and medieval world. It is quite a different book to *Janus*, but shares a central interest in race with an eugenic agenda. Petrie defined civilization on the grounds of artistic production and style, differentiating different periods of Egyptian, classical and medieval art through terms such as 'best', 'archaic' and 'decadent', which are verified by the naturalism of the art.

Beginning with the classical art of ancient Athens as an example of the pinnacle of civilization (Figure 9.2), Petrie galloped through the different styles of dynastic art from ancient Egypt. He placed them into eight successive periods according to their stage of development in civilization predicated on the glory and decay of art (Petrie, 1911: 47). He considered the earliest art of Dynasty I and II to be the best in terms of artistic excellence. The late

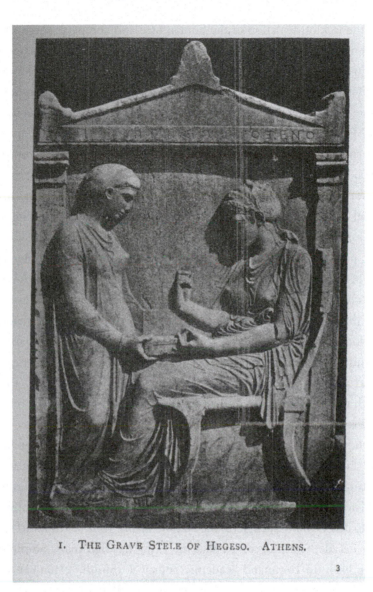

1. THE GRAVE STELE OF HEGESO. ATHENS.

3

Figure 9.2 'The grave Stele of Hegeso. Athens', Petrie (1911), *Revolutions of Civilization*, Plate I

period of the New Kingdom, he defined as showing 'continuous decay', while useful for portraiture and he mainly compared the heads of statues of various pharaohs as the point of comparison (Petrie, 1911: 37). Petrie described a Coptic depiction of the head as 'base', showing the 'decayed classical' (Petrie, 1911: 37). During the Islamic period of Egypt, Petrie used architectural style due to the lack of depiction of the human face and compares these styles to European equivalents, often concluding in favour of Islamic art. Like *Migrations*, Petrie turned from Egypt to Europe and drew on the work of Arthur Evans on the Cretan period, before considering Mycenaean and classical Greek art, in which he concentrated on technical aspects of work, such as the depiction of drapery. Petrie finished with European art in the medieval period before briefly considering other art forms, such as music and literature. In his concluding chapters, Petrie stressed the importance of race migration and displacement in the formation of artistic style. The system of government, Petrie argued, is crucial and artistic style can only exist in a democracy for so long before 'the majority without capital will eat up the capital of the minority' until 'the inferior population is swept away to make room for a fitter people' (Petrie, 1911: 124). Petrie also believed race fusion to be crucial for the production of art and civilization; the right racial mixing created conditions for new eras of activity through the production of people of ability. This is Petrie's main point in *Revolutions*. He argued for the future potential of eugenics to separate 'fine races' and 'prohibit continual mixture, until they have a distinct type, which will start a new civilization when transplanted' (Petrie, 1911: 131). The idea that such racial types could be separated and observed was partially informed by his discovery of heads showing different 'racial types' in Memphis.

Revolutions may have been reprinted many times since its first publication in 1911, but an obituary of Petrie, by Sidney Smith, described the work as illustrating a 'scientific bent' of mind looking for more 'positive guidance from history' than history can supply (Smith, 1945: 13). Commenting that it anticipated Oswald Spengler's *The Decline of the West* (1918 and 1922) by about a decade, Smith observed that the 'essay has had many admirers but is never likely to command academic approval' (Smith, 1945: 14). Petrie's political involvement in terms of joining organizations appears to have been, beyond letters to *The Times*, limited to between 1900 and 1914. He made little comment on events after World War One in his autobiography, though a passage describing the Great Strike of 1926 clearly illustrated where his sympathies lay:

> The most interesting event was the Great Strike, the greatest social struggle since 1649. The defiance given by the hand-workers to the head-workers was triumphantly answered by the head-workers doing the whole work,

and proving their ability, while no serious violence marred the spirit of the challenge. All other countries watched the clash, Italy most of all, and each said afterward that none but our own people would have come through it as well. The menace of social revolution was broken. (Petrie, 1931: 255)

In 1926 Mussolini, the Fascist leader of Italy, established his power, gradually dismantling democratic functions and banning strikes by trade unions. Petrie's point was not designed to support Mussolini but to illustrate that the British could break a strike through hard work and determination rather than legislation, which corresponds exactly with his ideas about the non-interference of the state.

There was a change to the direction of eugenics in Britain after World War One that was informed by the mass loss of young men in that war, the growing emancipation of women and universal suffrage (Soloway, 1995: 161). However, negative eugenics had a painful legacy across the world with many people, who were considered 'unfit' by political and health authorities, being sterilized. In Nazi Germany, 'euthanasia' programmes went one step further and the murder of people with learning disabilities and mental health problems led the way for genocide and medical experimentation in the name of eugenic science. The discovery of these crimes against humanity did not stop eugenic thinking and practice. Only last year, hearings in the American State of North Carolina heard from people who had been affected by the sterilization programme as late as the 1970s. Yet, in some ways, Karl Pearson's 'positive' form of eugenics – encouraging people to breed responsibly and improving living conditions – underpinned the Beveridge Report and the formation of the National Health Service and Welfare State in post-1945 Britain. Sir Keith Joseph, a frontrunner for the leadership of the Conservative Party in the mid-1970s, gave a speech in 1974 in which he promoted birth control as an antidote to the fertility and degeneration, as he saw it, of unmarried working class mothers (Soloway, 1995: 359). At the time, the furore over that speech cost Joseph the chance of running for Conservative Party leader and his protégé Margaret Thatcher ran for leader instead. The legacy of eugenic thinking in Britain is fraught and widespread.

It is too easy to look at the past and condemn attitudes that today we may find unpalatable without looking closely at our own assumptions and use of language. I am writing this book in 2012, in the aftermath of riots across

England during August 2011 in which the rioters were described by politicians and media commentators as belonging to a 'feral' class and 'sub-class'. Dan Stone has drawn attention to how language around the 'underclass' today parallels that of the 'sub-class' or 'under-man', and the idea of 'weeding', one hundred years ago, since 'it remains easier to blame the genes of individuals and groups for their social dispossession rather than to question the structures that make up divisive societies' (Stone, 2002: 139). The term 'chav' (council housed and violent) also seems to be an acceptable form of class prejudice in public and media use (Jones, 2012). Edwardian readers of *Janus* and *Revolutions* would recognize the implications of the term.

10

Heads

Among the numerous trays of terracottas from Memphis in the Petrie Museum collection is a drawer marked 'Memphis "Race" Heads' (Figure 10.1). This drawer contains 57 small heads, probably from terracotta figurines, that date from the Ptolemaic or Roman period. The occasional original typed label on yellowing paper lies by a head, such as 'Sumerian'. The heads and their Petrie Museum accession numbers are all listed in the Appendix along with their description by Flinders Petrie, where known. They are only a small fraction of about 300 heads preserved in the Petrie Museum collection, though no other drawer is similarly marked. It was while looking at these heads soon after starting to work at the Petrie Museum in 2007, that I realized how profound Flinders Petrie's interest in race and racial types was. This collection of "Race" heads was probably put together by Petrie for teaching purposes and it is clear that his early work on racial typologies influenced him so much that he believed students of Egyptian archaeology needed to understand the importance of establishing racial difference through looking at representations of the face.

The terracotta head UC33278 that Chapter 6 began with, is one of the heads of 'foreigners' from Memphis in the collection, though not included in the drawer of 'Memphis "Race" heads'. Petrie thought that these heads 'were the figures of more than a dozen races' made by Greco-Egyptian artists' carefully recording 'foreigners' in Memphis (Petrie, 1909b: 16). Sometimes he used contemporary examples from his own period to ascribe identities to these heads. He argued, for example, that one head (UC48515) is named 'Hebrew' due to the facial 'resemblance to a modern Jewish Type coming from Germany' (Petrie, 1909: 16) (Figure 10.2). Another head (UC8457), Petrie described as a Persian and commented that it shows the 'high-bred Aryan type', considering the Persian

Figure 10.1 Drawer of 'Memphis "Race" Heads', Petrie Museum of Egyptian Archaeology

Figure 10.2 'Hebrew' head, UC48515 © Petrie Museum of Egyptian Archaeology, UCL

Figure 10.3 'Aryan' head, UC8457 © Petrie Museum of Egyptian Archaeology, UCL

Empire as a 'magnificent creation' that established world peace from the Indus to the Balkans (Petrie, 1909: 16) (Figure 10.3). As we have seen, Petrie returned to these 'types' in his lecture to the Jewish Historical Society in 1922 on the migration into Egypt of different racial groups in the time of the Ptolemies:

The series of heads of foreigners found at Memphis shows how the Babylonian traders of the old Sumerian race flocked in, with Indians, Kurds, and a multitude of Scythian Cossacks, besides the ruling race of Persia itself. (Petrie, 1922: 22–3)

The production of these heads and figurines took place across the Hellenistic world from 350–40 BC. There are a vast collection of terracottas and terracotta heads from Smyrna in Asia Minor (now Izmir in Turkey) on display in the Musée de Louvre for example. These heads are displayed at the Louvre under different categories, including 'ethnic and realistic', 'hairstyles' or 'heroes and gods'. Some of these heads are termed 'grotesque' in a section at the Louvre. Many of these so-called grotesque images may be caricatures of rulers or the ruling classes, or genre types, such as the 'boastful soldier', from comedies. They may represent participants in ritual dances or they may represent medical pathologies. It is extremely difficult to position what their function was; it could have been votive, decorative, medical or a mixture of various functions. The heads found at Memphis belong to four different periods: Ptolemaic Egyptian, Hellenistic Greek, Romano-Egyptian and Roman. Sally-Ann Ashton has further categorized these heads into subject areas, such as Egyptian priests, divinities, rulers, caricatures, festival participants and actors (Ashton, 2003a: 171). Sally-Ann Ashton's book *Petrie's Ptolemaic and Roman Memphis* (2003) and chapter on 'Foreigners at Memphis? Petrie's Racial Types' in *'Never Had the Like Occurred': Egypt's View of its Past* (2003) has already vigorously interrogated Petrie's definitions of these heads.

We know from written evidence – from historians and papyri – that Memphis was a diverse city comprising groups of Jewish, Greek, Macedonian Greek, Egyptian, Persian and other peoples. These terracotta heads may give a glimpse of diversity in Ptolemaic Memphis. The exhibition *Alexander's Legacy – the Greeks in Egypt* (17 September 2010–20 March 2011), at the Allard Pierson Museum in Amsterdam, used dozens of similar heads from Alexandria and Memphis to illustrate the ethnic diversity and cosmopolitan hubs of Alexandria and Ptolemaic Egypt in 300–30 BC. The heads may show the caricatures of the ancient world or the stereotypes of the modern world; much depends on the viewpoint of the person looking at them. Petrie's emphasis on racial types in reading these heads and the lack of archaeological information about them makes our interpretation of them problematic. We have Petrie's vision of Ptolemaic Memphis, but how far does it correspond to what is known about Memphis during that period?

Greek and Egyptian Memphis

Petrie began excavating at Memphis in 1908 and finished there after successive seasons in 1913. Memphis had been occupied since the beginning of the Old Kingdom (c. 3000 BC) and was periodically the seat of administrative rule for ancient Egypt. The main deity of Memphis was Ptah, the god of arts and crafts. Excavations by Petrie revealed small workshops for a range of crafts, including faience and stone vessel production, mainly from the Late Period to early Roman Period. Petrie mainly excavated at the area around the palaces of Merenptah and Apries. The cost of excavating Memphis was high as the land needed to be leased and the water surrounding and covering the site, needed to be pumped out. The Ny Carlsberg Foundation in Denmark started supporting Petrie's work in 1908 and so Petrie could afford the high costs of this excavation (Bagh, 2011: 25). He was fascinated by the area around the Temple of Merenptah, which he believed to be the 'foreign or Greek quarter' dividing the city up much like the cities and towns of the Ottoman Empire were divided into Greek, Turkish and Frank quarters. This was partly because he found many of the heads in the Temple of Proteus (Merenptah) area, close to the Ptolemaic palace, though, as Ashton points out, many of the heads were collected by his workforce from across the site area (Ashton, 2003a).

Memphis changed with migration during the Greek-ruled period of Egypt. Dorothy Thompson has based her history of Ptolemaic Memphis on fragments of surviving evidence and outlined the changes made in the city through immigration and Greek rule:

> Throughout, my concerns are with the effects on the country and its population of the conquest of Alexander and of the imposition of Greco-Macedonian rule; with the effects more particularly on the city of Memphis of the foundation of a new Greek capital on the coast and all that this involved in terms of the balance of population within Egypt; and, finally, with the consequences of the introduction of new, immigrant outlooks and of the changed economic focus within the country. The context is important, for cities in Egypt were very different from those familiar to Mediterranean immigrants from the north. (Thompson, 1988: 5)

Immigration had taken place under the Persian rule, but then took place on a greater scale under Alexander the Great and his successor in Egypt, Ptolemy I, when Macedonians and other groups of Greeks were actively sought to settle in Egypt. Thompson notes that 'Petrie's racial typology of these heads is at times suspect' but 'the imagination' of those 'who produced them must have been fired by the racial mix of the community in which they lived' (Thompson, 1988: 92).One of the main pieces of ancient evidence that we have for the diversity of population in Memphis during the early Roman period, is from the geographer Strabo, who is more 'systematic in his description of the city' than Herodotus was 500 years earlier (Thompson, 1988: 9). In around 10–20 AD, Strabo

described the Palace, the temples, particularly the Sarapieion, as 'both large
and populous, ranks second after Alexandria, and consists of mixed races of
people, like those who have settled together at Alexandria' (Strabo, *Geography,*
Book XIII: 32). The Ptolemiac promotion of migration from Macedonia in
particular, as well as other Greek populations in the Mediterranean and North
Africa, such as, for example, Cyrene, radically altered the population.

Napthali Lewis argues that the policy of the Ptolemies around the different
cultures, which privileged those of Greek and Macedonian origin, was not
'racially motivated' but cultural and was concerned with keeping Greek status
as the highest in a country whose long history and religious traditions inevitably
over-shadowed that of the recent migrants (Lewis, 2001: 5). The Ptolemies
admitted Hellenized Egyptians into the civil service, as much for practical
needs as for cultural purposes. They knew (or learnt) the Greek language and
became assimilated into the upper class of government officials who ruled
Egypt. Lewis also points out that the idea of the 'Hellenization of Egypt', or the
Greek influence taking over the Orient and then the civilizing impulses of the
Greeks in the Near East being watered down, was an idea that was 'current in
the 1920s but is seen today as a product for the most part of a certain colonial
ideology in Western Historiography of those times' (Lewis, 2001: 159 f/n 4).
Lewis' point about the influence of 1920s' colonial ideology is important. It is
very difficult to consider the colonial identity of the ancient world, and, indeed,
how different ethnic groups are defined and described, without drawing on
modern assumptions. Denise Eileen McCoskey, in her overview of 'identity'
in Ptolemaic Egypt, points out that the ancient colonial structure not only
treated the categories of 'Greek' and 'Egyptian' as conceptually different and
'representative of inverse position of social power', but also that:

> Greek colonial identity, one expressed in great part through cultural forms,
> relied upon the uncomfortable and always disconcertingly incomplete
> expulsion of all Egyptian "elements" to the margin. (McCoskey, 2002: 15)

And yet, some aspects of Egyptian identity were at the forefront of establishing
the Ptolemaic dynasty as the true rulers and pharaohs of Egypt, such as the
cult of Isis and animal worship. Greek culture was mixed with an Egyptian
'otherness' at times when it suited the Ptolemaic rulers. Memphis was, then, a
city consisting of different cultures and groups of people and so to some extent

Petrie's drawer of 'Memphis "Race" Heads' may well reflect something of the diversity of the city during the Ptolemaic period.

Petrie's 'Race' heads

Petrie usually described the 'heads' as 'foreigners', that is foreign to Egypt, and ascribed difference to them according to their race as depicted in the physical characteristics of the face. In his autobiography, Petrie recalls the importance of the heads to him and repositioned the date of the heads to the earlier period of Persian rule:

> Of remarkable interest was the discovery of many terracotta heads, modelled, not from a mould, which represented many different types neither Egyptian nor Greek. These were only found in the foreign quarter of Memphis and belonged to the Persian age. In the first year the matter seemed to many people almost too strange for belief. The second season convinced all, that he had here the figurines of Indians Persians, Kurds, Scythians, Hebrews, Sumerians, Karian, Greeks of Asia Minor, Macedonian, and even Spanish or Sardinian portraits. A very few pottery heads were found, and those of Indians. (Petrie, 1931: 213)

The Louvre describes some of their collection of very similar heads from Smyrna as portraying ethnic difference. Ethnos or ethnicity is notoriously difficult to define. Uffe Østergård advocates a model for Ptolemaic Egypt based on one put forward by the Norwegian theorist Fredrik Barth in 1969:

> [Barth] proposed a social interaction model of ethnic identity that does not posit a fixed "character" or "essence" for the group but examines the perceptions of its members which distinguish them from other groups. (Østergård, 1992: 36)

This definition describes social and cultural shifting interactions and is not positioned on a biological basis. It takes on an independent dimension of social life, for example not necessarily linking ethnic identity to nation, and illustrates a continued interest in maintaining cultural boundaries as the main focus of defining ethnic identity. It is a description that better suits current ideas about cultural identity but is, however, a definition that is difficult to apply to 'unspeaking' material culture, which is why such material needs to be considered alongside other evidence, such as writing, from Ptolemaic Egypt. Physical appearance was not the only way of distinguishing ethnic groups in antiquity. It is impossible to adequately identify how different ethnic identities were perceived since contemporary scholars are bounded by the 'modern system of racial formation that the concept was associated with skin colour' and in Ptolemaic Egypt 'identities in antiquity seem to be based more systematically on practice and cultural traits, such as language' (McCoskey, 2002: 32). There is, though, more than skin colour defining race in the late nineteenth and early twentieth century but also the face (in all its detail), skull size and measurements, bone size, as well as language and custom. The Report on the 'Ethnographic Survey of the United Kingdom' at the 1895 Ipswich BAAS meeting considered all these areas in an effort to define racial identities in modern Britain.

The heads from Memphis do depict different types of face and people but the idea that they were by Greco-Egyptian artists carefully recording racial types around them is unlikely (Petrie, 1909b: 15). Comparison of some heads with royal portraiture of the Ptolemies period can be made, though it is still very much 'guesswork' (Bailey, 2008: 137). It is, in addition, clear that not all of these heads are 'Greek'. For example, the so-called Indians have been compared to figures of Harpocrates in the Roman period. Their garlanded headresses and raised left hand indicate that they 'may be revellers' as they are similar to the 'image of dancing dwarfs' or possibly depictions of Roman priests (Ashton, 2003b: 189). Sometimes a robe, hat or other form of garment or object seems to indicate what cultural group the head may belong to. The dating of these heads, as was noted by Petrie, is difficult but greater emphasis has been made on the techniques of construction and different types of clay used, which can indicate an Egyptian, Greek or Roman provenance. For example, Egyptian terracottas are 'traditionally solid and either hand-modelled or mould-made with a flat unmodelled back and base' out of coarse Nile silt (Ashton, 2003a: 72).

There are recognizable Greek-style heads, such as a number of 'Tanagra' style heads. Some of these in the Petrie Museum collection are from Memphis, some where the location is not known. As we have seen in Chapter 3, these 'Tanagra' figurines were found across the Hellenistic world and the heads at Memphis do not 'support Petrie's view that such images were intended to represent Greeks abroad, rather that they served a specific purpose, perhaps related to festivals' (Ashton, 2003b: 191). Another form of 'Greek' head found at Memphis is the so-called grotesque, though, again, such figurines were found across the Hellenistic world thus illustrating that such heads were not just produced in Memphis to record different racial types.

Petrie's discovery of these heads merited a mention in *The Times* in 1908 and can be set in the context of the contemporary interest of defining racial types during this period (*The Times*, 15 May 1908: 13). Writing about these heads in *Memphis II*, Petrie emphasized his continuing belief that character and race could be seen in the face:

> The absence of any collection of ancient portraiture of races, beyond that which I made in Egypt twenty-two years ago, leaves the identification of these very varied types to depend entirely upon chance observation. If any of the classical students would deal with this branch of Greek art, and collect a uniform series of photographs of every representation of racial types from sculpture and coins, a very necessary and important branch of study would take its proper place. Unfortunately archaeology, like literary scholarship, too often [. . .] leaves the weightier matters of the world's history neglected. There is not even any series of composite portrait heads from coins, which are greatly needed for the character study of celebrated kings. (Petrie, 1909b: 16–17)

Petrie referred back to the *Racial Photographs* that he had taken in 1886–7 and bemoaned the lack of impact they have had within classical archaeology. Although Galton began his composite experiments with photographs of different coins and medals of ancient rulers, such as Alexander the Great or Cleopatra VII, no classical archaeologist to Petrie's knowledge had continued this study.

The 'foreign' heads from Memphis that are in the Petrie Museum collection and were published and commented on by Petrie can be found in the Appendix. Here a few of Petrie's descriptions are featured with an image of the head in order to more fully understand his continuing emphasis on reading the face. The image of the terracotta head is shown next to Petrie's description.

UC48248 (Figure 10.4) is an example of using the style of hair to determine the cultural identity of the head and is here described as 'Macedonian':

> [...] with long ringlets shews a mode of hair which is familiar among the Ptolemaic queens, but not elsewhere. As they prided themselves on being Macedonians, this is probably the Macedonian type. (Petrie, 1909b: 17. Pl. XXXI, No. 102)

Figure 10.4 'Macedonian' head, UC48248 © Petrie Museum of Egyptian Archaeology, UCL

In this description of UC48452 (Figure 10.5), Petrie again bases his identification on the basis of garment rather than the face:

> The Karian (71) is named on the strength of the description of Herodotos, that the Karians wore helmets with a crest like a cock's comb. There is no other helmet type which would agree to this, and the Karian as being chief mercenary soldier race of the time, and settled in Egypt, must have been familiar in Memphis. (Petrie, 1909b: 17. Pl. XXVIII, No. 71)

In this head UC8981 (Figure 10.6), Petrie combines analysis of the garments and reference to a literary source with a judgement on the moral characteristics the facial features supposedly illustrate:

> Persian No. 18 is the cavalry officer, with the face swathed to keep off heat and dust, like the horseman on the Sidon sarcophagus (17). On the head is the lion's scalp, probably a regimental badge. Herodotos mentions of the

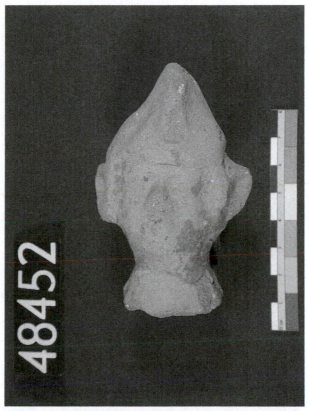

Figure 10.5 'Karian' head, UC48452 © Petrie Museum of Egyptian Archaeology, UCL

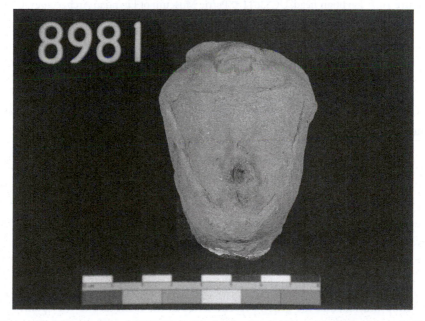

Figure 10.6 'Persian' head, UC8981 © Petrie Museum of Egyptian Archaeology, UCL

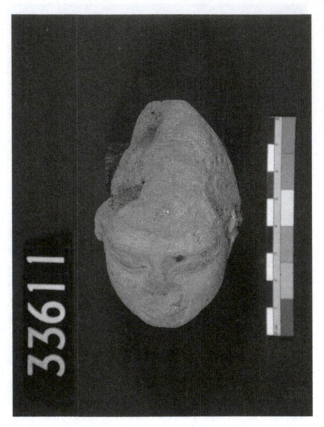

Figure 10.7 'Egyptian' head, UC33611 © Petrie Museum of Egyptian Archaeology, UCL

> Persian cavalry "that on their heads some of them wore brazen and wrought steel ornaments" (vii, 84). The face is delicate, and almost effeminate, in the slight brow and refined eyes. (Petrie, 1909a: 17. Pl. XXXVI, No. 18)

In this description of UC33611 (Figure 10.7), Petrie makes comparison with the depiction of hair on a tomb painting:

> Egyptian UC33611 No.2 is like the sturdy well-fed women of Middle Egypt; the swathing up of the hair when at work is seen in the tomb of Khnum-hotep at Beni Hasan. (Petrie, 1909a: 16. Pl. XXXV, No. 2)

Petrie describes this head UC48454 (Figure 10.8) as 'Iberian' based mainly on his perception that it resembles a modern Spaniard:

> The Iberian (70) is identified by the resemblance of the profile to the Shardana or Sardinian of the XIXth-XXth dynasty, in the long low head and the mutton-chop whisker, and the general resemblance of the front face to the Spanish

Figure 10.8 'Iberian' head, UC48454 © Petrie Museum of Egyptian Archaeology, UCLs

Figure 10.9 'Indian' head, UC33607 © Petrie Museum of Egyptian Archaeology, UCL

matador type at present. There is no other ancient race, so far as I remember, which has shaved in this fashion. (Petrie, 1909b: 17. Pl. XXVIII, No. 70)

Petrie thought that there must have been a large number of Indians, even Tibetans, in Memphis due to heads and figurines such as UC33607 (Figure 10.9):

36 is an Aryan Punjabi type; the attitude with the hip raised high on one side, the arms bent, and the loose lock of hair, are all Indian; but the band round the breast, the amulet hung round the neck, and the artificial navel line, are all strange and lack a comparison. (Petrie, 1909a: 16. Pl. XXXIX, No. 36)

Although, as Ashton argues, it is likely that such figurines represent priests or Harpocrates (Ashton, 2003b: 189). Petrie connects several heads to the Roman general Mark Anthony purely through comparison to portraiture and by reading his inherited features in the face, such as UC48173 (Figure 10.10):

The various types 125–132 are not yet connected with known localities. 128 has closely the Mark Anthony features; he did not get that type from Julia,

Figure 10.10 'Mark Antony', UC48173 © Petrie Museum of Egyptian Archaeology, UCL

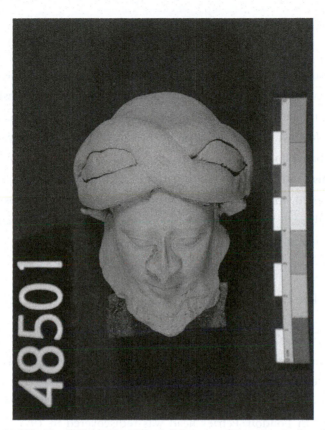

Figure 10.11 'The Kurd', UC48501 © Petrie Museum of Egyptian Archaeology, UCL

and if of the Antonia stock it might be sought among the Dorian Herakleidae from whom they claimed descent. The usual type of Herakles is somewhat like this. (Petrie, 1909b: 17. Pl. XXXIV, no. 128)

There are also problems with the evidence since the lack of a proper excavation history hinders identification of these heads and does not rule out fakes. This head UC48501 (Figure 10.11), in particular, has been identified as potentially being more modern due to its modelling and colour (personal conversation between Sally-Ann Ashton and the author), though further analysis is needed:

The Kurd (73) has the crossed turban which belongs to the Central Asian and Kurd race, but not to the Semitic peoples. Mr Hogarth informs me that the type of the face agrees to that of the modern Kurds, who were well known to the Greeks as the Karduchi. This is the finest piece of modelling among all the heads; the delicacy with which the features are worked, the detail of the

ear being pressed forward by the turban, wrinkling it on the inner side, and
the spirit of expression put this in the front rank. (Petrie, 1909b: 17)

Petrie's description of these heads range from the peculiar to the relatively
unproblematic, when predicated in identifying garment or fashions. In
describing the face, Petrie tends to rely on comparison with other portraits
of people, his own judgements around modern racial types or value-laden
adjectives based on his physiognomic reading of features. The ethnic diversity
of Memphis from 500 BC to AD 300, from which these heads probably date,
is not contested, but whether they truly identify the different groups of people
who lived there, is a difficult question and one which we are unlikely to ever
be able to answer.

The head of William Matthew Flinders Petrie

Almost 30 years after excavating and collecting heads at Memphis, Petrie died
in the Government Hospital at Jerusalem in July 1942 and his body is buried
in the Protestant cemetery on the summit of Mount Zion (Drower, 1995:
423). Petrie's head however is not. It is preserved in a jar in the Royal College
of Surgeons in London. Petrie's head was rediscovered in 1977 by Barbara
Adams, who was then assistant curator at the Petrie Museum. It was sent in
confused circumstances in the midst of World War II to the Royal College of
Surgeons (Chaplin, 1998: 391–4). According to Dr W. E. Thompson, the chief
bacteriologist of the hospital in which Petrie died, Petrie had asked for his
skull to be sent to the Royal College as a 'specimen of a typical British skull'
(Thompson to Keith, PMA: 9 October 1944). In response to this letter, Sir
Arthur Keith, on behalf of the Royal College of Surgeons, replied 'Flinders
Petrie was a very outstanding type in every respect in body and in mind
and deserves to have his last wishes made good' (Keith to Thompson, PMA:
undated). There is further confusion as to whether the brain was removed at
post-mortem or whether Petrie's intention was for his skull and brain to be
kept together in perpetuity as a perfect example of a 'British type'.

Petrie applied his racial and eugenic thinking to himself and clearly
believed that he was a perfect specimen of a 'British type'. His gift of his skull
and possibly his brain to science were 'entirely consistent with his long belief

in the power of race and heredity' (Silbermann, 1999: 70). A jar containing the head of Flinders Petrie in the Royal College of Surgeons is therefore a testament to Petrie's lifelong eugenic thinking and his belief in the power of the skull and face to illustrate what kind of person someone was in race, character and virtue. This, again, was not so unusual at the time in which Petrie most vividly articulated his eugenic thinking. In the early 1890s Burt Green Wilder, at Cornell University in New York, systematically started collecting brains for anthropometric comparison, while brains of 'great men and women' entered museum collections across Europe, America and Japan (Kwint, 2012: 14–15). It was, however, more unusual by the time that Petrie died in 1942 and Neil Asher Silbermann has pointed out that while Petrie's head was being removed in Jerusalem, eugenics was being used to justify and determine genocide across Nazi occupied Europe (Silbermann, 1999: 75). Silbermann cautions archaeologists to take a critical look at Petrie's theories of racial conflict before accepting the 'racial inequality that once filled Petrie's head' (Silbermann, 1999: 77).

Afterword

Until now, it has not been immediately evident that William Matthew Flinders Petrie, the famous archaeologist, was also an influential biometrician and eugenic supporter; however, as we have seen throughout this book, he was indeed central to the ideology and the science of eugenics. Although eugenics is, by and large, left out of published works about Petrie, the evidence in this book has brought into focus his eugenic work and his close professional relationships with eugenics pioneers, especially Francis Galton and Karl Pearson. Past historical and biographical studies largely have considered these three men separately. Pearson and Galton are often discussed together and are included extensively in one another's biographies; however, Petrie is seldom included (Galton, 1909: 97–100; Pearson, 1930a: 240; Pearson, 1930b: 515–17). Furthermore, Galton and Pearson, as close as they were to Petrie in his life, are barely mentioned by Margaret Drower, Petrie's most recent and most thorough biographer (Drower, 1995: 68, 222, 260, 302, 339). As a pair, Pearson and Galton were close colleagues as well as confidants; Petrie and Pearson were neighbours in Hampstead Heath; Galton visited Petrie on site at Abydos in 1900. The relationship among these men brought Petrie into the world of biology, anthropometrics and eugenics as early as 1883 (Chapter 3; Sheppard, 2010). Petrie's association with both these men, and the exchange of ideas, materials, and theories among them, was influential in his own practical and theoretical work on civilization, race and culture. Their work together was also important for the research Galton and Pearson were doing because Petrie supplied them with needed human data and aided them in their statistical analyses. We have seen that, over time, Petrie became convinced that organizing people by racial types was not only a useful means of directing the future of the human race but also essential when studying the features of humans from the past. It has been made clear in this book that Petrie used racial typing in his archaeological work.

Petrie published two books dealing specifically with civilization and its development, and the lessons Great Britain might learn from historical evidence: *Janus in Modern Life* (1907) and *The Revolutions of Civilisation* (1911). He probably based these two arguments on some of his earlier ideas presented in his 1906 Huxley Lecture at the Anthropological Institute, entitled 'Migrations' (1906a). As Challis has argued in Chapter 9, the lecture itself and print article that followed it dealt with the idea of the movements of human populations throughout history and what this meant for the appearance of human bony structure in the material remains. Through detailed statistical analysis of human remains from both Egyptian and European history, Petrie concluded that 'migrations are the inevitable means of supplanting the less capable races by the more capable' (1906b: 170). It was through long and difficult periods of 'weeding', Petrie argued, that was 'the only means by which improved races have come forward in the world' in each time and place (1906a: 220). Finally, his historically based solution for the present was that politicians, the state and society should help to clear up the present population in Britain 'with the least disturbance, the least pain and the most whole-hearted effect'. Demonstrating the centrality of Pearson's statistics to the science of eugenics, one reviewer at *Biometrika* – the official journal of the Eugenics Lab at UCL – thought that Petrie's lecture was 'spoilt by ... unsatisfactory statistical methods' (WPE, 1907: 480). Petrie's methods hardly mattered in the end because the reviewer stated that the researchers at the lab 'agree absolutely' with Petrie's conclusions, even though they might 'reach the result by a different method'.

In the end, it became clear that the statisticians and eugenicists – and especially Pearson – at the Anthropometric Lab, continually depended on and used Petrie's work (Pearson, 1901; Martin, 1936). In fact, it was in Petrie's conclusions that they put most of their emphasis to justify what they advocated. Pearson and Petrie agreed that over time, 'the mean of the population for a given character might be deliberately moved in an evolutionary line of eugenic advance' (Kevles, 1995: 37). For both, it was the small, gradual changes caused by the selection of favourable traits that had allowed and would continue to allow civilization to evolve in a eugenically favourable direction. It is significant that they came to the same conclusion, because until Petrie, this discussion had been confined to biology. Within biology and statistics, represented by Galton, Pearson and the UCL Eugenic Lab, these ideas were expressed through the eugenics movement. Within the discipline of archaeology, represented initially by Petrie, the mixing or weeding of preferred (or undesired) traits was expressed in the theoretical school known as diffusionism.

Diffusionism

In the early twentieth century, diffusionism as a theory of social development began to prevail over earlier ideas of social evolution (Kuklick, 1991: 125–33; Stocking, 1995: 210–12; Champion, 2003). In other words, peoples and their ideas had not evolved simply within particular environments, separate from many outside influences, but instead customs and ideas had been spread throughout the world primarily by the movement of and stimulus from outside groups. Petrie's colleague, UCL anthropologist Grafton Elliot Smith, sat at the helm of the staunchest supporters of the idea that any 'cultural similarities obtained among peoples were the result of diffusion' (Kuklick, 1991: 125). Not unlike other Egyptologists, Elliot Smith spent most of his time arguing that it was Egypt's 'unprecedented type of environment', which included harsh desert, a fertile river valley for agriculture, and its central geographic location, that allowed for the development of sciences, religion and civilization (Elliot Smith, 1928: 39). But, contrary to the established chronology of culture, the conclusion Elliot Smith reached was that Egypt was indeed the foundation of culture and thus all knowledge, beliefs and customs disseminated from Egypt to the rest of the world. Elliot Smith and others who argued these tenets are known to historians as hyperdiffusionists.

Hyperdiffusionists argued that it was in 'Egypt's great service to humanity, and of all that followed in its train' that justified a renewed effort to study Egypt and its part 'in moulding the world's civilization' (Elliot Smith, 1911: 7). This perspective differed markedly from the classical view that the primary influence on European culture had come from Greece and Rome; however, Elliot Smith believed that he had hard evidence to refute this claim. He had studied mummification in Cairo and Manchester, and he came away with a thorough comprehension of the processes required (Elliot Smith, 1906; Elliot

Smith and Dawson, 2002). Understanding that mummification was not only an Egyptian practice, but that it was also practiced by other cultures the world over, Elliot Smith 'convinced himself that [the procedures for mummification] were so complex that they could only have been invented once', thus leading him to the conclusion that knowledge and practice of the procedures had spread from Egypt (Champion, 2003: 129). He expanded his theory and in 1911 'he came out firmly in favour of diffusion over evolution and independent parallel development, laying the foundations for the short-lived domination of this theory in British social anthropology' (Champion, 2003: 128).

This first full articulation of diffusion was titled *The Ancient Egyptians and Their Influence upon the Civilization of Europe* (1911). In it, he maintained that 'no single factor has had an influence so great and so far-reaching as the discovery of metals', metal-working and the technology made possible by such tools, and that all of this development took place in Egypt (Elliot Smith, 1911: 2). Using these tools, Elliot Smith argued, Egypt 'raised civilization out of the slough of the Stone Age' (Elliot Smith, 1911: 6). Knowledge of science, such as astronomy, the ability to perform procedures such as mummification, the presence of institutions such as kingship and government and the ability to build megalithic monuments demonstrated the improbability of independent invention within cultures. Elliot Smith gave this reasoning to support his claim: 'No theory of parallel development can be seriously adduced to explain these curious changes' in other civilizations that, although geographically close to Egypt, were culturally dissimilar (Elliot Smith, 1911: 21). It was thus Egypt's superior knowledge combined with 'her peculiar geographical situation', which allowed it to be 'adequately isolated to be free to develop her own civilization without interference from outsiders, yet at the same time so closely in touch with the world at large' to be able to spread cultural influence broadly, even though Egypt was relatively small (Elliot Smith, 1911: 26–7). Elliot Smith's main point in this work was that 'the Egyptians, by the force of their example [and not through military force, such as that used by Rome], were able to lead their European relations out of the wilderness of the Stone Age into the promised land of the higher stage of civilization' (Elliot Smith, 1911: 6).

Critics of Elliot Smith's hypotheses were counted in the highest echelons of universities and anthropology and archaeology departments (Marett, 1927; Dawson, 1938: 54). Petrie also disagreed with him. The two had long been in dispute over the existence of cannibalism in early Egypt: as of 1910, Petrie believed there was evidence for the practice in Naqada, and Elliot Smith argued that there was none (Drower, 1995: 345–6).[1] As a result, Petrie was apparently 'much disgusted' with Elliot Smith's 1915 work, *The Migrations of Early Culture*, and notated his own personal copies of the book with comments such as 'No such thing!' and 'No evidence whatsoever' (Elliot Smith, 1915: 347). Is it possible that Petrie had taken personal offense to Elliot Smith's criticisms five years previous, and was now reacting to them? Yes. Moreover, Petrie's colleague Margaret Alice Murray claimed that Elliot Smith – who was no stranger to collegial feuds throughout his career – was the leader of a 'whispering campaign' in the College against Petrie, and the dispute that had begun in 1910 ended only after Elliot Smith's stroke in 1932 (Murray, 1963: 112, 165). However, Petrie's criticisms were common, and the question of evidence was certainly one that anthropologists and archaeologists had repeatedly asserted. Elliot Smith addressed these problems in his 1928 work, *In the Beginning*, where he presented much more evidence for Egypt being the cradle of civilization. The book is the first in a series entitled 'The Beginning of Things' and Elliot Smith instructed his reader that the series was 'based on the acceptance of the principle of the Diffusion of Culture', the case for which 'will only be fully revealed when the series is complete, by the piling up of evidence drawn from every subject and from every quarter of the globe' (1928: 1). He went into great detail about evidence such as calendars, clocks and writing in this work, arguing that the very act of his writing on 1 January 1928 at noon was only possible through the spread of Egyptian knowledge (1928: 10–16). Such evidence, he stated, would thus demonstrate that Egypt 'was the cradle, not only of agriculture, metallurgy, architecture, ship-building, the kingship and statecraft, but of civilization in its widest sense' (1928: 36). This evidence is, arguably, still being disputed (Crook, 2012).

Petrie did indeed agree with certain tenets of the diffusionist ideas. As late as 1939, he argued in *The Making of Egypt* that cultural changes in ancient Egypt came about because of 'new elements coming in from different directions' (Petrie, 1939: 55). On the other hand, Petrie's work focused on the change of prehistoric Egyptian civilization due to the influx of new peoples and cultures – thus due to the diffusion of cultural traits *into* Egypt from outside influences. He claimed that, in general:

[i]n changes of population there may be a general substitution (as by
Hulagu); or the killing of men and scattering of women (Melos); killing
of men and capturing women (Troy); enslaving men and taking women
(Belgium,[in]1914); victors ruling helots (Sparta); victors ruling over a
stable population (Turks); mixture of diverse peoples (Copts and Arabs);
assimilation of immigrants (England, Flemings and, later, Huguenots); or
there may be merely an adoption of foreign ideas (England, some from
Persia and Japan). (Petrie, 1939: 9)

Anatomical changes, grave goods and variations in carving motifs and
pottery styles marked the coming of new groups of peoples into Egypt. Even
though Petrie did not address changes in civilizations other than Egypt, the
attributes of diffusionism are evident in his claims. These claims were indeed
still prevalent in the late 1960s and early 1970s. The general framework, if not
the specific details, of hyperdiffusion found its way into the work of many
prominent anthropologists and archaeologists, thus assuring a much longer
period of popularity than current scholars would have us believe. Clearly, the
hyperdiffusionists were a significant influence within the human sciences.

Margaret Murray's ideas of cultural change seemed to have established
a middle ground between Elliot Smith's hyperdiffusionism and Petrie's
pseudo-diffusionist ideas. First she did so relationally, by forcing them to shake
hands and reconcile, then she did so in the scholarship (Murray, 1963: 165).
Murray was, in many ways, Petrie's student. Not only was he her first teacher
when she came to UCL in 1894, but she was influenced heavily by many of his
theories and methods in archaeology. She used his eugenic ideas much as he
did within archaeology, that is, to help explain the development of civilization
in Egypt. As Petrie's colleague, Murray believed that archaeology was the study
of the history of humanity, throughout all times and all areas of the earth. It was,
in fact, the diffusionists' attempt to 'provide a seamless narrative of the human
past' within a complex and generally applied framework of change that must
have drawn her to the ideas (Champion, 2003: 134). Murray was not a disciple
of Elliot Smith's as she was Petrie's, but she adopted some diffusionist views,
applying them to her work within Egypt and discussions of Egypt's history.
For the most part, for most Egyptologists, it was the movement of cultures
into Egypt that had caused substantial cultural and technological changes.
Like Petrie, Murray focused her central discussion on the cultural changes

brought about in Egypt's history 'in terms of mass migrations or the arrival of smaller groups who brought about cultural change by mingling culturally and biologically with the existing population' (Trigger, 1989: 154). Going further than this, however, Murray agreed with Elliot Smith and W. J. Perry that it was the spread of cultural traits *out* of Egypt that allowed for its disproportionate influence on the rest of the world (Perry, 1923).

Murray had first scribbled such ideas in her early lecture notes, writing in 1911 – the same year Elliot Smith's *Ancient Egyptians* had been published – that Egypt 'has exercised an influence on the history of the world out of all proportion to its size' (Murray, 1911). This power was not exerted through military means, nor did Egypt's influence begin with its 'rediscovery' by Europeans in the late eighteenth century. Egypt had begun civilizing centuries before the Greeks, and, Murray stated, the 'greatest Greeks acknowledged that they had learnt all from Egypt, that they were children in wisdom compared to the Egyptians' (ibid.). Although she taught these ideas in her classes at UCL for over 30 years, she did not publish them until much later, in *The Splendour that was Egypt*, in 1949. In the introduction to her *magnum opus*, she continued her argument that Egypt's authority was in its position as 'the first beginnings of material culture [. . .] the beginnings of the sciences . . . the beginnings of the imponderables' (Murray, 1949: xvii). The Egyptians were such fundamental forces that, shockingly, 'Egypt was to the Greek the embodiment of all wisdom and knowledge' (ibid.). The Greek culture then took what it learned from Egypt and 'they passed on to later generations that wisdom of the Egyptians which they had learnt orally from the learned men of the Nile Valley' (ibid.). It was in this way that '[i]n every aspect of life Egypt has influenced Europe, and though the centuries may have modified the custom or idea, the origin is clearly visible' (Murray, n.d. a). Like other diffusionists, she attributed Egypt's dominance culturally and scientifically to the unique environment of Egypt. She continued:

> Egypt always held a unique position among the ancient civilizations of the world. Geographically she was in touch with three continents, Europe and Asia were on her threshold, and she herself was situated in Africa. . . . Egypt was the supreme power in the Mediterranean area during the whole of the Bronze Age and a great part of the Iron Age; and as our present culture is directly due to the Mediterranean civilization of the Bronze Age it follows that it has its roots in ancient Egypt. (ibid., xviii)

In her lectures, Murray also told her students that in Egypt's eighteenth dynasty (roughly 1587–1414 BC), Egypt was the 'mistress of [the] known world ... [there have been] 3 great ruling nations, Eg[ypt], Rome, England' (Murray n.d.b, no page). Significantly, she used the very evidence Elliot Smith did – writing, writing utensils, clocks, calendars, astronomy and physics (Murray, 1949: 222–313). Although she did not cite them explicitly, many of Murray's ideas came directly from Elliot Smith, Perry and Petrie.

At the time, most of Murray's teaching agreed with widely accepted Egyptological theories, and in this case her ideas were not as far off-track as originally believed. The proposed hypothesis of cultural development described in the introduction to *Splendour* and many of her course lectures places Murray within range of the hyperdiffusionist school, led ideologically by Elliot Smith and Perry. However, unlike most in the hyperdiffusionist circle, Murray did not go so far as to say that Egypt's influence spread directly across the Pacific, like Elliot Smith and Perry believed, or that Egypt had any *direct* influence on any area outside the Mediterranean and Europe (Elliot Smith, 1928: 52–62). Furthermore, according to Champion, hyperdiffusionism was a 'fully and explicitly formulated expression of a more extreme version of [diffusionist] ideas that were common at the time' (2003: 139). Diffusionists are 'now largely ignored, or at best banished to a marginal place in the histories of archaeology or anthropology. [. . .] They are often regarded as indistinguishable from the lunatic fringe' (Champion, 2003). Thus, because many scholars tend to place this school of thought in the margins of the narrative, Murray's ideas are relegated there as well. For example, while Glyn Daniel accuses Elliot Smith of a 'violent advocacy of an Egyptocentric hyperdiffusion', some 'great' archaeologists, such as Petrie and V. Gordon Childe, are excused from their involvement in this group (Daniel, 1976: 317). Bruce Trigger argues that 'as late as 1940 Childe saw some merit in [Elliot] Smith's and Perry's' hyperdiffusionism, even though 'he rejected their specific historical speculations' (Trigger, 1980: 87–8). Furthermore, Sally Green states plainly that Childe may have been a little crazy when he agreed with Elliot Smith on certain points, but that '[i]n more normal times his sense of reality led him to oppose the excesses of hyper-diffusion' (Green, 1981: 97). To place hyperdiffusionists within the bounds of lunacy was, and still is, the popular position to take. Murray, I believe, never lost her 'sense of reality', as some would argue, when she was teaching her students the contemporaneously accepted model of cultural development for Egypt. Although her ideas were published after the extreme faction of the school allegedly had fallen into obscurity, *Splendour* was an outline of earlier lectures she had given to students and the general public alike, from 1905 to the mid-1940s, when the ideas were quite common (Sheppard, forthcoming).

Conclusions

The particular mingling of Petrie's works in both archaeology and eugenics brings both sciences into interdisciplinary studies. Including this facet of Petrie's life demonstrates that there are holes left in the literature about him; it also begins to shed some light on other aspects of the history of archaeology. More importantly, it reveals that Petrie was able to lend the authority of historical evidence to the eugenic movement. Some historians have characterized Petrie's involvement in the eugenics movement as 'unfortunate' and have claimed that he was 'badly misled' ('William Matthew Flinders Petrie', 2005: xv). I would argue instead that the omission of Petrie from the history and historiography of eugenics is unfortunate, and is perpetuated by those who are misled. In the history of eugenics, it is apparent that there are more than a few authors who believe that they should apologize for their subject's involvement in such a science. These apologies tend to inhibit in-depth work in the history archaeology and of eugenics, as is evidenced in the present study. We should not be afraid that our heroes' reputations will be tainted. Their influence should instead be embraced while respecting the outcomes of which they could not have known or expected.

Many archaeologists who subscribed to eugenicist viewpoints and translated those into theories of cultural development have also been marginalized, the degrees of marginalization depending on their subsequent reputation, of course. This, too, is a drastic misstep in the history of archaeology. Diffusionist ideas, as the ideas that preceded them in eugenics, should be analyzed within their appropriate context and be seen as an important step in the development of theories of historical, social and biological change. It is not a question of why these ideologies have been hidden, until now, but instead it is a question of what historians are doing to rectify the situation. *The Archaeology of Race* is an important step in the right direction – telling the whole story. Further work must be done in museum studies, biography, theoretical analysis, artefact analysis and more so historians can come to a better understanding of these ideas, their development and their impact on the study of human history.

Kathleen L. Sheppard[2]

Notes

1 The published version of this conversation is in *Nature*. See: Elliot Smith (1910) and Petrie (1910a; Elliot Smith, 1910; Petrie, 1910b–c); Petrie, 1910c.
2 I would like to thank Debbie Challis for putting together the exhibition on Petrie and Eugenics at the Petrie Museum of Egyptian Archaeology at UCL. I would also like to thank her for reading a number of drafts of this piece and providing invaluable comments and suggestions; any faults are my own. Thanks are also due to the staff at the PMA for always giving friendly and helpful support of my research in their archives and collections, especially Debbie Challis, Tracy Golding, and Stephen Quirke.

Appendix:
Heads from Memphis and their Racial Types[1]

Publications cited

W. M. Flinders Petrie (1909), *Memphis I*, London: School of Archaeology in Egypt.

W. M. Flinders Petrie (1909), *The Palace of Apries (Memphis II)*, London: School of Archaeology in Egypt.

W. M. Flinders Petrie (1910), *Meydum and Memphis III*, London: School of Archaeology in Egypt.

Drawer labelled 'Racial Types'

Accession number	Racial 'Type' (if given)	Description from the excavation report
UC30203	Greek	Terracotta head of Greek Type – shaven egg-shaped head; prominent eye brows and cheek bones; bulbous nose; wide open mouth; and prominent ears. Of grotesque form.
		Description on Petrie Museum catalogue.
UC48500	Roman/ Western	These heads seem to be more western in type. 47 is like the Roman figures, with the toga worn over the head, as in sacrificing and as the Fratres Arvales.
		Memphis I: 17
UC48501	Kurd	The Kurd (73) has the crossed turban which belongs to the Central Asian and Kurd race, but not to the Semitic peoples. Mr Hogarth informs me that the type of the face agrees to that of the modern Kurds, who were well known to the Greeks as the Karduchi. This is the finest piece of modelling among all the heads; the delicacy with which the features are worked, the detail of the ear being pressed forward by the turban, wrinkling it on the inner side and the spirit of expression put this in the front rank.
		Memphis II: 17
		Ptolemaic Period

---

1 Compiled with Alice Williams.

UC48502		Ptolemaic Period
UC48503		Second Persian Period
UC48504	Scythian	The tall pointed hood, the busy beard and the riding on horseback, all shew that we have the Sacae cavalry of the Persian army.
		Memphis I: 17
		Second Persian Period
UC48505	Scythian	As above.
		Second Persian Period
UC48506		Second Persian Period
UC48507		Second Persian Period
UC48508	Asia Minor	The type of face and tall cap seem to belong to Asia Minor. 113 is a peculiar type with apparently a flat folding cap having a flap or tasel at the side.
		Memphis II: 17
		Second Persian Period
UC48509		Second Persian Period
UC48510	Kurd	Ptolemiaic Period
UC48511	Unknown	The remaining heads cannot at present be identified, owing to the lack of any collection of ancient portraiture. Most of them are so distinctive that their complexion would be easily settled if we had the material for comparison.
		Memphis III: 46
		Late Ptolemaic Period
UC48512	Unknown	See above
		Late Period
UC48513		Ptolemaic Period
UC48514		Ptolemaic Period
UC48515	Hebrew	The Hebrew (72) is named only on the ground of resemblance to a modern Jewish type, coming from Germany.
		Memphis II: 17
		Middle Ptolemaic Period
UC48516	Not known?	*Memphis II*: 17
		Middle Ptolemaic Period

UC48517	Pergamene	Nos 151–2 have the rounded face and heavy jaw of the Pergamenes.
		Memphis III: 46
		Middle Ptolemaic Period
UC48518	Semitic Babylonian	No. 26 is a peculiar type, from the high flat forehead, and the short, prominent, sub-aquiline nose. It may perhaps be compared with the type of Khammurabu (25) which has the same form of forehead and lips, and only a slightly thicker nose. It may be regarded as a Semitic Babylonian, unless some closer resemblance may be found in the Persian empire.
		Memphis I: 16
		Second Persian Period
UC48519		Solid terracotta head with lock of Horus on the right side of the head and wearing a diadem with single rosette. The eyebrows and eyes are modelled; the nose is slightly snub in appearance; and the mouth is small with even lips. The ears are disproportionately large. The entire surface is covered in a white slip. Ptah priest.
		Late Ptolemaic Period
UC48520	Foreigner	Middle Ptolemaic Period
UC48521	Foreign women	Foreign women are very rarely found among these portraits, but the Rhodopes of the foreign colonies were known to Herodotus.
		Memphis II: 17
		Early Ptolemaic Period
UC48522		Early Ptolemaic Period
UC48523	Foreigner?	Late Period
UC48524	Foreigner?	Early Ptolemaic Period
UC48525	Foreigner?	Roman Period
UC48526		Late Period
UC48527		Dynasty 30
UC48528		Dynasty 30
UC48529	Mesopotamian	The head 116–24 are probably all from the Mesopotamian region, though perhaps of different races.
		Memphis II: 17
		Late Ptolemaic Period

UC48530	Unknown?	Late Period
UC48531	Greek	Nos 147–50 are of usual Greek types. *Memphis III*: 46 Late Period
UC48532		Late Period
UC48533	Foreigner?	Late Period
UC48534	Foreign woman (Rhodopes)	Foreign women are very rarely found among these portraits, but the Rhodopes of the foreign colonies were known to Herodotus. *Memphis II*: 17 Dynasty 30
UC48535	Foreigner	Second Persian Period
UC48536		Ptolemaic Period
UC48537		Late Ptolemaic Period
UC48538, UC48546	Unknown	The remaining heads cannot at present be identified, owing to the lack of any collection of ancient portraiture. Most of them are so distinctive that their complexion would be easily settled if we had the material for comparison. *Memphis III*: 46 Second Persian Period
UC48539		Second Persian Period
UC48540		Late Period
UC48541	Persian King as Egyptian ruler?	Head on a vase neck *Memphis II*: 17 Late Period
UC48542		Dynasty 27
UC48543		Ptolemaic Period
UC48544		Ptolemaic Period
UC48545		Ptolemaic Period
UC48547		Early Roman Period
UC48548		Ptolemaic Period

UC48549		Early Roman Period
UC48550		Early Roman Period
UC48551	Karian	The Karian is named on the strength of the description of Herodotus, that the Karians wore helmets with a crest like a cock's comb. *Memphis II*: 17 Early Roman Period
UC48552	Greek	Nos 169–71 are examples of how work decayed later, reducing the hair to a geometrical pattern. *Memphis III*: 46
UC48553		Fragment of terracotta figurine (head only). The figure is depicted with a headdress. Bears some similarity to imperial depictions. Late Roman Period

Other heads described by race cited in the excavation reports on Memphis that are in the collections of the Petrie Museum

Accession number	Racial 'Type' (if given)	Description from the publications/catalogue
UC49896	Egyptian	The large earring of No.1 is certainly Egyptian. *Memphis I*: 16. Pl. XXXV.1 Early Ptolemaic Period
UC33611	Egyptian	No. 2 is like the sturdy well-fed women of Middle Egypt; the swathing up of the hair when at work is seen in the tomb of Khnum-hotep at Beni Hasan. *Memphis I*: 16. Pl. XXXV.2 Ptolemaic Period
UC33609 (3) and UC33610 (4)	Egyptian	Nos 3 and 4 are of the southern type with prognathous face, and close curly hair. *Memphis I*: 16. Pl. XXXV.3 Ptolemaic Period
UC49895	Egyptian	*Memphis I*: 16. Pl. XXXV.5 Late Period

UC30187	Egyptian	Nos 5 to 13 are the regular Egyptian figures of a woman on a couch, sometimes with a child. Such were made as early as the XVIII dynasty, and on to Greek times; and they hardly belong to the general class of these ethnic types. *Memphis I*: 16. Pl. XXXV.6 Late Period
UC30186	Egyptian	As above.
UC33572	Egyptian	As above.
UC33578?/ UC33573?	Egyptian	As above.
UC48148	Egyptian	As above.
UC48149	Egyptian	As above.
UC30188	Egyptian	As above.
UC33612	Egyptian	No. 14 is Egyptian by the hair dressing, and the face is of higher-class type. *Memphis I*: Pl. XXXV.14 Ptolemaic Period
UC47754	Egyptian?	No. 15 would be probably Egyptian by the hair; but the type is not familiar. *Memphis I*: Pl. XXXV.15 Late Period
UC8457	Persian	In 16 we see the Persian Great King, with his bushy hair, close-fitting tiara and disc on the front; each of these distinctions may be seen on figures of Persian kings. The high-bred Aryan type is well shewn in the head. *Memphis I*: 16. Pl. XXXVI.15 Dynasty 27
UC8981	Persian	No. 18 is the cavalry officer, with the face swathed to keep off heat and dust, like the horseman on the Sidon sarcophagus (17). On the head is the lion's scalp, probably a regimental badge. Herodotos mentions of the Persian cavalry 'that on their heads some of them wore brazen and wrought steel ornaments' (vii, 84). The face is delicate, and almost effeminate, in the slight brow and refined eyes. *Memphis I*: Pl. XXXVI.18 Dynasty 27

UC33278	Hebrew/ Semitic Syrian	No. 20 is the most vigorously modelled head of all. It is carefully finished, the detail of the ears being precise. The flesh parts are coloured red, and the hair black. The type is that of the Semite, as shewn in the chief of the Amu at Beni-hasan (19), but sturdier and fatter owing to a settled life. It probably represents the Syrian or Jewish trader. *Memphis I*: Pl. XXXVI.20 Graeco Roman Period?
UC8982	Sumerian	No. 22 is of the old Sumerian or Akkadian type, as shewn by the limestone head from Babylonia (21). *Memphis I*: 16. Pl. XXXVII.22 Ptolemaic Period
UC47900	Foreigner	Nos 27 and 28 seem to be artificially flattened heads. *Memphis I*: 16. Pl. XXXVIII.27 Dynasty 30
UC49911	Foreigner	As above.
UC49897	Foreigner	*Memphis I*: Pl. XXXVIII, 29 Late Period
UC47873	Foreigner	*Memphis I*: Pl. XXXVIII, 30 Ptolemaic Period
UC49904	Foreigner	*Memphis I*: Pl. XXXVIII, 31 Late Period
UC49902	Foreigner	*Memphis I*: Pl. XXXVIII, 33 Late Period
UC49901	Foreigner	*Memphis I*: Pl. XXXVIII, 34 Late Period
UC17811	Tibetan	No. 35 is a Tibetan type, which is also found in Orissa. There is an ape on each side of the head. *Memphis I*: Pl. XXXIX.35
UC33607	Indian	No. 36 is an Aryan Punjabi type; the attitude with the hip raised high on one side, the arms bent and the loose lock of hair, are all Indian; but the band round the breast, the amulet hung round the neck and the artificial navel line, are all strange and lack a comparison. *Memphis I*: 16. Pl. XXXIX. 36 Roman Period

UC8788	Indian	As above. Memphis I: 16 Dynasty 27
UC8923	Indian	Nos 38 and 40 have the knees raised, and a scarf over the left shoulder. These attitudes are familiar in Indian art. *Memphis I*: 16–17. Pl. XXXIX.38 Roman Period
UC8931	Indian	As above.
UC8747	Indian	Nos 37 and 39 are seated cross-legged with drapery round the waist . . . these attitudes are familiar to Indian art. *Memphis I*: 16–17. Pl. XXXIX. 37
UC49906	Scythians	The other extreme of the Persian empire is seen in the figures of Scythians. The tall pointed hood, the bushy beard and the riding on horseback, all shew that we have here the Sacae cavalry of the Persian army. *Memphis I*: 17. Pl. XL.42 Late Period
UC48117	Scythians	As above.
UC48562	Italian and Greek?	*Memphis I*: 17. Pl. XLI.49 Ptolemaic Period
UC47878	Macedonian?	No. 50 should be compared with a glazed head found at Naukratis (*Nauk. Ii, xvii, II*), and the coins of Ptolemaic queens; it is perhaps a Macedonian. *Memphis I*: 17. Pl. XLI.50 Middle Ptolemaic Period
UC58577	Italian and Greek?	*Memphis I*: Pl. XLI.51
UC49900	Italian and Greek?	*Memphis I*: Pl. XLI.52 Late Period
UC47763	Greek?	*Memphis I*: Pl. XLI.53 Ptolemaic Period

UC49912	Italian and Greek?	*Memphis I*: Pl. XLI. 54 Ptolemaic Period
UC49905	Greek	Here are distinctly Greek figures . . . 56 is of the archaic Greek type of face and hair, but not made by a Greek of that age; it is rather the Egyptian version of an early Greek. *Memphis I*: 17. Pl. XLII.56 Ptolemaic Period
UC33411	Greek	The graceful little figure, 57, is of a usual type; the instrument played upon is the Syrian kinyra. *Memphis I*: 17. Pl. XLII.57 Graeco Roman Period
UC48494	Greek	Nos 57 to 60 are all modelled hollow. *Memphis I*: 17. Pl. XLII.58 Early Graeco Roman Period.
UC48444	Greek	As above.
UC48194	Greek	As above.
UC49913	Greek	These are the later Greek works. *Memphis I*: 17. Pl. XLIII.61 Ptolemaic Period
UC49909	Greek	These are the later Greek works, some apparently grotesque, as 64, 66, 67, 69. Such are often found in Ptolemaic sites. *Memphis I*: 17. Pl. XLIII.66 Ptolemaic Period
UC49910	Greek	As above.
UC49899	Greek	*Memphis I*: Pl. XLIII.68 Late Period
UC48575	Greek	These are the later Greek works, some apparently grotesque, as 64, 66, 67, 69. Such are often found in Ptolemaic sites. *Memphis I*: 17. Pl. XLIII.69 Ptolemaic Period

UC48458	Iberian	The Iberian (70) is identified by the resemblance of the profile to the Shardana or Sardinian of the XIX–XX dynasty, in the long low head and the mutton-chop whisker and the general resemblance of the front face to the Spanish matador type at present. There is no other ancient race, so far as I remember, which has shaved in this fashion.
		Memphis II: 17. Pl. XXVIII,70
		Ptolemaic Period
UC48452	Karian	The Karian (71) is named on the strength of the description of Herodotos, that the Karians wore helmets with a crest like a cock's comb. There is no other helmet type which would agree to this, and the Karian as being chief mercenary soldier race of the time, and settled in Egypt, must have been familiar in Memphis.
		Memphis II: 17. Pl. XXVIII,71
		Late Period
UC48154 (74) UC48510 (75) UC47762 (76) UC48155 (77)	Unidentified	The heads 74–7 cannot be identified. *Memphis II*: 17. Pl. XXIX.78
UC48156 (78)	Scythian	In 78 we have probably an eastern Scyth by the Mongolian slope of the eyes.
		Memphis II: 17. Pl. XXIX.78
		Second Persian Period
UC30155 (79)	Scythian	Scythians are again found in the heads 78–81. *Memphis II*: 17. Pl. XXIX.78
UC48045 (80)	Scythian	No. 80 appear to be partly Persian, by the better profile and the clubbing of the hair in a rounded mass.
		Memphis II: 17. Pl. XXIX.80
		Second Persian Period
UC30156 (81)	Scythian	
UC48063 (82)	Scythian	No. 82 shows the jockey attitude of riding, and is probably Scythian, like all the other horsemen.
		Memphis II: 17. Pl. XXIX.82
		Late Period

UC48039 (84)	Scythian	No. 84 is the usual Scythian horseman, with the round shield. *Memphis II*: 17. Pl. XXIX.84 Second Persian Period
UC48157 (85)	Scythian?	Nos 85–7 are not identified. *Memphis II*: 17. Pl. XXIX.85 Ptolemaic Period
UC48574 (87)	Scythian?	As above.
UC48179 (88) UC48564 (89) UC48158 (90) UC48521 (91)	Foreigner	Nos 88–91 are an interesting class, having much expression and character. They seem to be all female heads, and not Egyptian. Foreign women are very rarely found among these portraits, but the Rhodopes of the foreign colonies were known to Herodotos. *Memphis II*: 17. Pl. XXX.88 Ptolemaic Period
UC48159 (92) UC48160 (93) UC48534 (94)	Foreigner	Nos 92–4 are less carefully wrought, but seem to be also women. *Memphis II*: 17. Pl. XXX.92 Late Period
UC48472 (95)	Foreigner	Nos 95–7 are the usual Greek type of Asia Minor. *Memphis II*: 17. Pl. XXX.97 Early Ptolemaic Period
UC48161 (96)	Foreigner	As above.
UC48479 (97)	Foreigner	As above.
UC48162 (98)	Greek: Ionian Type	Nos 98 is a Greek head of the Ionian type, as seen in terracottas from the Smyrna region.
UC48163 (99)	Greek: Mausolus type	*Memphis II*: 17. Pl. XXXI
UC48165 (100)	'Familiar' Greek types	*Memphis II*: 17. Pl. XXXI
UC48248 (102)	Macedonian type	No. 102 with long ringlets shews a mode of hair which is familiar among the Ptolemaic queens, but not elsewhere. As they prided themselves on being Macedonians, this is probably the Macedonian type. *Memphis II*: 17. Pl. XXXI

UC48247 (103)	Macedonian type?	No. 103 appears to have the same profile, but it is a later head, as it is moulded hollow, and modelled solid. *Memphis II*: 17. Pl. XXXI
UC48492 (106) UC48118 (107)	Greek types	Nos 104–7 are also Greek types, which I cannot locate at present.
UC48424 (108)	Foreigner	No. 108 is remarkable for having a royal Egyptian cloth head-dress, and yet being bearded. It is on the neck of a vase, and is painted with purple stripe. Can it possibly be a Persian king in his costume as Egyptian ruler? *Memphis II*: 17. Pl. XXXII.108 Ptolemaic Period
UC48177 (109)	Foreigner	No. 109 bears an extraordinary helmet, which from its shape and folds seems made of leather. Perhaps the slits were attached to a moveable vizor which is here shewn folded back, but which could be drawn down over the face. *Memphis II*: 17. Pl. XXXII.109 Ptolemaic Period
UC48541 (110)	Foreigner	No. 110 is another head on a vase-neck. *Memphis II*: 17. Pl. XXXII Late Period
UC48167 (111)	Assyrian?	No. 111 has a helmet with long cheek pieces. From the heaviness and the straightness of the form it was probably of iron like the Norman pot helmet and this points to the Assyrian side, but the source of the form as yet to be found. *Memphis II*: 17. Pl. XXXII
UC47765 (112)	Asia Minor	No. 112 may probably be represented with a felt cap. The type of face and tall cap seem to belong to Asia Minor. *Memphis II*: 17. Pl. XXXII
UC48508 (113)	Asia Minor	No. 113 is a peculiar type with apparently a flat folding cap having a flap or tasel at the side. *Memphis II*: 17. Pl. XXXII Second Persian Period

UC48176 (114)	Asia Minor	No. 114, though very roughly made, is distinctive in the slope of the head backwards, the hair and short beard, like any other head. *Memphis II*: 17. Pl. XXXII
UC48168 (116) UC48169 (118) UC48169 (120) UC48269 (121) UC48171 (122) UC48176 (123) UC48529 (124)	Mesopotamian	The head 116–24 are probably all from the Mespotamian region, though perhaps of different races. The shaved head does not seem to be found anciently outside of that basin, except in Egypt where such physiognomy is not found. *Memphis II*: 17. Pl. XXXIII
UC48560 (119)	Sumerian	No. 119 is closely like the Sumerian heads of last year, 22, 24. *Memphis II*: 17
UC48172 (125) UC48459 (126) UC48516 (127) UC48173 (128) UC48174 (131) UC48175 (132)	Not known localities.	The various types 125–32 are not yet connected with known localities. No. 128 has closely the Mark Anthony features; he did not get that type from Julia, and if of the Antonia stock it might be sought among the Dorian Herakleidae from whom they claimed descent. The usual type of Herakles is somewhat like this. *Memphis II*: 17. Pl. XXXIV
UC33431	Egyptian	Nos 133–5 (134 is UC33431) are apparently Egyptians; 134 and 135 are of limestone, very few Egyptian heads being found in pottery. Memphis III: 46. Pl. XLII
UC8926 UC8927 UC8933 UC8928 UC8929 UC8930	Sumerian	No. 139 (UC8926) is Sumerian, and probably 141 to 145 also. *Memphis III*: 46. Pl. XLII
UC8932	Indian	No. 140 (UC8932) is an Indian, similar to that found before (36), as seen by the wreath, the position of the arms, the large amulet and the deep umbilical line. Memphis III: 46. Pl. XLII
UC48254	Herakles type	*Memphis III*: 46. Pl. XLIII
UC47779 (147) UC48204 (148)	'Usual Greek types'	*Memphis III*: 46. Pl. XLIII

UC48203 (151) UC48517 (152)	Pergamenes	Nos 151 and 152 have the rounded face and heavy jaw of the Pergamenes. *Memphis III*: 46. Pl. XLIII
UC47866 (153) UC47871 (154)	Mausolus type	*Memphis III*: 46. Pl. XLIII
UC48189 (155) UC48485 (157) UC48190 (158) UC48490 (159) UC48471 (160) UC48474 (161)	Usual Greek type.	*Memphis III*: 46. Pl. XLIV
UC48496 (163)	Usual Greek type	No. 163 gives an indication of the meaning of these figures bearing jars. On the jar, retrograde, is HP above and DI below, probably referring to Hera and Dios (Zeus) and showing that this represents a jar-bearer in a festival of those gods.
UC33430 (164)	Greek?	No. 164 is a limestone head, with a veil like that of Arsinoe Philadelphos. *Memphis III*: 46. Pl. XLIV
UC48146 (167)	Arsinoe Philadelphos	Nos 166–7 are of the same type, not identified elsewhere. *Memphis III*: 46. Pl. XLIV
UC48151 (169) UC48552 (170) UC48150 (171)	?	Nos 169–71 are examples of how work delayed later, reducing the hair to a geometrical pattern. *Memphis III*: 46. Pl. XLIV
UC48583 (172) UC48511 (173) UC48143 (174) UC48512 (175) UC48145 (176) UC48530 (177) UC48147 (178) UC48531 (179) UC48142 (180) UC47897 (182) UC48144 (184) UC48452 (185) UC48546 (187)	Not identified	The remaining heads, 172–88, cannot at present be identified, owing to the lack of any collection of ancient portraiture. Most of them are so distinctive that their connexion would be easily settled if we had the material for comparison. *Memphis III*: 46. Pl. XLV

Bibliography

Archives

Galton Archive, UCL Special Collections

Mylne to Galton: Margaret Mylne to Francis Galton 29 March 1869, Galton Archive, 120/3.

Petrie to Galton: Letter from Finders Petrie to Francis Galton, 12 February 1885, Galton Archive, Galton 297.

Petrie to Galton: Letter from Flinders Petrie to Francis Galton, 29 October 1886, Galton Archive, Galton 297.

Petrie to Galton: Letter from Flinders Petrie to Francis Galton, 1 November 1886, Galton Archive, Galton 297.

Petrie to Galton: Letter from Flinders Petrie to Francis Galton, 11 November 1886, Galton Archive, Galton 297.

Petrie to Galton: Letter from Flinders Petrie to Francis Galton, 2 April 1887, Galton Archive, UCL, Galton 297.

Petrie to Galton: Letter from Flinders Petrie to Francis Galton, 14 September 1887, Galton Archive, Galton 297.

Petrie to Galton: Letter from Flinders Petrie to Francis Galton, 15 October 1887, Galton Archive, Galton 297.

Petrie to Galton: Letter from Flinders Petrie to Francis Galton, 25 April 1888, Galton Archive, Galton 297.

Poole to Galton: Letter from Reginald Stuart Poole to Francis Galton, 26 October 1886, Galton 299/1.

Press Cuttings and Reviews of *Hereditary Genius,* Galton Archive, 120.

Griffith Institute, University of Oxford

Petrie, W. M. Flinders (1887), Notebook 16/1/2: The Nile / Dahshur Journals 1886–7.

Petrie, W. M. Flinders (1887), 'Inscriptions copied from Theban temples – Luxor, Medinet Habu, Ramesseum and Royal Tombs – Seti II'. Notebook 123.

National Gallery Archive (NGA)

Petrie to Burton: Letter W. M. Flinders Petrie to Sir Frederick Burton, 4 August 1888, National Gallery Archives, NG7/105/5.

Petrie to Burton: Letter W. M. Flinders Petrie to Sir Frederick Burton, 20 July 1888, National Gallery Archives, NG7/105/3.

Mond: Copy of Dr Ludwig Mond's Will with list of pictures, National Gallery Archives, NG7/380/6.

Mackay to Holroyd: Postcard from Ernest Mackay to Sir Charles Holroyd, 2 September 1912, National Gallery Archives, NG7/411/16.

Palestine Exploration Fund (PEF) Archive

Palestine Excavation Fund Minute Book, 4 October 1887, Palestine Excavation Fund Archive.

Palestine Excavation Fund General Committee Meeting, 3 July 1888, Palestine Excavation Fund Archive.

Petrie Museum Archive (PMA)

Flower to Petrie: Letter from W. M. Flower to Flinders Petrie, 12 October 1889, PMA 16/5/1 (1–3).

Godfrey to Petrie: Letter from Thomas Godfrey to Flinders Petrie, 31 July 1907, PMA 16/6/1(3a).

Galton to Petrie: Letter from Francis Galton to Flinders Petrie, 17 December 1899, PMA 18/8/1(13).

Hubbard to Petrie: Letter from Arthur John Hubbard to Flinders Petrie, 14 August 1907, PMA 16/6/1(3a).

Pearson to Petrie: Letter from Karl Pearson to Flinders Petrie, 13 March 1907, PMA 16/6/1(1).

Pearson to Petrie: Letter from Karl Pearson to Flinders Petrie, [Undated – 1895?], PMA 115/5/2.

Pearson to Petrie: Letter from Karl Pearson to Flinders Petrie, 17 June 1895, PMA 115/5/2.

Pearson to Petrie: Letter from Karl Pearson to Flinders Petrie, 11 August 1895, PMA 115/5/2.

Pearson to Petrie: Letter from Karl Pearson to Flinders Petrie, 12 August 1895, PMA 115/5/2.

Petrie to Edwards: Letter from Flinders Petrie to Amelia Edwards, 2 July 1888, PMA 16/3/1.

Petrie to Edwards: Flinders Petrie to Amelia Edwards, 12 July 1888, PMA 16/3/1.

Petrie to Edwards: Flinders Petrie to Amelia Edwards, 10 July 1888, PMA 16/3/1.

Virchow to Petrie: Letter from Rudolf Virchow to Flinders Petrie, 14 April 1888, PMA 16/3/1.

? to Petrie: Letter from Name [Undecipherable] to Flinders Petrie, 14 July 1907, PMA 16/6/1 (3a).

Bibliography

Adburgham, A. (1975), *Liberty's: A Biography of a Shop,* London: George Allen & Unwin Ltd.

Alberti, S. J. M. M. (2011), *Morbid Curiosities: Medical Museums in Nineteenth-Century Britain.* Oxford: Oxford University Press.

Alberti, S. J. M. M., Bienkowski, Pietr and Chapman, Malcolm J., (2009), 'Should We Display the Dead?', *Museum and Society,* 7/3: 133–49.

Ambridge, L. J. (2012), 'Imperialism and Racial Geography in James Henry Breasted's *Ancient Times, a History of the Early World', Journal of Egyptian History,* 5: 12–33.

Appenzeller, O. (2002), 'An Ancient Eye', *Archives of Neurology,* 59/3: 480–1.

Appenzeller, O., Amm, M. and Jones, H. (2004), 'A Brief Exploration of Neurological Art History', *Journal of the History of the Neurosciences,* 13/4: 345–50.

Appenzeller, O., Stevens, J. M., Kruszynski, R. and Walker, S. (2001), 'Neurology in Ancient Faces', *Journal of Neurology, Neurosurgery, and Psychiatry,* 70: 524–9.

Arendt, H. (1944), 'Race-Thinking before Racism', *The Review of Politics* 6/1: 36–73.

Arnold, B. (1990), 'The Past as Propaganda: Totalitarian Archaeology in Nazi Germany', *Antiquity,* 64/244: 464–78.

Ashrafian, H. (2005), 'William Penny Brookes (1809–1895): Forgotten Olympic Lord of the Rings', *British Journal of Sports Medicine,* 39: 969.

Ashton, S. (2003a), *Petrie's Ptolemaic and Roman Memphis,* London: Institute of Archaeology, UCL.

— (2003b), 'Foreigners at Memphis? Petrie's Racial Types', in John Tait (ed.), *'Never Had the Like Occurred': Egypt's View of its Past,* London: UCL Press, 187–96.

Asleson, R. (2000), *Albert Moore,* London: Phaidon Press Ltd.

Bagh, T. (2011), *Finds from W. M. F. Petrie's Excavations in Egypt in the Ny Carksberg Glyptotek,* Copenhagen: Ny Carlsberg Glyptotek.

Baigent, E. (2004), 'Bent, (James) Theodore (1852–97)' in Matthew, H. C. G and
   Harrison, B. (eds.), *Oxford Dictionary of National Biography*, Oxford: Oxford
   University Press.
Bailey, D. M. (2008), *Catalogue of Terracottas in the British Museum. Volume IV:
   Ptolemaic and Roman Terracottas from Egypt*, London: The British Museum Press.
Barclay Smith, E. (October 1919), 'Professor Alexander Macalister M.D., F.R.S.,
   1844–1919', *Journal of Anatomy*, 54/1: 96–9.
Bard, K. A. (1996), 'Ancient Egyptians and the Issue of Race' in Mary Leftkowitz and
   Gary Maclean-Rogers (eds), *Black Athena Revisited*, Chapel Hill: University of
   North Carolina, pp. 103–11.
Bates, A. W. (2008), '"Indecent and Demoralising Representations": Public Anatomy
   Museums in Mid-Victorian England', *Medical History*, 1: 52/1: 1–22.
— (2010), *The Anatomy of Robert Knox. Murder, Mad Science and Medical Regulation
   in Nineteenth Century Edinburgh*, Eastbourne: Sussex Academic Press.
— (2011), 'The Anatomy of Beauty in Nineteenth-Century England', *Hektoen
   International: A Journal of Medical Humanities*, 3/1:www.hektoeninternational.
   org/Anatomy_of_beauty.html [accessed 30 June 2102].
Bent, T. J. (1892), 'The Ruins of Mashonaland and Explorations in the Country',
   Proceedings of the Royal Geographical Society and Monthly Record of Geography,
   14/5: 273–98.
— (1893), 'On the Finds at the Great Zimbabwe Ruins (With a View to Elucidating
   the Origin of the Race that Built Them)', *The Journal of the Anthropological
   Institute of Great Britain and Ireland*, 22: 123–36.
Beresford, J. (2011), 'Eugenics in Egyptology', *Minerva*, September/October: 46–8.
Bernal, M. (1987), *Black Athena: The Afro-Asiatic Roots of Classical Civilization*,
   London: Free Association Books.
Biddiss, M. D. (April 1976), 'The Politics of Anatomy: Dr Robert Knox and Victorian
   Racism', *Proceedings of the Royal Society of Medicine*, 69: 245–50.
Bierbrier, M. (1997), 'The Discovery of the Mummy Portraits', in Walker and Bierbrier
   (eds), *Ancient Faces*, pp. 23–4.
Bindman, D. (2002), *Ape to Apollo: Aesthetics and the Idea of Race in the Eighteenth
   Century*, London: Reaktion Books.
Blackman, A. M. (1917), 'The Nugent and Haggard Collections of Egyptian
   Antiquities', *The Journal of Egyptian Archaeology*, 4/1: 39–46.
Blake, C. C. (1871), 'The Life of Dr. Knox: Review', *Journal of Anthropology*, 1/3: 332–8.
Blanchard, P., Boëtsch, G. and Snoep, N. J. (2011), *L'invention du Savage. Exhibitions*,
   Paris: Musée du quai Branly.
Boime, A. (2002), 'William Holman Hunt's *The Scapegoat*: Rite of Forgiveness/
   Transference of Blame', *The Art Bulletin*, 81/1: 94–114.

Bolt, C. (1971), *Victorian Attitudes to Race*. London: Routledge and Kegan Paul.

Bonnett, A. (2008), 'Whiteness and the West', in Claire Dwyer and Caroline Bressey (eds), *New Geographies of Race and Racism*, Aldershot: Ashgate, pp. 17–28.

Bradley, M. (2010), 'Approaches to Classics and Imperialism', in Mark Bradley (ed.), *Classics and Imperialism in the British Empire*, Oxford: Oxford University Press, pp. 94–120.

Brand, P. (2011), *The Theban Mapping Project* website: www.thebanmappingproject.com/sites/browse_tomb_831.html [accessed 17 May 2011].

Brauer, F. (2008), 'Introduction: making eugenic bodies delectable', in Brauer, F. and Callen, A., *Art, Sex and Eugenics. Corpus Delecti*, Hampshire: Ashgate publishing, pp. 1–34.

Brave, R. and Sylva, K. (2007), 'Exhibiting Eugenics: Response and Resistance to a Hidden History', *The Public Historian*, 29/3: 35–51.

Brooks, M. M. and Rumsey, C. (2007), '"Who knows the fate of his bones?" Rethinking the body on display: object, art or human remains?' in Simon Knell, Suzanne Macleod and Sheila Watson (eds), *Museum Revolutions: How Museums Change and Are Changed*, London: Routledge, pp. 343–54.

Brook, W. H. (1981), 'Advancing Science: The British Association and the Professional Practice of Science' in Roy Macleod and Peter Collins (eds), *The Parliament of Science: The British Association for the Advancement of Science*. Northwood, Middx: Science Reviews Ltd, pp. 89–117.

Brown, K. D. (1976), 'The Anti-Socialist Union, 1908 –49', in Kenneth D. Brown (ed.), *Essays in Anti-Labour History: Responses to the Rise of Labour in Britain*, London: The Macmillan Press.: pp. 234–61

Brück, H. A. and Brück, M. T. (1988), *The Peripatetic Astronomer: The Life of Charles Piazzi Smyth*, Bristol: Adam Hilger.

Burbridge, D. (1994), 'Galton's 100: An Exploration of Francis Galton's Imagery Studies', *The British Journal for the History of Science*, 27/4: 443–63.

Campbell, G. (1886a), 'Presidential Address' to Section H: Anthropology, *Report of the British Association for the Advancement of Science: Birmingham 1886*, London: John Murray, 826–32.

— (1886b), 'What is an Aryan?', *Report of the British Association for the Advancement of Science: Birmingham 1886*, London: John Murray, 842.

Carcos, A. F. (2005), *The Myth of the Jewish Race: A Biologist's Point of View*, Cranburg: Associated University Presses.

Carey, N. (2011), *The Epigenetics Revolution. How Modern Biology is Rewriting Our Understanding of Genetics, Disease and Inheritance*, London: Icon Books Ltd.

Caton-Thompson, G. (1929), 'Zimbabwe', *Antiquity*, 3: 424–33.

Challis, D. (2008), *From the Harpy Tomb to the Wonders of Ephesus: British Archaeologists in the Ottoman Empire 1840–1880*, London: Duckworth.

— (2010), '"The Ablest Race": Ancient Greek Art and Victorian Racial Theory', in Mark Bradley (ed.), *Classics and Imperialism in the British Empire*, Oxford: Oxford University Press, pp. 94–120.

— (2011), 'The Race for a Healthy Body: The Ancient Greek Physical Ideal in Victorian London', in Barbara Goff and Michael Simpson (eds), *Thinking the Olympics: The Classical Tradition and the Modern Games*, London: Bloomsbury Academic: pp. 141–55.

Champion, T. (2003), 'Egypt and the Diffusion of Culture' in D. Jeffreys (ed.), *Views of Ancient Egypt since Napoleon Bonaparte: Imperialism, Colonialism and Modern Appropriations*, London: University College London Press, pp. 127–45.

Chaplin, S. (1998), 'Appendix A: Donation of Remains of Sir William Matthew Flinders Petrie', Peter J. Ucko 'The Biography of a Collection: The Sir Flinders Petrie Palestinian Collection and the Role of University Museums', *Museum Management and Curatorship*, 17/4: 351–99.

Christensen, L. K., Grinder-Hansen, Paul, Kjeldback, Eshen and Rasmusen, Bodil Bundgaard (2012), *Europe Meets the World*, Copenhagen: National Museet.

Cohen, D. (October 2002), 'Who was Who? Race and Jews in Turn of the Century Britain', *The Journal of British Studies*, 41/4: 460–83.

Conlin, J. (2006), *A History of the National Gallery*, London: Pallas Athene.

Coombes, A. (2004), 'Museums and Formation of National and Cultural Identities' in Donald Preziosi and Claire Fargo (eds), *Grasping the World: The Idea of the Museum*, Aldershot: Ashgate, 278–97.

Coombe, A. E. (1994), *Reinventing Africa: Museums, Material Culture and Popular Imagination in Late Victorian and Edwardian England*, London: Yale University Press.

Cowan, R. S. (1972), 'Francis Galton's Statistical Ideas: The Influence of Eugenics', *Isis*, 63/4: 509–28.

Cowling, M. (1989), *The Artist as Anthropologist: The Representation of Type and Character in Victorian Art*, Cambridge: Cambridge University Press.

Crook, P. (2012), *Grafton Elliot Smith, Egyptology, and the Diffusion of Culture: A Biographical Perspective*, Eastbourne, UK: Sussex Academic Press.

Cunningham, P. (2002), *Reforming Women's Fashion, 1850–1920. Politics, Health and Art*, Ohio: Kent State University Press.

Currie, A. S. (1932), 'Robert Knox, Anatomist, Scientist and Martyr', *Section of the History of Medicine*, 26(1): 39–46

Daniel, G. (1976), *A Hundred and Fifty Years of Archaeology*, Cambridge, MA: Harvard University Press.

Darwin, C. (1871), *The Descent of Man and Selection in Relation to Sex. Volume Two.* London: John Murray.

Dawson, J. W. (1886), 'Note on Photographs of Mummies of Ancient Egyptian Kings, Recently Unrolled at Boulak', *Report of the British Association for the Advancement of Science: Birmingham*, London: John Murray, 845.

Dawson, W. R. (1938), 'A General Biography', in W. R. Dawson(ed), *Sir Grafton Elliot Smith: A Biographical Record by His Colleagues*, London: Jonathan Cape, pp. 17–110.

de Waal, E. (2010), *The Hare with Amber Eyes. A Hidden Inheritance,* London: Chatto & Windus.

Deadly Medicine. Creating the Master Race (2004), United States Holocaust Memorial Museum website:www.ushmm.org/museum/exhibit/online/deadlymedicine/ [accessed 5 July 2012].

Desmond, A. and Moore, J. (2009), *Darwin's Sacred Cause: Race, Slavery and the Quest for Human Origins.* London: Allen Lane.

Disraeli, B. (1881), *Lothair,* London: Longmans Green & Co.

Donohue, A. A. (2005), *Greek Sculpture and the Problem of Description*, Cambridge: Cambridge University Press.

Doyal, L. and Muinzer, T. (2011), 'Should the Skeleton of the "Irish Giant" be Buried at Sea?', *British Medical Journal*, 343d: 7597.

'Dr Knox on the Races of Men', *The Manchester Times and Gazette*, 28 September 1847.

'Dr Knox Responds to Criticism from T. T', *Manchester Times and Gazette*, 26 June 1847.

'Dr Knox's Lectus', *The Manchester Times and Gazette* (issue 87), 27 June 1848.

Drower, M. S. (1995), *Flinders Petrie: A Life in Archaeology.* Madiscon: University of Wisconsin Press.

Du Maurier, G. (1994), *Trilby*, Middlesex: Penguin Books

Dubow, S. (1995), *Scientific Racism in Modern South Africa.* Cambridge: Cambridge University Press.

Ebers, G. (1893), *The Hellenic Portraits of the Fayum at Present in the Collection of Herr Graf,* New York: Appleton and Company.

Edwards, A. B. (1891), *Pharaohs, Fellahs and Explorers*, London: James R. Osgood, McIlvaine & Co.

Edwards, E. (2001), *Raw Histories: Photographs, Anthropology and Museums.* Oxford: Berg.

— (2009), 'Evolving Images: Photography, Race and Popular Darwinism', in Diana Donald and Jane Munro (eds), *Endless Forms: Charles Darwin, Natural Science and the Visual Arts.* London: Yale University Press, pp.167–93.

'Egyptian Portraiture of the Roman Period', *Academy*, 7 July 1888, 34/884: 15.

Ehrman, E. (2011), 'Women's Dress', in Stephen Calloway and Lynn Federle Orr (eds), *The Cult of Beauty: The Aesthetic Movement 1860-1900,* London: V&A Publishing, 2011, pp. 206-7.

Elliot Smith, G. (1906), *A Contribution to the Study of Mummification in Egypt*,
    L'Institut Egyptien, Cairo.
— (1910), 'Early Burial Customs in Egypt', *Nature*, 84/2137: 461–2.
— (1911), *The Ancient Egyptians and Their Influence upon the Civilization of Europe*,
    New York: Harper Brothers.
— (1915), *The Migrations of Early Culture: A Study of the Significance of the
    Geographical Distribution of the Practice of Mummification as Evidence of the
    Migrations of Peoples and the Spread of Certain Customs and Beliefs*, Manchester,
    UK: Manchester University Press.
— (1928), *In the Beginning: The Origin of Civilization*, Gerald Howe Ltd., London.
Elliot Smith, G. and Dawson, W. R. (2002 [1924]), *Egyptian Mummies*, New York:
    Kegan Paul.
Elsner, J. (July 1997), 'Ancient Faces at the British Museum', *Apollo*, LXLVI/25: 48–9.
— (2007), *Roman Eyes. Visuality and Subjectivity in Art and Text,* Princeton:
    Princeton University Press.
Erskine, A. (1993), 'Culture and Power in Ptolemaic Egypt: The Museum and Library
    of Alexandria', *Greece & Rome*, 42/1: 38–48.
'Eugenics and the Jew: Interview for the *Jewish Chronicle* with Sir Francis Galton', *The
    Jewish Chronicle*, 20 July 1910: 16.
Fabian, A. (2010), *The Skull Collectors: Race, Science and America's Unburied Dead*.
    Chicago: University of Chicago Press.
Falconer, J. and Hide, L. (2009), *Points of View: Capturing the 19th Century in
    Photographs*, London: The British Library.
Fasick, Laura, (1994), 'Charles Kingsley's Scientific Treatment of Gender', in Donald
    E. Hall (ed.), *Muscular Christianity: Embodying the Victorian Age,* Cambridge:
    Cambridge University Press, pp. 91–113.
Feldman, David (1994), *Englishmen and Jews: Social Relations and Political Culture
    1840–1914*. London: Yale University Press.
— (November 2010), 'Equality, Race and the Jewish Problem', *Inaugural Lecture: Pears'
    Institute of Anti-Semitism,* Senate House, University of London.
Fenton, J. (July 1997), 'The Mummy's Secret', *The New York Review of Books*.
Field, J. A. (1911), 'The Progress of Eugenics', *The Quarterly Journal of Economics*, 26/1:
    1–67.
Fluehr-Lobban, C. and Rhodes, Tharyssa (eds) (2004), *Race and Identity in the Nile
    Valley: Ancient and Modern,* Eritea: The Dead Sea Press.
Forbes-Robertson, J. (1889), 'Graeco-Roman Portraiture in Egypt. A Recovered Page
    in the History of Painting', *Magazine of Art*, 12: 177–80.
Galanakis, Y. and Nowak-Kemp, M. (2011), 'Ancient Greek Skulls in the Oxford
    University Museum, Part II: The Rhousopoulos-Rolleston Correspondence',

Journal of the History of Collections, first published online January 10, 2011. doi:10.1093/jhc/fhq040 [accessed 26 June 2012].

Galton, David J. (1998), 'Greek Theories on Eugenics', *Journal of Medical Ethics*, 24: 263–7.

Galton, D.J. and Galton, C. J. (1998), 'Francis Galton and Genetics Today', *Journal of Medical Ethics*, 24/2: 99–105.

Galton, F. (1869), *Hereditary Genius: An Inquiry into Its Laws and Consequences*. London: Macmillan & Co.

— (1872; 5th edn), *The Art of Travel or Shifts and Contrivances in Wild Countries*. London: John Murray.

— (April 1885a), 'Photographic Composites', *The Photographic News,* 243–5.

— (1885b), 'Presidential Address' to Section H: Anthropology, *Report of the British Association for the Advancement of Science: Aberdeen 1885*, London: John Murray, 1206–15.

— (1907), *Inquiries into Human Faculty and Its Development* (2nd edn), London: J. M. Dent & Co.

— (1908), *Memories of My Life*, London: Methuen.

— (1909), *Essays in Eugenics*, London: The Eugenics Education Society.

Gere, C. (2007), *The Tomb of Agamemnon*, London: The Profile Press.

Gilbert, P. K. (2007), *The Citizen's Body: Desire, Health and the Social in Victorian England,* Columbus: The Ohio State University Press.

Gilham, N. W. (2001), *A Life of Sir Francis Galton: From African Exploration to the Birth of Eugenics*, Oxford: Oxford University Press.

Gilman, S. (1992), *The Jew's Body*, London: Routledge.

Goff, B. (ed.) (2005), *Classics and Colonialism*, London: Duckworth.

Gosden, C., Larson, F. with Petch, A. (2007), *Knowing Things: Exploring the Collections of the Pitt Rivers Museum 1884–1945,* Oxford: Oxford University Press.

Gould, S. J. (1996), *The Mismeasure of Man,* New York: W. W. Norton & Co.

Graham-Dixon, A. (May 1997), 'Immortal longings', *The Independent*, Visual Arts, 4.

Green, D. (1984), 'Veins of Resemblance: Photography and Eugenics', *Oxford Art Journal,* 7/2: 3–16.

Green, S. (1981), *Prehistorian: A Biography of V. Gordon Childe*, Bradford-on-Avon, UK: Moonraker Press.

Greenaway, F. (2008), 'Mond Family (per. 1867–1973)', *Oxford Dictionary of National Biography,* Oxford: Oxford University Press, 2004: www.oxforddnb.com/view/article/51124 [accessed 24 February 2010].

Gunn, B. and rev. Gurney O. R. (2004), 'Sayce, Archibald Henry (1845–1933)', *Oxford Dictionary of National Biography*, Oxford: Oxford University Press:www.oxforddnb.com/view/article/35965 [accessed 9 May 2011].

Haggard, H. R. (2001), *She*, London: Penguin Books Ltd.

Hamilton, R. and Hargreaves R. (2001), *The Beautiful and the Damned. The Creation of Identity in Nineteenth-Century Photography*, London: Lund Humphries / National Portrait Gallery.

Harlan, D. (2011), 'The Cult of the Dead, Fetishism and the Genesis of an Idea: Megalithic Monuments and the Tree and Pillar Cult of Arthur J. Evans', *European Journal of Archaeology*, 14/1: 213–33.

Harris, J. (2004), 'Spencer, Herbert (1820–1903)', *Oxford Dictionary of National Biography*, Oxford: Oxford University Press: www.oxforddnb.com/view/article/36208 [accessed 17 March 2012].

Harrison, Simon J. (2008), 'Skulls and Scientific Collecting in the Victorian Military: Keeping the Enemy Head in British Frontier War', *Comparative Studies in Society and History*, 50/1: 285–303.

Hatt, Michael (2001), 'Thoughts and Things: Sculpture and the Victorian Nude', in Alison Smith (ed.), *Exposed: The Victorian Nude*, London: Tate Publishing, pp. 36–49.

Haweis, Eliza (1878), *The Art of Beauty*, New York: Harper & Brothers.

Heuman, Gad (2004), 'Eyre, Edward John (1815–1901)', *Oxford Dictionary of National Biography*. Oxford: Oxford University Press; online edn, January 2008: www.oxforddnb.com/view/article/33060 [accessed 17 March 2012].

Hewitt, Martin (1996), *The Emergence of Stability in the Industrial City: Manchester 1832–67*, HANTS: Scolar Press.

Higgins, Reynold (1990), *Tanagra and the Figurines*, London: Trefoil Books Ltd.

Hoffman, Michael A. (1980), *Egypt Before the Pharaohs: The Prehistoric Foundations of Egyptian Civilization*, London: Routledge & Kegan Paul.

'Human Remains Workshop: How Do We Display Human Remains with Respect?', Unpublished proceedings, Petrie Museum of Egyptian Archaeology, 29 September 2011.

Huxley, Thomas (1870), 'On the Geographical Distribution of the Chief Modifications of Mankind', *The Journal of the Ethnological Society of London*, 2/4: 404–12.

International Health Exhibition: Official Guide (1884), London: William Clowes and Sons Ltd.

Isaac, Benjamin (2004), *The Invention of Racism in Classical Antiquity*, Princeton: Princeton University Press.

Jacobs, Joseph (1885), 'A Comparative Estimate of Jewish Ability', *Report of the British Association for the Advancement of Science: Aberdeen*, London: John Murray, 1220.

— (1886), 'On the Racial Characteristics of Modern Jews', *The Journal of the Anthropological Institute of Great Britain and Ireland*, 15: 23–62.

Jenkins, Tiffany (2011), *Contesting Human Remains in Museum Collections: The Crisis of Cultural Authority*, London: Routledge.

Jones, Owen (2012), *Chavs: The Demonisation of the Working Class*, London: Verso.

Jones, Steve (1994), *The Language of the Genes: Biology, History and the Evolutionary Future*. London: Flamingo.

Keita, S. O. Y. (1992), 'Crania', *American Journal of Physical Anthropology*, 87: 245–54.

Kemp, Martin and Wallace, Marina (eds) (2000), *Spectacular Bodies: The Art and Science of the Human Body from Leonardo to Now*, Berkeley: University of California Press.

Kenna, J. C. (1964), 'Sir Francis Galton's Contribution to Anthropology', *The Journal of the Royal Anthropological Institute of Great Britain and Ireland*, 94/2: 80–93.

Kennedy, Maev (June 1997), 'She Died 2,000 Years Ago But Fatima Has a Smart New Face', *The Guardian*, 9.

Kershen, Anne J. (2004), 'Jacobs, Joseph (1854–1916)', *Oxford Dictionary of National Biography*, Oxford: Oxford University Press:www.oxforddnb.com/view/article/51106 [accessed 15 December 2010].

Kevles, Daniel J. (1995), *In the Name of Eugenics: Genetics and the Uses of Human Heredity*, London: Harvard University Press.

Kidd, Jenny (2011), 'Challenging History: Reviewing Debate within the Heritage Sector on the "Challenge of History"', *Museum and Society*, 9/3: 244–8.

King, E. (1883), *Exhibition of Rational Dress*, London.

Kingsley, Charles (1874), *Health and Education*, New York: D. Appleton and Company.

— (1880), *Sanitary and Social Lectures and Essays*, London: Macmillan and Co.

— (1894), *Hypatia*, New York: J.F. Taylor & Company.

— (1901), *Two Years Ago. Vol. 1*, London.

Kingsley, F. E. (1877), *Charles Kingsley: His Letters and Memories of His Life Vol. II*, London: Henry S. King and Co.

Knox, Robert (1852), *A Manual of Artistic Anatomy for the Use of Sculptors, Painters and Amateurs*, London: Henry Renshaw.

— (1862), *The Races of Men: A Philosophical Enquiry into the Influence of Race over the Destinies of Nations*, London: Henry Reshaw.

Kostal, R. W. (2004–12), 'Jamaica Committee (act. 1865–1869)', *Oxford Dictionary of National Biography*, Oxford: Oxford University Press.

Kuklick, Henrika (1991a), *The Savage within: The Social History of British Anthropology, 1885–1945*, Cambridge, UK: Cambridge University Press.

— (1991b), 'Contested Monuments: The Politics of Archaeology in Southern Africa', in George Stocking Jr. (ed.), *Colonial Situations: Essays on the Contextualisation of Ethnographic Knowledge. History of Anthropology. Vol. 7*, Wisconsin: University of Wisconsin Press, pp. 135–69.

Kwint, Marius and Wingate, Richard (2012), *Brains: The Mind as Matter*, London: Wellcome Collection.

Lape, Susan (2010), *Race and Citizen Identity in the Classical Athenian Democracy*, Cambridge: Cambridge University Press.

Lawrence, Christophe (1988), 'Alexander Monro "Primus" and the Edinburgh Manner of Anatomy', *Bulletin of the History of Medicine*, 66/2: 193–214.

Legassick, Martin (2006), 'From Prisoners to Exhibits: Representations of Bushmen of the Northern Cape, 1880–1900', in Annie E. Coombes (ed.), *Rethinking Settler Colonialism History and Memory in Australia, Canada, Aotearoa New Zealand and South Africa*. Manchester: Manchester University Press, pp. 63–84.

Legge, F. (1919), 'The Society of Biblical Archaeology', *Journal of the Royal Asiatic Society of Great Britain and Ireland*, January: 25–36.

Leighton, Frederic (1896), *Addresses Delivered to Students of the Royal Academy*, London: Kegan Paul, Trench, Trubner & Co.

Lenman, Bruce P. (2009), *Enlightenment and Change: Scotland 1746–1832*, Edinburgh: Edinburgh University Press.

Leoussi, A. S. (1999), 'Nationalism and the Antique in Nineteenth-Century English and French Art', in Michael Biddiss and Maria Wyke (eds), *The Uses and Abuses of Antiquity*, Bern: Peter Lang, 79–106.

Lewis, Naphtali (2001), *Greeks in Ptolemaic Egypt: Case Studies in the Social History of the Hellenic World*, Oakville: American Society of Papyrologists.

Lilian Thuram Foundation Website, www.thuram.org [accessed 20 June 2012].

Lodge, David (2012), *A Man of Parts: A Novel*, London: Vintage Books.

Lonsdale, Henry (1870), *A Sketch of the Life and Writings of Robert Knox: The Anatomist*, London: Macmillan and Co.

Lorimer, Douglas A. (1978), *Colour, Class and the Victorians: English Attitudes to the Negro in the Mid-Nineteenth Century*, Leicester: Leicester University Press.

— (1997), 'Science and the Secularization of Victorian Images of Race', in Bernard Lightman (ed.), *Victorian Science in Context*. Chicago: University of Chicago Press, pp. 212–33.

Lynch, Bernadette and Alberti, Samuel J. M. M. (2010), 'Legacies of Prejudice: Racism, Co-Production and Radical Trust in the Museum', *Museum Management and Curatorship*, 25/1: 13–35.

MacKenzie, Donald (1976), 'Eugenics in Britain', *Social Studies of Science*, 6/3: 499–532.

Maclaren, I. (2000), 'Robert Knox MD, FRCSEd, FRSEd 1791–1862: The First Conservator of the College Museum', *The Royal College of Surgeons of Edinburgh, Journal of the Royal. College of Surgeons of Edinburgh*, 45/6: 392–7.

Macleod, Roy (1981), 'Introduction: On the Advancement of Science', in Roy Macleod and Peter Collins (eds), *The Parliament of Science. The British Association for the Advancement of Science*. Northwood, Middx: Science Reviews Ltd., pp. 17–42.

Malamud, Margaret (2009), *Ancient Rome and Modern America*. Oxford: Oxford University Press.

— (2011), 'Black Minerva: Antiquity in Antebellum African American History', in Daniel Orrells, Tessa Roynon, Garminder Bhambra (eds), *African Athena: New Agendas*, Oxford: Oxford University Press: pp. 71–89.

Malik, K. (1996), *The Meaning of Race: Race, History and Culture in Western Society*, New York: New York University Press.

Marett, R. R. (1927), *The Diffusion of Culture: The Frazer Lecture in Social Anthropology*, Cambridge, UK: Cambridge University Press.

Marsh, J. (2005), *Black Victorians. Black People in British Art 1800–1900*, Hampshire: Lund Humphries.

Marstine, Janet (2011), 'The Contingent Nature of the New Museum Ethics', in Janet Marstine (eds), *The Routledge Companion to Museum Ethics: Redefining for the Twenty-First Century Museum*, London: Routledge, pp. 3–25.

Martin, E. S. (1936), 'A Study of an Egyptian Series of Mandibles, with Special Reference to Mathematical Methods of Sexing', *Biometrika*, 28: 1/2: 149–78.

Massing, Jean Michel and Ashton, Sally-Ann (2011), *Triumph, Protection and Dreams. East African Headrests in Context,* Cambridge: Fitzwilliam Museum.

Mathieux, Neguine (2010), 'Tanagras in Paris: A Bourgeois Dream', in *Tanagras: Figurines for Life and Eternity*, Paris: Musée du Louvre: pp. 17–19

Maxwell, Lucy May, Musson, Suzzanah, Stewart, Sarah, Talarico, Jessica and Taylor, Emily (2012), *Haarfarbentafel GALT040*, MA Collections Curatorship Project, UCL.

Mazlish, B. (1993), 'A Triptych: Freud's The Interpretation of Dreams, Rider Haggard's She and Bulwer-Lytton's The Coming Race', *Comparative Studies in Society and History: An International Quarterly*, 35/4: 726–44.

McCornick, John (1982), 'Introduction: The Prime Minister', in Anthony Trollope, *The Prime Minister,* Oxford: Oxford University Press: xi–xxii.

McCoskey, Denise Eileen (2002), 'Race before "Whiteness": Studying Identity in Ptolemaic Egypt', *Critical Sociology*, 28/1–2: 13–39.

Meijer, Miriam Claude (1999), *Race and Aesthetics in the Anthropology of Petrus Camper (1722–1789)*, Amsterdam: Editions Rodopi.

Meltzer, Edmund S. (2012), 'Egyptologists, Nazism and Racial "Science"', *Journal of Egyptian History*, 5: 1–11.

Miller, Judith (2008), *An Appraisal of the Skulls and Dentition of ancient Egyptians, Highlighting the Pathology and Speculating on the Influence of Diet and Environment,* BAR International Series 1794, Oxford: Archaeopress.

Montserrat, Dominic (1998), 'Unidentified Human Remains: Mummies and the Erotics of Biography', in Dominic Montserrat (ed.), *Changing Bodies, Changing Meanings: Studies on the Human Body in Antiquity*, London: Routledge, pp. 162–97.

— (July 1999), "'To Make Death Beautiful": The Other Life of the Fayum Portraits', *Apollo*, CL/449: 18–28.

— (2000), *Akhenaten: History, Fantasy and Ancient Egypt,* London: Routledge.

Moran, William L. (ed. and trans.) (1992), *The Amarna Letters*, London: The John Hopkins University Press.

Mosrop, John James (1999), *Measuring Jerusalem: The Palestinian Exploration Fund and British Interest in the Holy Land*, Leicester: Leicester University Press.

Moyr Smith, J. (1882), *Ancient Greek Female Costume,* London: Sampson Low.

'Mr Flinders Petrie's Egyptian Antiquities', *The Times*, 2 July 1888 (32427), 6 col. A.

Murray, Margaret (1911), 'Lecture I: Predynastic Period', MS ADD 387, A-561, Series 1, Special Collections, University College London, London.

— (1949), *The Splendour That Was Egypt: A General Survey of Egyptian Culture and Civilisation*, New York: Philosophical Library.

— (1963), *My First Hundred Years*, London: William Kimber.

— 'Lecture I: Egypt & Europe – Introductory & Prehistory', MS ADD 387, A-561, Series 1, Special Collections, University College London, London.

— 'Lecture II: Dyn. XVIIIth (contd)', MS ADD 387, A-561, Series 2, Special Collections, University College London, London.

Murray, Tim (1993), 'Archaeology and the Threat of the Past: Sir Henry Rider Haggard and the Acquisition of Time', *World Archaeology*, 25/2: 175–86.

'National Olympic Festival', *Penny Illustrated Paper,* 11 August 1866 (issue 254), 81.

Neubauer, A. (1886), 'Notes on the Race-Types of the Jews', *The Journal of the Anthropological Institute of Great Britain and Ireland*, 15: 16–23.

Newberry, Percy E. (1943), 'William Matthew Flinders Petrie, Kt., F.R.S., F.B.A.', *The Journal of Egyptian Archaeology*, 29: 67–70.

Newton, S. M. (1974), *Health, Art and Reform: Dress Reformers of the Nineteenth Century*, London: John Murray.

Novak, Daniel A. (2008), *Realism, Photography and Nineteenth-Century Fiction*, Cambridge: Cambridge University Press.

Nowak-Kemp, Malgosia and Galanakis, Yiannis (2012), 'Ancient Greek Skulls in the Oxford University Museum, Part I: George Rolleston, Oxford and the Formation of the Human Skulls Collection', *Journal of the History of Collections* 24/1: 89–104.

'Obituary: Robert Knox', *The Lancet,* 81/3 January 1863.

O'Gorman, Francis (2003), "'To See the Finger of God in the Dimensions of the Pyramid": A New Context for Ruskin's "The Ethics of the Dust" (1866)', *The Modern Language Review*, 98/3: 563–73.

Østergård, Uffe (1992), 'What is National and Ethnic Identity?' in Per Bilde, Troels Engberg Pedersen, Lise Hannestad and Jan Zahle (eds), *Ethnicity in Hellenistic Egypt*, Aarhus: Aarhus University Press, pp. 16–38.

Patch, Diana Craig (ed.) (2011), *Dawn of Egyptian Art,* New York: The Metropolitan Museum of Art.

Pearson, Karl (1901), 'On Some Applications of the Theory of Chance to Racial Differentiation', *Philosophical Magazine,* 110–24.

Pearson, Karl (1914), *The Life, Letters and Labours of Francis Galton, Vol. 1: Birth 1822 to Marriage 1853,* Cambridge, UK: Cambridge University Press.

— (1924), *The Life, Letters and Labours of Francis Galton, Vol. 2: Researches of Middle Life,* Cambridge, UK: Cambridge University Press.

— (1930a), *The Life, Letters and Labours of Francis Galton, Vol. 3A: Correlation, Personal Identification and Eugenics,* Cambridge, UK: Cambridge University Press.

— (1930b), *The Life, Letters and Labours of Francis Galton, Vol. 3B: Characterization, especially by Letters, & Index,* Cambridge, UK: Cambridge University Press.

Pearson, Karl (ed.) (1912), *Treasury of Human Inheritance Vol. 1.,* London: Dulau and Co. Ltd.

Peckham, R. S. (2001), *National Histories, Natural States: Nationalism and the Politics of Place in Greece,* London: I.B. Tauris.

Perl, Jed (Summer 1997), 'Drastic Realism', *Modern Painters,* 38–41: 40.

Perry, W. J. (1923), *Children of the Sun: A Study in the Early History of Civilization,* London: Metheun & Co.

Petrie, W. M. Flinders (1878), 'Alternate and Stereoscopic Vision', *Nature,* 18/448: 115–16.

— (1887), *Report of the Committee, consisting of Mr. Francis Galton, General Pitt-Rivers, Professor Flower, Professor A., Mcalister, Mr F. W. Rudler, Mr R. Stuart Poole and Mr Bloxam (secretary), appointed for the purposes of procuring, with the help of Mr Flinders Petrie, Racial Photographs from the Ancient Egyptian Pictures and Sculptures,* London: British Association for the Advancement of Science.

— (1892), *Tell el Amarna,* London: Methuen & Co.

— (1895), 'President's Address: Section H – Anthropology', *Sixty-Fifth Meeting for the British Association for the Advancement of Science, Ipswich,* London: John Murray, 816–24.

— (1896a), *A History of Egypt: The Seventeenth and Eighteenth Dynasties,* London: Methuen & Co.

— (1896b), *Naqada and Ballas,* London: Bernard Quartch.

— (1899), 'On our present knowledge of the Early Egyptians', *The Journal of the Anthropological Institute of Great Britain and Ireland,* 202–03: 28.

— (1900), 'Address', *Egypt Exploration Fund Report of the Fourteenth Ordinary General Meeting 1899–1900,* London: Egypt Exploration Fund.

— (1901), 'Correction', *Naqada and Ballas,* London: Bernard Quartch.

— (1906a), *Migrations: The Huxley Lecture of 1906,* London: Anthropological Institute of Great Britain and Ireland.

— (1906b), 'Migrations: Being an Abstract of the Seventh Annual Huxley Memorial Lecture of the Anthropological Institute, Delivered on November 1st, 1906', *Man*, 6: 170.

— (1907), *Janus in Modern Life,* London: G. P. Putnam.

— (1909a), *Memphis I,* London: British School of Archaeology in Egypt, UCL.

— (1909b), *The Palace of Apries (Memphis II),* London: British School of Archaeology in Egypt, UCL.

— (1910a), 'Early Burial Customs in Egypt', *Nature*, 84/2135: 401.

— (1910b), 'Early Burial Customs in Egypt', *Nature*, 84/2138: 494.

— (1910c), 'Early Burial Customs in Egypt', *Nature*, 85/2141: 41.

— (1911, repr. 1941), *Revolutions of Civilization*, New York: Peter Smith.

— (1922), *The Status of the Jews in Egypt*, London: George Allen & Unwin Ltd.

— (1931), *Seventy Years in Archaeology*, London.

— (1939), *The Making of Egypt*, London: The Sheldon Press.

— (2007), 'Extracts from the Petrie Journals', selected and collated by Paul C. Roberts and Stephen Quirke in Janet Picton, Stephen Quirke and Paul C. Roberts (eds), *Living Images: Egyptian Funerary Portraits in the Petrie Museum*, Walnut Creek, CA: Left Coast Press, pp. 83–104.

Pict, Daniel (1989), *Faces of Degeneration: A European Disorder, c. 1848–c. 1918,* Cambridge: Cambridge University Press.

— (1994), 'Introduction: Trilby', George Du Maurier, *Trilby*, Middlesex: Penguin Books: pp. vii–xl.

Picton, Janet, Quirke, Stephen and Roberts, Paul C. (eds) (2007), *Living Images: Egyptian Funerary Portraits in the Petrie Museum*, Walnut Creek, CA: Left Coast Press.

Pluciennik, Mark (2006), 'From Primitive to Civilised: Social Evolution in Victorian Anthropology and Archaeology', in Richard Pearson (ed.), *The Victorians and the Ancient World: Archaeology and Classicism,* Cambridge: Cambridge Scholars Press, pp. 1–24.

Poole, Reginald Stuart (1887), 'The Egyptian Classification of the Races of Man', *The Journal of the Anthropological Institute of Great Britain and Ireland*, 16: 370–9.

Porter, Theodore M. (2004), *Karl Pearson: The Scientific Life in a Statistical Age,* Princeton: Princeton University Press.

Prettejohn, Elizabeth (2007), *Art for Art's Sake: Aestheticism in Victorian Painting,* London: Yale University Press.

Pringle, Heather (2006), *The Master Plan: Himmler's Scholars and the Holocaust,* London: Harper Perennial.

Quirke, Stephen (2010), *Hidden Hands: Egyptian Workforces in Petrie Excavations and Archives 1880–1924,* London: Duckworth.

— (2011), 'Petrie's Photographs of Egypt', *Petrie's Photographs of Egypt: Landscape, Monuments, People. A database of photographs taken by Flinders Petrie in Egypt in 1886-7*. Griffith Institute Online Database.www.griffith.ox.ac.uk/gri/4elres.html [accessed 9 August 2011].

— (January 2012), 'Inaugural Lecture', Unpublished, Institute of Archaeology.

Quirke, Stephen (ed.) (2000-3), *Digital Egypt for Universities website,* www. digitalegypt.ucl.ac.uk [accessed 30 June 2012].

Rausch, David A. (1978), 'Our Hope: Protofundamentalism's Attitude toward Zionism, 1894-1897', *Jewish Social Studies*, 40/3: 239-50.

Reid, Donald Malcolm (2002), *Whose Pharaohs? Archaeology, Museums and Egyptian National Identity from Napoleon to World War One*, London: University of California.

Richards, Evelleen (Fall 1989), 'The "Moral Anatomy" of Robert Knox: The Interplay between Biological and Social Thought in Victorian Scientific Naturalism', *Journal of the History of Biology*, 22/3: 373-436.

Richardson, Ruth (1987), *Death, Dissection and the Destitute,* London: Routledge & Kegan Paul.

Richter, J. P. (1910), *The Mond Collection: An Appreciation Vol. II*, London: John Murray, 599-600.

Ridge, T. S. (1993), *Dr Barnardo and the Copperfield Road Ragged Schools,* London: Ragged School Museum.

Roberts, Paul C. (2007), 'An Archaeological Context for British Discoveries of Mummy Portraits in the Fayum', in Picton, Janet, Quirke, Stephen and Roberts, Paul C. (eds), *Living Images: Egyptian Funerary Portraits in the Petrie Museum*, Walnut Creek, CA: Left Coast Press.

Ronnick, Michele Valerie (2000), 'William Sanders Scarborough: The First African American Member of the Modern Language Association', *PMLA*, 115/7: 1787-93.

— (2004), 'Early African–American Scholars in the Classics: A Photographic Essay', *The Journal of Blacks in Higher Education*, 43: 101-5.

— (2005), *The Autobiography of William Sanders Scarborough. An American Journey from Slavery to Scholarship*, Detroit: Wayne State University Press.

Sanchez, Sonia (1987), 'Nefertiti: Queen to a Sacred Mission', in Ivan van Sertina (ed.), *Black Women in Antiquity*, New Brunswick: Journal of African Civilizations: pp. 49-55.

Sandell, Richard (2007), *Museums, Prejudice and the Reframing of Difference,* London: Routledge.

Sayce, A. H. (1887), 'Section H: President's Address', *Report of the British Association for the Advancement of Science, Manchester 1887*, London: John Murray, 885-95.

— (1923), *Reminiscences*, London: Macmillan.

— (1925), *The Races of the Old Testament*, London: The Religious Tract Society.

— (1931), 'The Antiquity of Civilised Man: The Huxley Memorial Lecture for 1930', *The Journal of the Anthropological Institute of Great Britain and Ireland*, 60: 269–82.

Schneer, Jonathan (1999), *London 1900*, London: Yale University Press.

Schneider, Thomas (2012), 'Ägyptologen im Dritten Reich Biographische Notisen anhand der sogenannten "Steindorf-Liste"', *Journal of Egyptian History*, 5.

Searle, Adrian (May 1997), '2,000 Years on from the paintings above, we give prizes for portraits like this. What's gone wrong?', *Guardian*, Features T 14.

Sedra, Paul (2004), 'Imagining an Imperial Race: Egyptology in the Service of Empire', *Comparative Studies of South Asia, Africa and the Middle East*, 24/1: 249–59.

Sen, Satadru (2009), 'Savage Bodies, Civilized Pleasures: M. V. Portman and the Andamanese', *American Ethnologist*, 36/2: 364–79.

Severson, Kim (2012), 'Payments for Victims of Eugenics are Shelved', *New York Times*, 20 June 2012,www.nytimes.com/2012/06/21/us/north-carolina-eugenics-co mpensation-program-shelved.html [accessed 5 July 2012].

Sewell, Brian (June 1997), 'The marvels that must not be hidden from view', *Evening Standard*, 28–9.

Sheppard, Kathleen L. (2010), 'Flinders Petrie and Eugenics at UCL', *Bulletin of the History of Archaeology*, 20/1: 16–29.

— (forthcoming), *A Woman's Work in Archaeology: The Life and Legacy of Margaret Alice Murray*.

Silberman, Neil Asher (1999), 'Petrie's Head: Eugenics and Near Eastern Archaeology', in Alice B. Kehoe and Mary Beth Emmericks (eds), *Assembling the Past: Studies in the Professionalisation of Archaeology*, Alberquerque: University of New Mexico Press: pp. 69–79.

Simon, Virginia Spottswood (1987), 'Tiye: Nubian Queen of Egypt', in Ivan van Sertina (ed.), *Black Women in Antiquity*, New Brunswick: Journal of African Civilizations: pp. 56–63

Smith, Shawn Michelle (2000), '"Looking at One's Self Through the Eyes of Others": W. E. B. Du Bois's Photographs for the 1900 Paris Exposition', *African American Review*, 34/4: 581–99.

Smith, Sidney (1945), 'William Matthew Flinders Petrie, 1853–1942', *Obituary Notices of Fellows of the Royal Society*, 5/14: 3–16.

Snowden, Frank Jr (1996), 'Bernal's "Blacks" and the Afrocentrics', in Mary Leftkowitz and Gary Maclean-Rogers (eds), *Black Athena Revisited*, Chapel Hill: University of North Carolina, pp. 112–28.

Soloway, Richard Allen (1982a), 'Counting the Degenerates: The Statistics of Race Deterioration in Edwardian England', *Journal of Contemporary History*, 17/1: 137–64.

Soloway, Richard Allen (1982b), 'Feminism,Fertility and Eugenics in Victorian and Edwardian England' in Seymour Drescher, *Political Symbolism in Modern Europe: Essays in Honor of George L. Mosse,* New Brunswick: Transactions Inc., pp. 121–45.

Soloway, Richard Allen (1995), *Demography and Degeneration: Eugenics and the Declining Birthrate in Twentieth-Century Britain*, London: University of North Carolina Press.

Spencer, P. (2011) 'Petrie and Discovery of Earliest Egypt' in E.Teeter (ed), *Before the Pyramids: The Origins of Egyptian Civilization,* Chicago: Oriental Institute Museum Publications: pp. 17–24.

Stack, David (2008), *Queen Victoria's Skull: George Combe and the Mid-Victorian Mind,* London: Hambledon Continuum.

Stansky, Peter (1995), 'Anglo-Jew or English/British? Some Dilemmas of Anglo-Jewish History', *Jewish Social Studies, New Series,* 2/1: 159–78.

Stevenson, J. (1998), 'Nacktleben' in Montserrat, D. (ed.), *Changing Bodies, Changing Meanings. Studies on the Human Body in Antiquity,* London: Routledge, pp. 198–211.

Stocking, G. W. (1995), *After Tylor: British Social Anthropology, 1888–1951*, Madison: University of Wisconsin Press.

Stone, Dan (2002), *Breeding Superman. Nietzsche, Race and Eugenics in Edwardian and Interwar Britain*, Liverpool: Liverpool University Press.

Strabo, *Geography,* Loeb Classical Library Edition, 1932.

Swain, Simon (ed.) (2007), *Seeing the Face, Seeing the Soul: Polemon's 'Physiognomy' from Classical Antiquity to Medieval Islam,* Oxford: Oxford University Press.

Sweet, Matthew (2011), 'Introduction: Kantsaywhere', *Francis Galton's Kantsaywhere,* UCL Special Collections website:www.ucl.ac.uk/library/special-coll/ksw.shtml [accessed 4 July 2012].

Taines, Richard (2005), *Sporting London: A Race Through Time*, London: Historical Publications Ltd.

Tangri, Daniel (1990), 'Popular Fiction and the Zimbabwe Controversy', *History in Africa*, 17: 293–304.

'The British Association', *Birmingham Daily Post*, Saturday 3 September 1887, issue 9106. 19th Century British Library Newspapers.

'The British Association', *The Standard*, Saturday 3 September 1887, issue 19702, 2. 19th Century British Newspapers: Part II.

'The Latest Acquisitions of the National Gallery', *The Times*, 28 August 1888 (32476), 4 col. E.

The National Gallery Annual Report April 1993–March 1994, London: National Gallery Publications, 1994, Appendix C.

Thompson, Dorothy J. (1988), *Memphis under the Ptolemies*, Princeton: Princeton University Press.

'To the Editor of the Manchester Examiner', *Manchester Times and Gazette*, 3 August 1847 (issue 87).

'Toleration versus Dr Knox', *Manchester Times and Gazette*, 18 June 1847 (issue 77).

Tomkins, Henry George (1889), 'Remarks on Mr. Flinders Petrie's Collection of Ethnographic Types from the Monuments of Egypt', *The Journal of the Anthropological Institute of Great Britain and Ireland*, 18: 206–39.

Toohey, K. and Neal, Anthony James (2007), *The Olympic Games: A Social Science Perspective*, Walingford: ABI.

Trigger, Bruce G. (1980), *Gordon Childe: Revolutions in Archaeology*, New York: Columbia University Press.

— (1989), *A History of Archaeological Thought*, Cambridge: Cambridge University Press.

Trollope, Anthony (1982), *The Prime Minister*, Oxford: Oxford University Press.

Tromans, Nicholas (2008), 'The Holy City', in Nicholas Tromans (ed.), *The Lure of the East: British Orientalist Painting*, London: Tate Publishing, pp. 162–97.

Tylor, Clare L. (2004), 'Robert Knox (1791–1862), Anatomist and Ethnologist', *Oxford Dictionary of National Biography*, www.oxforddnb.com/view/article/15787 [accessed 10 January 2005].

Ucko, Peter J., Sparkes, Rachael Thyrza and Laidlaw, Stuart (2007), *A Future for the Past: Petrie's Palestinian Collection*, London: Left Coast Press.

Van Wyck Smith, Malvern (2001), *The First Ethiopians: The Image of Africa and Africans in the Early Mediterranean World*, Johannesburg: Wits University Press.

Vance, Norman (2004–08), 'Kingsley, Charles (1819–1875)', *Oxford Dictionary of National Biography*, Oxford: Oxford University Press, on line edn: www.oxforddnb.com/view/article/15617 [accessed 10 April 2008].

Von Binsbergen, W. M. J. (ed.) (1997), *Black Athena: Ten Years After*, Talanta: Dutch Archaeological and Historical Society.

Waldron, H. A. (2000), 'The Study of the Human Remains from Nubia: The Contribution of Grafton Eliot Smith and His Colleagues to Palaeopathology', *Medical History*, 44: 363–88.

Walker, Susan and Bierbrier, Morris (1997), *Ancient Faces: Mummy Portraits from Roman Egypt*, London: British Museum Press.

Wallace, Jennifer (2004), *Digging the Dirt: The Archaeological Imagination*, London: Duckworth.

Wallace, M. and Kemp, M. (2000), *Spectacular Bodies. The Art and Science of the Human Body from Leonardo to Now*, London: Hayward Gallery Publishing.

Warren, Ernest (1897), 'An Investigation on the Variability of the Human Skeleton with Especial Reference to the Naqada Race, Discovered by Professor Flinders Petrie in his Excavations in Egypt', *Proceedings of the Royal Society of London*, 61: 398–401.

Wee, C. J. W.-L. (1994), 'Christian Manliness and National Identity: The Problematic Construction of a Racially "Pure" Nation', in Donald E. Hall (ed.), *Muscular Christianity: Embodying the Victorian Age*, Cambridge: Cambridge University Press, pp. 66–88.

Weeks, Kent R. (2005), *The Treasures of Luxor and the Valley of the Kings*, Vercelli, Italy: Whitestar S.P.A.

Wells, H. G. (1902), *Anticipations of the Reaction of Mechanical and Scientific Progress upon Human Life and Thought*, London: Harper Brothers.

Whitehead, C. (2009), *Museums and the Construction of Disciplines: Art and Archaeology in Nineteenth-Century Britain*, London: Duckworth.

Worboys, Michael (1981), 'The British Association and Empire: Science and Social Imperialism 1880–1940', in Roy Macleod and Peter Collins (eds), *The Parliament of Science: The British Association for the Advancement of Science*. Northwood, Middx: Science Reviews Ltd, pp.170–87.

WPE (1907), 'Review: Migrations: The Huxley Lecture for 1906', *Biometrika*, 5/4: 480.

'William Matthew Flinders Petrie' (2005), in *Excavating Egypt: Great Discoveries from the Petrie Museum of Egyptian Archaeology, University College London*, (eds) B. Teasley Trope, S. Quirke and P. Lacovara, Michael C. Carlos Museum at Emory University, Atlanta, p. xv.

Yeo, Richard (1981), 'Scientific Method and the Image of Science 1831–1891' in Roy Macleod and Peter Collins (eds), *The Parliament of Science: The British Association for the Advancement of Science*. Northwood, Middx: Science Reviews Ltd, pp. 65–88.

Young, Robert (1995), *Colonial Desire: Hybridity in Theory, Culture and Race*, London: Routledge.

— (2008), *The Idea of English Ethnicity*, Oxford: Blackwell Publishing.

Index